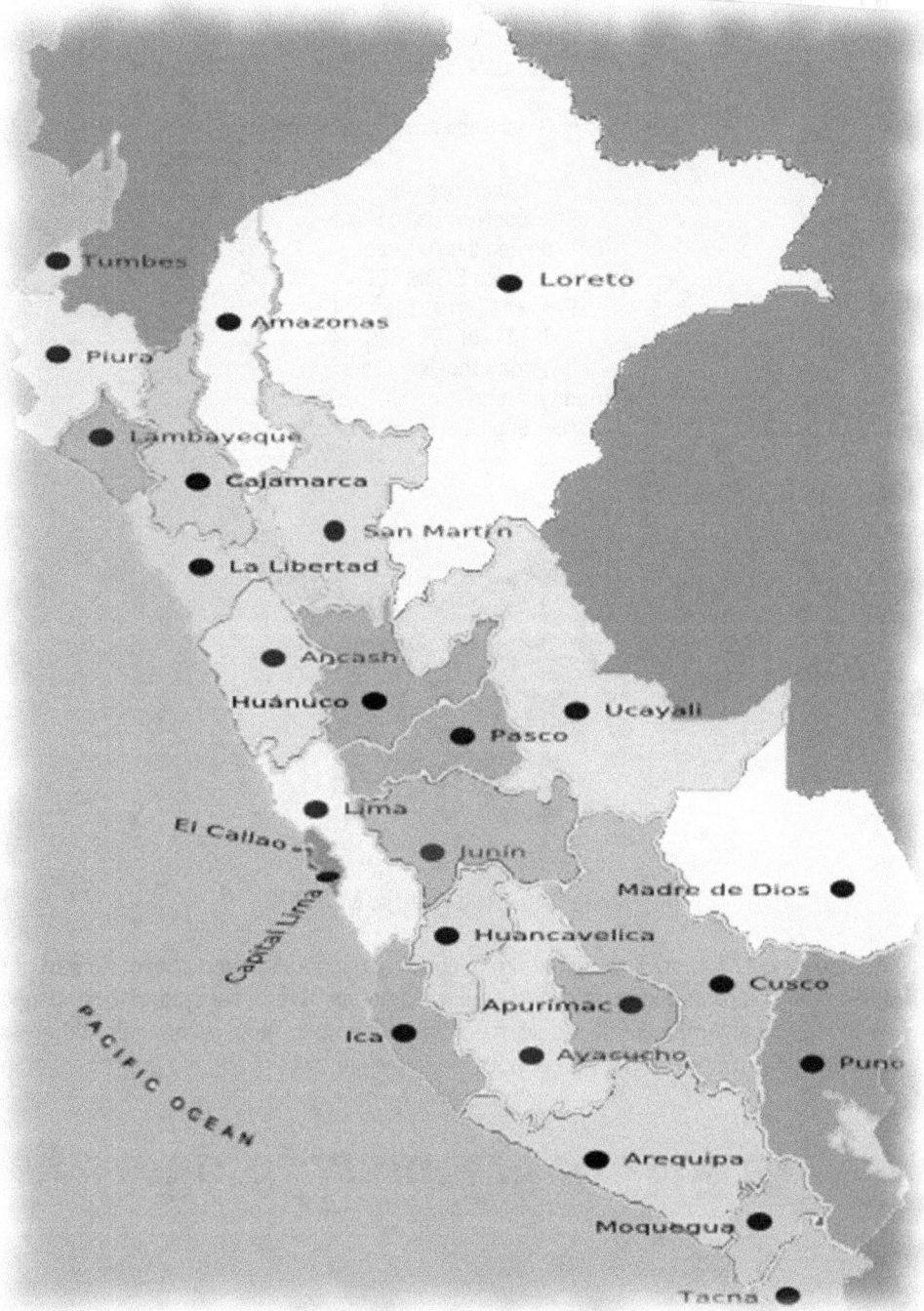

Tumbes

Loreto

Amazonas

Piura

Lambayeque

Cajamarca

San Martín

La Libertad

Ancash

Huánuco

Ucayali

Pasco

Lima

El Callao

Junín

Madre de Dios

Capital Lima

Huancavelica

Cusco

Apurímac

Ica

Ayacucho

Puno

PACIFIC OCEAN

Arequipa

Moquegua

Tacna

Typeset by Harry Wadham,
Cover and Layout by SPiderKaT for CFZ Communications
Using Microsoft Word 2000, Microsoft Publisher 2000, Adobe Photoshop CS.

Published in Great Britain by Gonzo Multimedia

c/o Brooks City,
6th Floor New Baltic House
65 Fenchurch Street,
London EC3M 4BE
Fax: +44 (0)191 5121104
Tel: +44 (0) 191 5849144
International Numbers:
Germany: Freephone 08000 825 699
USA: Freephone 18666 747 289

ISBN: 978-1-908728-98-2

Thanks to Jonathan for seeing the vision.

Thanks to Danilo for drawing it out.

Thanks to Beatrice, for being the most badass motherf' ing matriarch a son could ever have.

Prologue

The half-naked dwarf waving the butcher's knife in my face has really got me thinking. He barks like a feral dog, rotted fish breath and saliva spewing out from his red Dancing Devil mask. His low-slung centre of gravity feels like being sumo wrestled to death by a rabid fire hydrant.

And me? Thick glasses. Lax muscles. Pencil-thin wrists. Too much video game keyboard time lost in a virtual lifestyle.

Yet this is no game. This mismatch is all too real, and the hopeless thoughts are creeping in again.

But let me tell me something. This time, I'm dead wrong.

Dirt-stained fingernails scratch my cheek as he tries gouging out my eyes. We strain for control of the blade. Instinctively, I grab his elbow and twist and roll over on top of him next to the splintered chair. We bang into the knotted wood table, knocking over potted plants and beer bottles. He gropes for my face. A sick, metallic taste fills my mouth as I bite down on his fingers, turning his guttural wolf howls into wailing pig squeals. He rips his bloody hand away, lowering his guard. I drop my forehead square into his nose, full force. A sharp crack and a dribble of blood.

He's a goner. . .

Not.

"Ow!"

That damn mask is harder than it looks.

In these push-comes-to-shove moments in life, we can all be stronger than we think.

Wresting the knife from his grip, his ribs crack as I heave my entire buck-fifty of fighting force onto him. I wrap my right hand around his windpipe and squeeze. His eyes bulge open as he struggles, grunting and baring teeth like a stuck swine.

Gravity and weight prevail, and the blade descends slowly, pointing straight for his collarbone. Screams of horror echo in my skull. "SHHHhhhhhhh."

With panicked breaths, he jabs at my face as I push down on the knife's handle for the death blow, puncturing his throat. "SHHHHHhhhhhhh. SHHHHhhhhhhhh."

Blood gushes out the devil mask and he gurgles up a final, pathetic cry. I twist the knife for good measure. His arms convulse in spastic circles. Then, all strength leaves him. "SHHHhhhhhhh."

I spring up, rubbing the pain from my forehead and gasp for breath. A quick scan to my right at the dishevelled kitchen strewn with Inca Kola bottles and glass carboys filled with gelatinous sludge. To my left, beyond the large painting of a disfigured woman blindfolded and bearing a torch against a black storm background, Marcello's skeletal frame is stuck in his chair. His eyes are rolled up, locked in a distant gaze towards the ceiling. Yellow bile sloughs from his twitching lips as he finishes O.Ding.

Catching my breath, I creep to the dwarf's lifeless body, carefully avoiding the pooling blood as I kick his foot. "No. No. No! Can't be! This can't be. You can't be. . . real."

Yes, it's true. Really. There is so much more we can do in our world. All it takes is the right. . . frame of mind.

Portland, Oregon

ALGARROBINA
(Pisco Egg Nog)

Ingredients:
2 ounces Pisco
1/2 ounces Algarrobina syrup
1 ounce Evaporated milk
1/2 ounces Simple syrup
1/2 ounces Egg white
Ice
Ground cinnamon for garnish

Preparation:
To make the simple syrup, mix 1/2 cup sugar with 3 tablespoons of water. Bring to a slow boil, and simmer until the sugar dissolves   completely. Set aside to cool.

Mix all the ingredients in a blender, adding enough ice to double volume of the mixture. Blend for 2 minutes. Serve and decorate   with a sprinkle of cinnamon.

"Peru!"

"What?" Startled, I adjust my glasses and stare into Gus' face as he blinks at the orgy of rainbow-colored video poker lights. His Argentinian beret covers long, greying hair hiding bloodshot eyes.

"¡JesuCristo!" Ol' Gooseman sparks yet another cigarillo. His tongue clicks between the gaps in his teeth. "Portland Town just no is for you, Duck. . . You gotta get the fluck outta here."

"Here you go, Dougie." Redhead Gayle hands me a note and sing-songs, "She speaks English."

All I can manage is a lame, "Cool!" while holding up my empty beer glass. "How about another one?"

"No, thanks." Gayle shakes her pigtails and strides past me, giggling with a tray full of beers in tow for the weed smokers playing pool in the back of the bar.

Crossing himself three times, Gus whacks a button, betting another line. Sharp blasts of technicolors and funride sounds erupt before. . . another dollar down the electric money drain.

With a theatrical drum roll and button slap, he curses in Spanish and taps out his game. After adjusting his plaid flannel jacket, he bounces up, steadying his drink. "Qua-Qua-Qua-Qua."

The strains of Bananarama's 'You're My Obsession' wind down while we glide through the menthol-flavored haze of bleary faces before nestling into our well-worn 'writer's booth'.

Gus raises his glass for a grandiose toast. "Here's to quitting your job at the extract plant. ¡Viva Peru!"

Is he drunk already? The bar just opened. I chime in just as the music shifts to Toto's 'Africa'. "Why Central America?"

"Aye." A pained expression. "It's South America, Duck. For a geek you sure make no sense of geography. Dios Mío."

"Points taken. Anyways, what about Peru?"

"Ah. It's fabuloso. My brother has a friend whose buddy knows a lady whose auntie-in-law, after Peru's last ex-presidentes got sent to prison. . ."

"Prison?"

"Yeah. Is like a tradition down there."

"That's reassuring."

"Claro. Anyways this auntie, she's in her forties, about your age. She could show you around: Iquitos--"

"Is that her first or last name?" I squint and cock my head to an angle.

"Ee-kee-tos. Is the biggest city in the world you can't drive to. A half a millions peoples living in the lush, green Amazon. You must go. The Nazca Lines. Machu Picchu."

He's crazy. "Heard of the last one. I dunno, Gus. I've never even been South of the border before. At least not sober."

"I know. Is just your scene. Machu Picchu's very spiritual. Up there is the pure air. You will loves it. Besides, you always wanted to practice your Spanish."

Gus squelches his lips into a staccato whistle. "A month or two and you is speaking more betters than me."

How long have I been going to this bar, listening to this? "Sounds nice. Might be a year before I can carve out enough vacation time. Maybe a four-day look-see?"

Gus leans over and forces a solemn look. "Duck, is time you quit letting others thinks for you and grab your lifes by its brass cojones."

"You mean like you?" My tone's incredulous. But then again, at least Gus seems happy. A life lived in accord with its freest spirits.

"Exactamente." Gus crudely smears the cigarillo into the ashtray, then gazes up at me. "I knows just what you need."

Here it comes.

As Gus' voice drones on about his theories on worldwide transcendental meditation and how ancient aliens transcribed dolphin language into Aramaic, I sip my beer, mulling over the two decades I've misspent at my dead-end job. And now I'm taking spiritual advice from the town drunk. Perhaps I'm doomed?

I take stock of the watering hole's fauna, imagining the rest of my grim life locked into perpetual unenjoyment. Yava, the three-hundred-thirty pound Fijian bouncer, sits on an absurdly tiny chair near the entrance while gazing at his cell phone as he wolfs down forkfuls of mashed potatoes and salisbury steak through his lion's mane of a beard.

Over at the bar, Tim sits stiff as an ironing board, his bloodshot and bloated face transfixed on the football game on TV as he pours another boilermaker down his gullet. His rosy-cheeked brother of the bottle, Jon, thin as a scarecrow, cranes his head around, unable to focus his blurry thoughts.

They're all beaten down, resigned to waiting life out in this bar together until their livers slough off.

And then I see it. A fresh scrawl above the booth in magic marker:

'TOYNBEE IDEA
IN MOVIE '2001
RESURRECT DEAD
ON PLANET JUPITER
REMEMBER YOUR CREATOR,
IN THE DAYS OF YOUR YOUTH'

Strange? Was that there last night? Is that my handwriting?

Leaning back on the worn red cushions, Gus rips open a new cigarillo pack, theatrically tamps it down, then lights a brand new, juicy cancer stick. "You always fancies yourself a writer."

A meek laugh dribbles from my lips. "Yeah?"

Gus bends over the table, pointing at me with his Swisher Sweet. "Together, you and me are gonna writes the best traveled book of all times."

He pauses, crosses himself, then looks up lovingly at the grimy ceiling fan. "Well, since the Bibles of course." Gus slams his fist, then raises his empty

glass and whistles to Gayle behind the bar. "Hola, señorita. Dos cervezas, por favor."

She continues stacking steaming glasses just plucked from the dishwasher under the liqueur rack. He smirks and sprays a giant raspberry. "Pffffththththahh! Aye, she ignores to me again."

"Imagine that." Turning in my seat with a rapid hand wave. "Excuse me, Gayle? Could I get two more beers, please?" She whips her head around at me, then nods quietly.

Gus shakes his head. "Why is she always likes that?"

Now I know he's messing with me. "Because you're drunk."

"With the passion." He coughs and spits out a loud belch, bathing the stained table in frothy spittle. "Just be my eyeballs on the ground. I will fill in the blanks of your mind. Like I is your professor."

"So, I'm your peon pupil?" I shake my head and sigh. "Marvellous. Finally, my life's dream fulfilled. And where will you be?"

"Pffffththththahh! I will be here finding my muse. But don't you worry, Duck, I'll be down there in spirit."

Gus grins like a de-fanged wolf, then peeks past me.

Gayle stares balefully at me, cocking her head stiffly to the side. A nasally, scathing, "This game again, little Dougie?" She plies me with another drink, then shakes her head and clucks a 'tsk tsk' without looking.

Gus belly laughs. "And gets him some fish tacos."

She snorts, then straightens, deadpan. More chortling. What's so funny? I try a weak "Hi." but Gayle's already marching away with that sharp cadence of hers. A shapely martinet in red Converse.

Gus snaps his fingers. "You know I can master that savage language of yours. Is like I'm flucking William Shakespeare."

I pull a sip of beer. "This is insane."

After thumbing his glass while he gazes at his reflection, Gus looks me over, his mouth forming that familiar grin. The face of an elderly child seeking attention.

Okay. I'll budge. "What is it, Mister Wizard?"

"Nada. Forget about Gayle, Lonesome Duck. She's not into guys like you."

"Like me?"

"Sí. You know, guys that look like Bill Gates with leprosy."

I shudder. *A harsh truth.* "Thanks."

He laughs. "No offense."

"Oh, none taken." *There's nothing for me here.*

"You got a pasaporte?"

"Somewhere." *Everyone at the bar's turning on me. Including my one, true friend. For his pleasure.*

Gus nods and raises his glass for a toast.

I instinctively raise mine. *I'm tired of being their plaything.* "Huh?"

Clink. Clink.

"I pick you up Monday."

"Monday? What's this Monday?"

#

I kick my travel gear to keep the blood nourishing numb toes. Steamed breath whorls from my frozen lips. An early winter morning in Portland, Oregon. How do they say winter en espanol? El invierno? Damn memory. When will you speak to me, fluently?

A glance at my phone. Gus is a no show. Again. Maybe there's still time to turn tail and head to work? If I'm late, tell my asshole manager I woke up to the smell of rotting eggs. No sense having my condo blown to smithereens from stove gas.

Grabbing the handle of my Rockland wheeled suitcase, bite my lips, and turn towards my faded-blue apartment building. Back to my bummer of a job.

Aaaaaahhhhht. Aaaaahhhht. Aaaaaaaahhhhhhht.

Down the row of yellow streetlights, a scarlet convertible MINI Cooper hurtles my way, blasting its car horn and waking the entire neighborhood. The driver races like some Patagonian wild man caught in a tornado, confirming my deepest hopes. It's Gus, dressed in a half-assed gaucho Red Baron getup, waving and smiling like he's driving a parade float on Thanksgiving.

My bags fall to my side as the convertible twists into the parking lot, brakes screeching. "Duck. You're here? I didn't think you'd show."

"What?" Annoyed, I toss in my lightweight backpack.

"Whaddya think?" Gus snickers as he looks through the rearview mirror at my struggle heaving my heftiest luggage into the back seat.

"Think?"

"This brand new two-thousand-twelve flaming diarrhea red MINI. Splitting image of the ones you own."

My face puckers as I wedge in my last suitcase with a good shove. "Imagine that."

I sag into the suicide seat. Gus wipes his glasses, then stares at me, hunched over, gripping the full backpack on my lap like a small child clutching his favorite blanket. "You okay, Duck?"

A big sigh. "Rough night."

The MINI lurches through Portlandia's neo-workweek gridlock, severely overloaded with the top down. I pack too much when I travel. It's the raw, pre-airport jitters and lack of organizational skills.

My voice yells over the wind scream. "I still think we should try putting the top up. I can see my breath."

Ignoring me, Gus fidgets with the radio dials and pounds the horn at the traffic horde brawling its way through the Monday morning commute. Xerxes had better odds fighting the ocean.

"Gus?"

"Aye."

I press my 'I No Hablo Stupid' ball cap tight, trying to warm my ears. "My face is frozen and everybody's staring at us. We look like assholes."

"Duck?"

"Yeah."

"Pfffffthththhahh!"

So we're locked in traffic with the Mini's top down in December. My teeth rattle as I wipe frost off the windshield.

My first thought is that Gus has given in to his usual eccentricities, but after we fumble through the Mini's user manual, he blathers about how the roof's motor sensor jammed because of too much damn luggage.

Best to just play it out. We both smile, pretending we're two middle-aged morons tooling around on a seventy degree spring day before Gus turns to me. "I hates driving on Mondays, but before I blacked out at the bar last night, I remembered our solemn oath over cheap beers."

"Thanks?"

He takes a big cigarillo drag and blows the smoke my way. "I am unemployable, Duck, not irresponsible." Satisfied, he cocks his head and grins. "Besides, is only a little cold and no rain."

I look up at the blackening storm clouds, then back at the dashboard clock. Not much time. In my mind I've already detonated this charade. We can still take the next off-ramp and dart through the warren of back roads to my work. Sure, I'd look like a rube showing up dressed as a fashion-addled gringo on vacation in Puerto Rico, but I can deal with that. Small harm, small foul.

It's right after the I-205 Freeway off ramp that the stench hits me. At first I can't place it. Like there's some big pig shit farm, hidden away just over the horizon.

A few seconds later, Gus' nostrils flair up. "Carajo."

"What is that smell? Is something rotting?"

"Ohh jayy. I think some squirrels or a rat or one of them dogdamn nutria thingees crawled insides the engine to keep warm and maybe died. Is been making smells like this for two weeks now."

"Two weeks? Did you check under the hood?"

"Na. Is bad for my kundalini," Gus replies with a shrug.

"Christ, I can taste it. What if it's still alive? It's probably chewing through the timing belt right now? We'll be stuck out here?"

"Pfffffthththhahh!"

Gus tightens his steering wheel grip, spinning the MINI out of traffic and accelerating onto the right shoulder, mere inches from a concrete wall.

My fingernails dig into the backpack's straps. Visions of using it as some sort of an airbag/parachute combo plate dance through my mind. "What the fuck is this?"

Gus cranes his neck and squints. Assessing. Honking. Blasé. "A passing lane, I guessed?"

"You guessed?"

"No worries." Gus shrugs, completely disinterested, casually smoking his Swisher Sweet and flipping the bird at the honking traffic. I'm silent as a stone, feeling at my numb ears while taking in big gulps of stinking, icy air.

Finally, after the honking has crescendoed to a deafening roar, he clutches the wheel with both hands and violently jabs the MINI in front of a Peterbilt, forcing it to lock its brakes to keep from rear-ending us into a Goth soccer mom driving a Volvo with a rainbow-colored 'KEEP PORTLAND NORML' bumper sticker.

#

The rainstorm lets loose just before Gus wheels into the covered short-term parking garage, bleating the MINI's horn while pushing into the ticket lane.

After jerking to an abrupt halt, I jump out and squeeze the water from my soaked shirt, then turn to my carry-on bags. Gus pushes me aside, yanking out the heavier luggage with surprising vigour.

I'm taken aback. "You're coming in?"

Dabbing his face with a greasy snot-green bandana, Gus points his elbow at the pouring rain. "You wants me to drive back in this?" He gums a drunken Cheshire Cat grin. "Besides, is six in the AMs. Times to make my daily fit-shace."

My lips pinch to the left while I pace along in thought. My potentially ex-work shift just started. Am I really going through with this?

"No free hour?" Gus stops dead in his tracks, reading the parking sign overhead: Hourly Parking (Short-Term Parking Garage)/Rate: $3 Per hour/$27 Per Day. "I'm telling you, Duck, why even gets outta bed for Mondays?"

I look down and stifle a chuckle. "Nice shoe."

Gus looks down with a pained expression. A lone, red, decrepit girl's shoe lies at his feet as if waiting for its soulmate on the cold, hard concrete of the airport parking garage.

"What?"

"Terr-ee-bleh. You see? Usually they comes in pairs."

"Unless she was an amputee."

"No. Is serious. This place has fallen into the wicked juju." Gus grimaces and shuffles slowly around the offending shoe. "I bet some depraved icehole's keying my MINI. I can feels it."

"Yeah, probably that same googly-eyed fucker you cut off coming in here."

"And I just stole it, too."

I give a good tug at the rolling luggage. "C'mon, I'll buy you a coffee you goof." I point my head to the yellow sign over the skybridge entrance.

"No coffee." Gus' voice pitches upward to a whiny tone. "Life's so unfair."

Gus' superstitious mood turns even weirder when a well-coiffed matriarch and her mega-brood meatplows in front of us at the airport's revolving glass doors. We watch helplessly as they bog down.

"Fuck it." I bound towards the lone side door.

"Duck, wait! Is bad luck going in there."

Too late. I trundle on through with Gus following behind, staring back in slackjawed horror at the masses of flesh straining to pancake their way through the turnstile. Gus snuffs out his cigarillo on the escalator handrail, then crosses himself rigidly as we drag our bags down to the airline check-in.

"This is way too much bad karma for a Monday, Duck. Dios mío."

After ticketing, we saunter into the airport bar, greeted by a small cortege of waitstaff in Hawaiian shirts flashing plastic-lollipop smiles and barraging us with 'Hellos' and 'Good Mornings'.

"Aha." Gus marches towards a firepit table lined with chairs, not a stone's throw from the server's station at the bar. We sit down and Gus' eyes widen in surprise when I pull out a notebook and a weighty tome about Peru from my backpack.

"You is really taking charge of this change-of-lifestyle thing, hey Duck?" He whistles approvingly.

"You bet your bippy." I start thumbing pages. "Lima is the second biggest city in the world that's technically a desert even though it sits on the coast? Isn't that amazing?"

"Increíble."

"It's because of the Humbolt Current."

Gus rolls his eyes, yawns and lights a Swisher Sweet. "JesuCristo. Do I needs to use the white courtesy phone to get a drinks around here?"

Shaking my head. "Please don't. And you know you can't smoke in here."

"No. Is okay 'cuz no one ever stops me." After a big, satisfied puff, Gus looks around and squeaks a sharp whistle, trying to get the attention of the closest waiter, who's helping a Japanese couple order in English by raising his voice several decibels and pantomiming.

My phone rings. "Dammit. It's my work. What do I do?" I set the phone on the table like it's contagious.

Gus tilts forward at me. "You know, Duck, I has a theory."

This can't be good. We have a staring contest while the phone continues ringing. After some seconds, I give in. "Okay, what's the theory?"

He gestures like a street hustler performing a card trick. "They is two types of hombres in this flucked up world: the ones who gets weird and the ones who work. Which hombre is you, Duck?"

I should have known better. "Really, Gus."

"Sí. Most guys ditching work use lame fluckarounds like I gots the flu, or my grandmother just dies again. That's all wrong."

"Yeah?"

"Aye, them weak-sauce flake outs might gain an extra long drunkfest in Vegas or Cancun, but for an extended reprieve from your working class shitehole, you needs something extra special."

"I can tell you've put a lot of thought into this."

"Pffffthththththahh! Of course I has. I is unemployed. I has all the times in the worlds. The points is to let your imaginations run wild. Hows about you gots Hairy black tongue disease from eating an infested hamburger. Wouldn't that be a nice?"

I wipe Gus' spittle off my face. "Charming."

"Or. . ." He sticks out his tongue. Sweet, musty smoker's breath hits me in the face. "Aye. Or maybes your fecal replacement surgery got boshed. That's a real game-changer."

The phone rings.

"Or Exploding Heads Syndrome. You just·wakes up y that little noggin of yours, Pffffthththththahh! pops like a zit, exploding in two!"

"Unbelievable." I snatch the phone and get up from my notebook. "Watch my stuff and get me a coffee."

"A Cuba Libre?"

"Coffee."

"I is just kidding. Don't take life so seriously you dumb ding dong, Duck." Gus chortles, then pulls out his bandana and blows his nose.

I dodge foot traffic past a statue of ex-governor Vic Atiyeh. "Hu. . . hello?" **Dammit. Get that milquetoast tone out of your voice, Doug.** The secretary's chewing gum habit pops through the receiver. I can almost smell the spearmint. "Doug?"

A fake a half-assed coughing fit. "Sorry I couldn't make it into work this morning. I'm feeling a bit under the weather. The. . . sniffles." *Crap.*

The gum smacking stops. "Aw. Does somebody have a case of The Mondays?"

A case of The Mondays? "Oh, heck no, Linda. Uh, I would never. . . it's just. . . I've got a headache." Cringy.

"A headache? Well, pop a Tylenol and buck up, little soldier."

"Head cold. I meant head cold. Like the flu."

"Well, which is it?"

"I'm not sure." A couple more coughs for good measure. "I was so out of it when I checked myself into urgent care."

"Urgent care? Which hospital?" She sounds genuinely concerned.

Good question. "Ah. . ." Heck if I know. "I was. . . catatonic when they brought me in." The gum-chewing starts in. "Wait a minute? I thought you just said you checked yourself in?"

Double crap. "Maybe both? You know doctors, Linda. Buncha dorks in white coats."

A deep voice from behind. "Fuck you!"

Wheeling around, a huge, mohawk-sporting bodybuilder-type in a white jacket and matching loafers barges past me and scowls. I cover the phone with my palm. "Sorry, sir. I meant that it looks great on you."

Linda's voice. "Is that your doctor?"

"Yes. His bedside manner is quite. . ." I watch Lord Humongous flip me off while marching down the hallway. "Intense."

Chewing gum popping, then a breathless, "What's his name?"

I'm pacing around. Don't panic. Stay sharp.

"Your doctor's name?"

Leaning over, I squint at the golden statue's plaque. "Vic. Vic Atiyeh."

"You mean the dead ex-governor?"

Why does she have to bad so damn smart? Our educational system sucks. I inspect the plaque again. When did this poor bastard die? "I think it's his, uh, grandson, actually."

"Doug, this sounds like another one of your--"

"How long have we worked in Hell together, Linda?"

She draws in a big breath. "Forever and a long day."

"Exactly. And I've always been consistent and, uh. . ."

"Weird."

"Quirky."

"Fair enough."

"Consistently quirky. You know what it's like to be trapped day after miserable day with Larry and the suck up twins, Tom and Jerry."

"Yeah, buddy. Ugh."

"Exactly. Listen, any idiot can do my job."

"Any idiot has done your job. Hahaha."

"Haha. Very funny. Please, I just need some time to find myself. I'm begging you."

"And what if you can't find yourself, Dougie?"

"Well, then you'll never have to hear from my consistently--"

"Weird."

"Quirky self, again."

A pause on the other end. "Just call in tomorrow."

CLICK.

I walk back to find Gus smiling impishly while taking a plug off a bottle of Corona.

I sit down in front of another beer bottle on top of my notebook. "What's this?"

Gus gesticulates wildly, then pulls in close enough so I can smell his wino breath between the gaps in his teeth. "It's magic! They ran out of coffees."

"Uh. Huh." I drag out the two beats, skeptically, before taking a sip. He's read my mind. Anything to help me sleep on the plane.

A big, carnie geek chortle from Gus. "Aye. How'd the work call go?"

"Like I sucker-punched myself in the balls. I'm guessing with sick time and a few well-executed excuses like this last one. . ."

Dammit. Lord Humongous and his equally-buffed wife seat themselves at the table next to us and start perusing menus. Has he seen me? I scoot my chair until my back's to them. ". . . two, maybe three weeks, tops?"

"What's done is done, Duck."

"What's so funny?"

I peer down at my Peru notebook:

Fact 6: Macchu Picchu, one of the Seven Wonders of the World. It is the largest tourist attraction with over 2 million visitors annually.

Fact 7: There are over 4,000 native varieties of Peruvian potatoes cultivated in the Andes. Major agricultural products are cotton, sugarcane, coffee, cocoa and rice.

Fact 8: Mining and fishing are the main sources of employment in Peru.

Then, in a wild, jagged scrawl in black magic marker lettering:

#Fact 8.5: We just got backs from deepest jungle after my friend got bittened by that big, ugly bat. He is in the baño, bleeding out his eyeballs, and turning into a Pishtaco. Only God saves us all.

"What the fuck?"

Gus spits out a fountain stream of beer between the gaps in his teeth. "¿Qué?"

"What the fuck's a Pishtaco?" I say, wiping beer spray from my face, then holding up the notebook.

"Andean vampire. Carves its victim's fat off with a big knife and eats it. That gabaucho waiter was being all nosy, looking over my shoulders after he takes our order. I had to makes him leave."

"Christ. I thought he looked at me funny when I walked back in." As I pull back my beer, it foams over, spilling all over my crotch.

Gus flashes his gapped-tooth smile. "JesuCristo, Duck, you is such a gloob."

Shaking my head, I scoot my chair closer to the firepit. "What? You think I did this on purpose like it's some sort of fashion statement?"

Gus chuckles to himself while surrounding customers pretend not to stare at us. "No worries. Passengers pissing themselves is the least of security's problemas. Not after last weeks."

I take the bait, blotting my pants with a paper napkin. "What happened last weeks?"

Gus gulps more beer. "They find the, uh, dead pilot's corpse stuffed in a bathroom's stall."

"Damn."

"Sí. His skins completely peeled off his face and stuffed in a murse filled with bath salts and anus chemicals."

"Anus?" That can't be right? "Heinous?" I sure hope so.

Gus continues. "Yeah, heinous. So this dwarf is--"

"Little person."

"¿Que? Like munchkin?"

"No, they like to be called little people." He watches me scowl as he sips his beer.

"In Spanish they is called enanos."

"That sounds better."

"Okay. This enano is all whacked off his gourd, all sweaty like he's flucking a Neanderthal, with a 'SOUTHWEST AIRLINES' pilot's nametag pierced to his bloody left tit, munching on one of Captain Stubing's ears like is a breakfast burrito. They finally captures him pissed out naked on luggage carousel ten."

"Jesus. Sounds like one of my nightmares." The hopeless thoughts are creeping in again.

"Aye. Somethin' to look forward to on your deathbed." Gus probes my scowl and reacts with a huge, sick smile. "I'm telling ya', Duck, this is your lifes exchanging message from God." Gus solemnly looks up while crossing himself. "With vibes like this, how can you not moves to Peru?"half-drunk bottle of Corona.

We both sip our beers and ponder what a terribly weird world we live in, before Gus shows off a sinister smile.
"Word is the bath salt dwarf's the head mechanic for one of the major airlines."
My phone rings again. My maybe ex-manager's number. Click.
"Gus, I don't know how you did it, but you did. I just can't afford to sweat the small stuff anymore. Well, until in the future sometime when I die a horrible death, of course."
"Is there any other types of death to die, Duck?"
I hoist up my Corona for a toast. "To Orville Wright. 'The Airplane stays up because it doesn't have time to fall.'"
The beer bottles clink and Gus' eyes light up. "Unless the Bath Salt Dwarf's working on your plane."

Not what I needed.

Gus studies my reaction with a grim smile. "Or is nine-eleven. Or that German flight where the co-pilot gots all depressed and rammed the airliner into a mountain. Or Malaysian Airline Flight 370, which, poof--"

Gus chugs his beer as our favorite waiter walks by us balancing a full tray. He furtively glances our way like he's just seen the ghost of Vic Atiyeh roaming the tarmac, then averts his eyes without breaking stride.

I sit paralyzed, my mind locked in a gedanken thought bummer about suicidal pilots and a fiery crashes at terminal velocity. *That's it. No tip.*

"--vanished like a fart into the Andaman Sea."

With a hefty wheeze, I sag deeper into my chair. "Thanks. I was feeling so much better."

"De nada. 'Course where you is going, there's Uruguayan Air Force Flight 571."

"How do you know all this stuff?"

"I like the carnage. It relaxes my soul. They crashed into the Andes. The survivors resorts to cannibalism."

I lean back, horrified. "Jesus."

He shrugs and crosses himself. "What can you do? Is a filthy habit."

"That's it." I grab all my stuff and begin awkwardly rolling my luggage to the security check-in point. "Thanks for depressing the shit out of me, Gus," I reply, not looking back.

"Hey, Duck!" His tone cuts through my spine.

Stopping dead in my tracks, I turn around, listening to the sound of my luggage crashing to the floor.

There's Gus staring back, completely carefree, toasting me with my own half-drunk bottle of Corona.

"I hopes you find your pieces of your mind in Peru. And maybe a nice señorita alongs the way."

"You know my luck with that stuff." I stiffly grab my things and turn around. I'm on my way. Nothing can stop me.

Over my shoulder Gus bellows, "Enjoy your flights and remember, Duck, 'Take lots of notes'. We is gonna makes me the next Mario Vargas Llosa!"

"Who?"

Not what I needed.

Gus studies my reaction with a grim smile. "Or is nine-eleven. Or that German flight where the co-pilot gots all depressed and rammed the airliner into a mountain. Or Malaysian Airline Flight 370, which, poof--"

Gus chugs his beer as our favorite waiter walks by us balancing a full tray. He furtively glances our way like he's just seen the ghost of Vic Atiyeh roaming the tarmac, then averts his eyes without breaking stride.

I sit paralyzed, my mind locked in a gedanken thought bummer about suicidal pilots and a fiery crashes at terminal velocity. *That's it. No tip.*

"--vanished like a fart into the Andaman Sea."

With a hefty wheeze, I sag deeper into my chair. "Thanks. I was feeling so much better."

"De nada. 'Course where you is going, there's Uruguayan Air Force Flight 571."

"How do you know all this stuff?"

"I like the carnage. It relaxes my soul. They crashed into the Andes. The survivors resorts to cannibalism."

I lean back, horrified. "Jesus."

He shrugs and crosses himself. "What can you do? Is a filthy habit."

"That's it." I grab all my stuff and begin awkwardly rolling my luggage to the security check-in point. "Thanks for depressing the shit out of me, Gus," I reply, not looking back.

"Hey, Duck!" His tone cuts through my spine.

Stopping dead in my tracks, I turn around, listening to the sound of my luggage crashing to the floor.

There's Gus staring back, completely carefree, toasting me with my own half-drunk bottle of Corona.

"I hopes you find your pieces of your mind in Peru. And maybe a nice señorita alongs the way."

"You know my luck with that stuff." I stiffly grab my things and turn around. I'm on my way. Nothing can stop me.

Over my shoulder Gus bellows, "Enjoy your flights and remember, Duck, 'Take lots of notes'. We is gonna makes me the next Mario Vargas Llosa!"

"Who?"

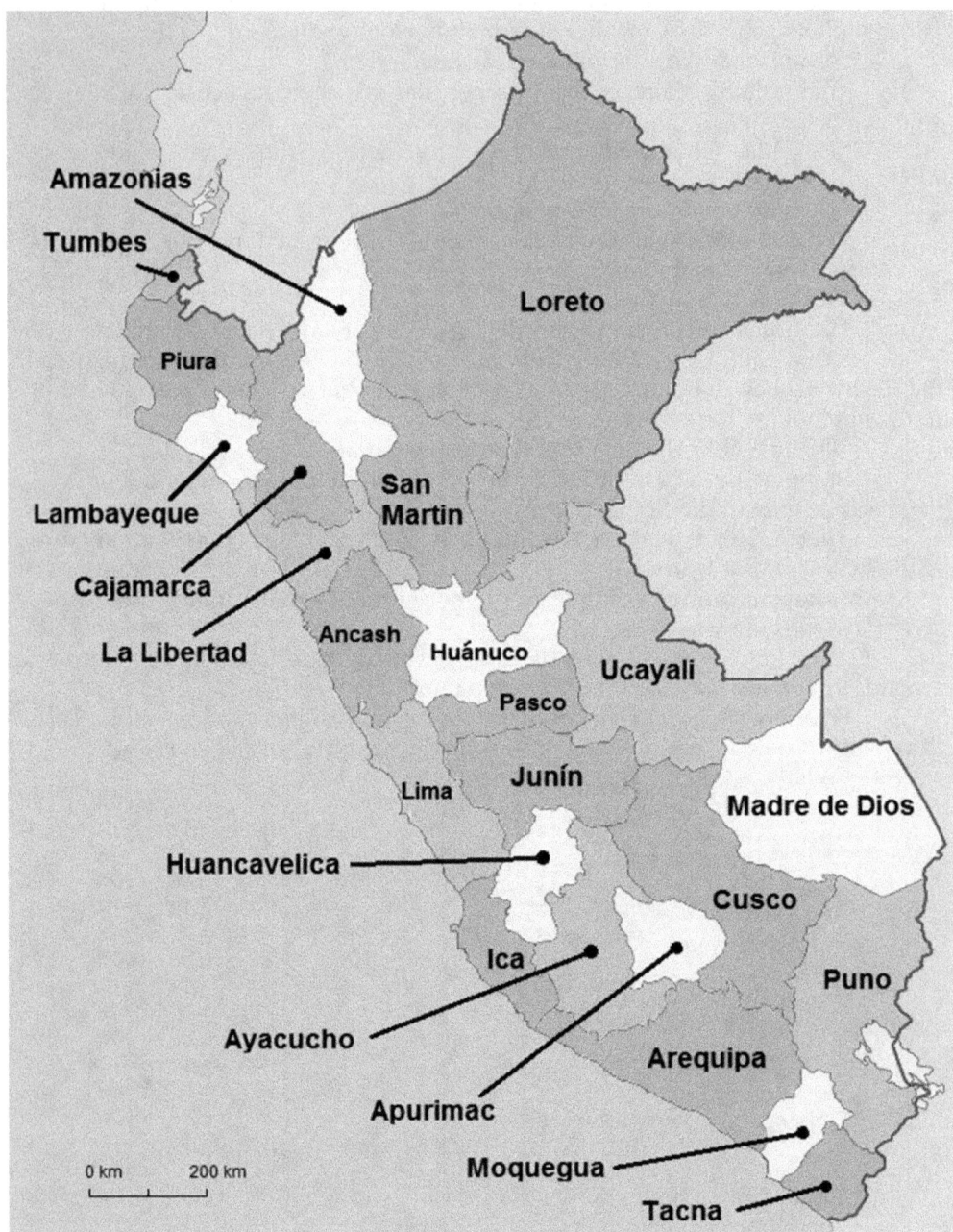

Amazonias

Tumbes

Loreto

Piura

San
Martin

Lambayeque

Cajamarca

La Libertad

Ancash

Huánuco

Ucayali

Pasco

Junín

Lima

Madre de Dios

Huancavelica

Cusco

Ica

Puno

Ayacucho

Apurimac

Arequipa

Moquegua

Tacna

0 km   200 km

Once upon a Lima Dawn

PISCO SUNRISE

Ingredients:
2 ounces of pure pisco
5 ounces of orange juice
1 ounce grenadine syrup

Preparation:
In a long glass, add about 4 ice cubes.
Add the pisco, orange juice and grenadine syrup - carefully, so that the ingredients do not mix.
Garnish with a slice of orange and a cherry (optional).

A thousand eighty-proof needles burning through my skull. Another hangover.

Sliding off the fancy hotel bedspread, I walk on lamb's legs to the Cusqueña beer cans stacked like a tabletop modern art exhibit. All empty. Oh well. I look around and grab an opened Inca Kola bottle, then head out to the terrace to check out the skyline.

Basking in the sunrise from the preteenth floor at one of Lima's finest hotels, I spy a man in the park down below. He appears to be enjoying an impromptu drunken Tai Chi and burpee workout, dressed like a refugee from an eighties South American discoteca. His ample gut bounces out of his multi-colored leisure suit when he dances unsteadily in the middle of a greenbelt that's undoubtedly the favored toilet for every stray dog within a three mile radius. After a five-minute performance, our hero finishes his wine bottle with a flourish, before collapsing into a stone cold deep sleep.

Between flat belches of Inca Kola, I rub my aching temples like a savantless idiot. Cross-cultural shock therapy. I've launched myself smack dab into the capital of a country I know nothing about. What's next?

What were those god-awful noises bellowing throughout the night? The

sounds of my Pisco-soured brain imploding? Or perhaps Peru has lurched into a state of anarchy? Maybe a nice South American coup like the ones the mainstream propaganda outlets like to gloss over?

I imagine myself bunkered down inside the giant egg-shaped jacuzzi, training an AK-47 past the 'Love Ewe' sex doll and bricolage of toiletries towards the front door. On the other side, a steely-eyed 'El Generalisimo' stands to the front of his death squad, twerks his pencil-thin mustache and yells through gold-plated teeth in a Ricky Ricardo accent, "Openz up, Americano! We know you are in there! Viva la Revolucion!"

I knew I should've put that 'Do Not Disturb' sign back on the door.

Time to appraise the room. I paid for a one-time, fuck-it-all send up to greet the country in style, and this suite delivers. It boasts a public-cinema-sized wall-mount TV, a modern polycarbonate chair with a remote control I'm deathly afraid to touch, and a giant purple bed with a ceiling mirror in case I want to blow kisses to myself while I masturbate.

I place the Inca Kola bottle on the table next to the oversized bed and take a chair. A deep breath of stale, hotel air. Sweat beads roll down my cheeks. The nagging, negative vibe just won't die. My stomach moans, then a burp fills my mouth with an acid-washed slurry.

Toilet time. Now.

Siphonic flushing sounds. The Big Spit's over. Finally. The porcelain is so cold, yet so comfortable. I rise like a zombie king from the throne, wipe my watery eyes, and stare into the bathroom mirror. A stooped cartoon caricature of my father squints back at me:

A paunch that's lost its will to defy gravity, wafer-thin lips, a greying hairline, a bony nose, huge bags under blood-red slits for eyes, all composed on a pufferfish face that makes me look like a sick mole.

Pretty normal, methinks.

Have I committed the biggest blunder in my life? My surroundings are hip, yet I feel like I'm some modern day Falstaff on a Truman Show reality TV channel entitled 'Doug's Fucked Up!'.

I plop down into the club chair, wiping spittle off my chin with a grimy bath towel. Am I genetically predisposed to these lame fuckarounds? Cursed? A botched DNA experiment between a near-sighted hermit crab and a eurotrash pimp?

How did I get here?

#

I distinctly remember following the passenger megaherd to the Llegadas internacionales luggage carousel at Juan Chavez International Airport, listening to the sexy female intercom voice greeting 'Welcome to Lima Airport. . .'

Auntie M, Gus' tour guide conscript, is missing on arrival. Even worse, owing to a battery charging catastrophe, my phone has run out of electric go juice, so I'm flying incommunicado.

But I feel good about my Spanish, belting out confident "Holas" and "Graciases" to the bored customs officials at the currency exchange post. With every monosyllabic Spanish answer, my confidence grows. I took two years of the language in my high school, did I not? What could possibly go wrong?

And then I step into the clusterfuck of Juan Chavez Airport's Arrivals area. With over ten million people, Lima is the second-largest city in South America, and it sounds as if they all showed up at the airport to heckle me.

A complete sensory overload of reeking armpits and guttural shrieks, it's like stepping out into some Emilio Westphalen-inspired version of a '90s grunge music video. Bug-eyed security dorks and airport employees look around anxiously as taxi drivers, chauffeurs, and genuine batshit crazies push and scream at the top of their lungs while holding up placards with exotic names on them. I'm shell-shocked, unable to grasp even the simplest syllable tossed my way, hoping to find Auntie M's friendly face amidst the mosh pit of frenzied faces.

Doug, you're not in Portland, anymore.

People of all stripes ask me unintelligible things, but my brain's locked up, overloaded with Spanish verb conjugations. Calm down. Remember basic language training. Name. Rank. And make up a serial number.

By my fifth lap around the airport, I stink of the shitmist of defeat, and even cabbies shun me like I've keistered an ibogaine suppository prior to arrival and now I'm doomed to walk in circles around the airport for the rest of my days like a Golem with PTSD.

Is this the punchline in one of Gus' sick jokes? 'Aye Duck, fluck you and your stupid stories'. I search around, seeking a savior, but there's nothing but a blur of faces. What's plan B? Pissing myself silly, then playing "Hide and Seek" in a locked public toilet stall until the next flight out arrives? Maybe?

Then I see it. A tortured scrawl on a piece of cardboard in a maelstrom of whirling bodies. My port in this storm. A slightly built, tall twenty-something with the faint beginnings of a porn mustache firmly holds up the sign reading 'LaLaLa Tours for DOuG' with the 'u' squished between the 'O' and the 'G' like an afterthought.

It's now or never.

"Hola."

He turns around, squints, then forces a grin.

"¿Qué tal? Doog?"

No Doog. Doug."

A scowl and a burst of light-speed Spanish encoded in a hyperdrive filled with slang. My eyes glaze over. Say something. "¿Cuánto cuesta. . . uh. . . ?"

"You is. . . for Auntie M?"

Oh thank God. "Sí."

He grabs the lightest pieces of luggage and we head out to his taxi. I have no clue where we're going. Rolling out of the parking lot, it hits me just how vulnerable I am. Visions dance through my head of being cast in the starring role of a drug lord's snuff film somewhere in the Amazon.

I gained an important insight, however. My Spanish skills truly suck.

Reader Warning: You may have some James Bond-type of training. You may be a NASCAR champion. You may have taken up ice road trucking as a relaxing hobby. In a former life, you may have been a world-renowned war correspondent or done three tours in Iraq. Or maybe you had to stitch your buddy's legs back together after his wingsuit escapade went awry.

None of that tame horseshit will ever prepare you for the adrenalized extreme sport of driving in Peru.

Scientists theorize that the smallest distance in the universe is Planck length. It isn't. The smallest measurable distance in the universe is the amount of space a Limeño feels they can squeeze their car into during rush hour traffic.

And squeeze they will, so learn to acclimate to having hundreds of Mini heart seizures from all the four-wheeled metal coming at you.

There is no road rage down here. Only survivors' grief. Death via head-on pile up on a four-way stop is a natural part of life in Lima, and should be embraced, not feared.

At first blush, Peru is a nation of walking suicides. Pedestrians crouch behind parked cars, a silent prayer in their throats, only to make the big leap of faith into the crosswalk, which looks like the Omaha Beach scene in 'Saving Private Ryan' with blaring car horns for a soundtrack.

Learn to enjoy darting perilously close to a tanker truck full of materiales combustibles, whose driver is throwing up on himself from a pisco hangover. Think of the bragging rights you'll have after you tell your friends that you've just been sideswiped by a semi truck and your boring Subaru station wagon has instantly been converted into a convertible. Did I shit my pants? Who has the time? I haven't even left my driveway yet.

After checking my pulse, I notice my taxi driver's annoyance at all the traffic distracting him from the phone app game he's playing. But really, who can blame him? After all, if you're almost certainly going to get into a head-on collision today, why fight it? Maybe throw the opposing drivers off balance and complete your morning by commuting in reverse?

Bracing for impact, the taxi driver races past ten cars waiting on a newly minted green light. We dart into head-on traffic, past a woman on a unicycle juggling bowling pins for spare change, before quickly cutting off the lead car, leaving car horn blasts behind us.

#

The cab bucks to a stop on a lively two-way street with a of couple neighborhood farmacias. Is this the place where they bury the touristas? Should I flee? Say something. "Uh, finito?"

The driver pulls his phone down from his face. "Sí."

Car horns blare from behind as I bungle paying the cab fare. Scooting my travel gear towards a pasteleria, I watch the taxi bolt off, becoming just another four-wheeled missile in Lima's public highway arsenal. Then, a sudden, primal urge to kiss the sidewalk for blessed, sweet life.

"How was your ride?" A heavily-accented female voice.

"Huh?"

A lithe Peruvian in her early twenties. "I'm Maria, Auntie M's niece. How was your ride?"

I wanna play it off casual, but all I can muster is a nervous smile.

"Uh. . . I'm here."

A hearty laugh. She wipes the long bangs from her green-rimmed glasses, then opens a heavily fortified door to a cramped, open air courtyard where a black Toyota Yaris is parked.

She points with her chin up at a spiral staircase beyond another small gate and yells above the buzz of traffic. "We're going up."

Taking in the climb with a sigh, I drop my traveling gear next to a hanging bike rack.

As we ascend, Maria explains how a last-second job and Lima's unyielding traffic conspired against Auntie M meeting me at the airport. Stymied, she tried out some seat-of-the-pants improvisation and called in for the taxi reinforcement.

Maria leads me into a small second floor apartment, and casually points down the hall. "Second room on the left, but be quiet. She's in her Hobbit House."

"Hobbit House?"

A furball Pomeranian pup latches onto my Achilles tendon like a blood-lusting pit bull. "Owww!"

"Oh, Pimienta." Maria lovingly picks the bundle of monstrosity up, making baby talk as it licks her nose. After shaking out my leg and shaking off my pride, I step up to the doorway, before turning to Maria.

She cradles Pimienta in one arm, then places her pointer finger to her mouth. "SHHHhhhhhhh."

Nodding, I tease the door open, then carefully poke my head in. The Hobbit House is a sound baffle and cardboard recording space nestled in a nooklet the size of a ventriloquist dummy's walk-in closet. Tiptoeing in, I listen to a beautiful voice lilt in a smooth Spanish sing song as she acts out the copy material.

Swift typing hands clack at a keyboard from inside the makeshift studio. Dead tired, I slowly drape myself on the frilly white bed. A voice from the tiny fortress of silence. "Hola?"

"Auntie M?"

She carefully pops open a Hobbit House ceiling panel, stands up off her chair and pokes her head out. A broad, reassuring face set on a round chin. "Dougito!"

"Hi."

The small door opens, and Auntie M's diminutive frame steps out. She looks like a human blueberry, wearing cotton pajamas covered with little indigo llama patterns. Unkinking her neck, she stretches out her hand. "Bienvenidos a Peru, Mi-stah Dougito. Welcome to my office."

I give an admiring look-see over at the Hobbit House, then back at her and smile. "I like it." A glance down at her fluffy llama-head slippers, each sporting goofy eyes and ruby-red felt tongues.

She grins, showing off her full cheeks as she beams at her slippers, then back at me. "Perks of the job."

"I thought you were my tour guide?"

"My other job." Her smile disappears as she scans me up and down. "Did you wear that on the plane?"

Looking down self-consciously at my brown corduroy pants and silver and red checkerboard sneakers, I wince. "Yeah."

"Interesting." The smile reappears. "Better take what you need for your hotel."

I nod. "It's all downstairs."

"Perfecto." She fishes her car keys out of a small change jar.

Blood drains from my face. "We're going back out there?" My voice misbehaves like it's going through a second puberty.

She chuckles, showing deep dimples, like a forty-year-old school girl. "You came here to see my country, no?"

#

Auntie M's aggressively calm behind the wheel. I'm quietly freaking out, counting near-fatal misses from the passenger's seat.

"What brings you to Peru?"

"Life change."

A quick burst of stifled laughter.

"What was that?"

She smirks. "Nothing." Then lays on the car horn at an ancient truck pulling into her lane. "¡Asu mare!"

I pry my fingers from the dashboard and show off a friendly grin. "What do you mean, nothing?"

Auntie M scrutinizes me, before pausing to compile the English words. "Es just every gringo that comes down here es looking for a change." Her expression lightens when she sees my concern. "No worries. I is sure you will find what you es looking for."

Shrieks of traffic as Auntie M barely avoids rear ending a mototaxi. The driver yells. She snarls, "¡No me jodas!" Then calmly looks over at me.

My eyes are saucers. "Do you always drive this way?"

A boisterous laugh. "Tranquilo."

We stop off at a bank to exchange U.S. dollars for Peruvian soles, then dip next door to a small neighborhood "catch-all" store in the hopes of finding me a cheap phone charger.

"Stay here."

Auntie M heads in to expertly handle the purchase while I stretch my legs and fumble around in circles, coughing as I soak up exhaust from all the passing cars. Leaning against a lamp post, I yawn into my shirt sleeve, then crane my neck and gape at all the small stores sharing space with houses behind tall fences and concertina wire. What's the meaning of all these well-worn hospital signs dotting the street? Weird.

I'm lost in wonder. Auntie M appears next to me. "Es yours," she says, handing me the charger.

"Thanks. Hey, I'm impressed."

"Huh?"

"The. . . hespedajes in your country. They're everywhere," I say, pointing to the street of hospitals. "You must have the best healthcare system in the entire world."

She stares through me. "Hospedaje es hostel, Doug. No es hospital."

Damned if Gus wasn't right. I am helpless down here. After racking up about twenty-seven Mini heart attacks, we leave the festival of claxons, parking on a side street next to a gaudy, purple and faux-gold-plated casino. Las Vegas writ small.

Passing a panoply of sparkling signs and gambling machines, the rumble of incoherent voices thickens as we glide up to the second floor on a brightly lit escalator.

I lean over to Auntie M. "What are we doing here, again?"

"Meeting my friends." She looks ecstatic.

"Really?" Crowds are a horror show for me. No matter what the pretense, I always manage to make a fool of myself.

"Only a few. No es nada," she says in a thick, halting accent. Auntie M taps my arm as we make a left turn, and even before the attentive waiter opens the glass double doors, I know I'm fucked.

Jet lagged, I had hoped for a small, quiet table nestled in the corner and some light conversation over cheap appetizers with maybe a Coke to wash it all down. So, after seeing three massive dining hall tables chock-full of gussied up Limeños, I sweat where I didn't even know glands existed.

Auntie M's greeted by a lineup of hugs, "Holas" and "Qué tals", and kisses on the cheek, the apparent linchpins of Peruvian custom. It's a far cry from my customary handshake or, preferably, just a nod.

I pump out clammy handshakes, greeted with curious smiles, like I'm some foreign object floating in the penguin exhibit at the Lima zoo. Tired, I'm confounded by a blur of happy, drunk, and amiable partygoers introducing themselves: a comedienne, an extroverted media specialist, an actress, a naval officer in uniform, a smiling lady dressed in blue with a blue birthmark, a puffy-faced musician, a tanned bodybuilder from the Isle of Man and his winsome Peruvian girlfriend.

A younger, well-dressed woman greets me and says in halting English. "You smell American."

Oh-kay? Her smile implies this isn't malicious. Maybe something's lost in translation? Or could it be from the thirteen-hour plane ride with layovers? Maybe the early onset of old man smell?

The confusion builds. She misunderstands about every eighth word in English and I understand about every tenth word in Spanish. Finally, after a klutzy pantomime of an attempted conversations, Auntie M performs the save, cheerfully steering me away from more muddlement.

"Do I smell American to you?" I sniff around, taking in Auntie M's alluring perfume.

"Nah. I think in any country your scent is unique."

"Thanks. I like your friends, but I stick out like a sore thumb. It reminds me of high school."

"Y what es that like?"

"Like being trapped in an insane asylum for the hormonally supercharged. Eight semesters of Lord of the Flies horseshit games and popularity contests. A singularly deformative experience."

She puckers her lips and crows. "Pobrecito. Don't be eh-scared." Before I can protest, she plops me into a chair. "I will find peoples who can talk to you."

After an encouraging wink, she veers back into the ensemble. I'm all alone, at the lone corner seat on the farthest table, like the awkward teenager seated at the kids' table during Thanksgiving dinner.

Auntie M talks to various people and points to me. Is she arranging seating based on English skills? Or mocking me from afar? All's I know is that this party's going to get real tedious, being stuck here in its outer orbit with my head up my ass. In between the socializers, waiters pop in and out of existence, placing exotic foods onto the tables.

Oh well. If you can't join 'em, write about 'em. I pull out my notebook and a pen.

"Hola."

Who said that? Looking up, I see a large, well-dressed Peruvian guy with a strangely powerful grin. Not forced, but rather locked in place, like he cracked a smile from a recess joke in grade school and it just froze that way.

"Habla español?" The smile continues. Unchanging.

Don't stare. "Poquito."

"Poquito." He nods and sits down next to me. "My name is Marco. What brings you to Lima?" he says in impeccable English.

I shift in my seat. "Oh, I dunno. I guess because my American Dream is dead, and I wonder if I can make another dream somewhere else." "Good luck, my friend. I hope you find your way." Marco puts his hand on my shoulder and widens his shark tooth smile. The intent seems reassuring, but up close the effect is terrifying.

Marco sits back and pats his ginormous belly, pulsing out like an expectant anaconda after she just swallowed a Clydesdale.

The toothy smile grows more intense. "How do you like the traffic?"

"Incredible." But not as incredible as a talking shark.

"You know how can you tell a second in Lima?"

I place a hand to my chin and fake think, then vigorously shake my head.

"It's the amount of time after a green light before the honking starts."

I laugh as Gabi, the energetic comedienne in her thirties, leans over to hand me a pisco sour.

"So Daaaaahhhhgg-ah, do you e-speak eh-Spanish?" She smiles while lighting a cigarette.

"Poquit-"

"Poquito." She's already deep in thought, the smoke plume gently defying the gravity around her face. She raises her voice above a cramped conversation behind her. "I seeee. Y how do you know Maaagda?"

"Uh, where I'm from in Oregon."

She cups her hand around her ear and leans in, puffing a big cloud of smoke at my face. "Uh, where?"

I sneeze, eliciting a chorus of "Salud" from everyone nearby. "Thank you. . . Gracias." After shaking my head in semicircles from another sneezing fit, I turn back to Gabi. "Oregon. I'm from Oregon. You see, I know this guy named Gus and. . . I guess he knows her. . . or knows someone that knows someone that knows her. . . I think?"

Mixed laughter from Gabi and Marco.

It goes on like this. Peruvians politely listening to me butcher their language while they ply me with pisco sours in the hopes the alcohol will lubricate my foreign language cortex. Wouldn't bet on it. With every empty glass in front of me, I'm feeling sweatier and pastier.

By the fifth double shot, my skull feels like an empty vessel and even English is sounding alien to me. The brainless gringo novelty factor wears. I fumble with parts of speech like I'm having aneurysms, so the guests begin forming disparate groups to socialize amongst themselves.

Marco rips through a big plate of ribs like a Great White sucking down chum on 'Shark Week'. Are those extra rows of teeth? Can't be. He looks down at my empty pisco sour glasses. "¿Te gusta?"

I belch out a well-lubricated. "Yeah."

"Our national drink. One of your countrymen helped invent it."

"Really?"

"Oh yes." A high, simpering laugh. "An American named Morris left Gringolandia in the early twentieth century to work in Peru. A few years later he opened up Morris' Bar in Lima. It became a popular spot for the Peruvian upper class and English-speaking foreigners. The pisco sour went through several changes before a Peruvian bartender working for Morris named. . ." Marco swishes around his half-full wine glass. ". . . ah, shit. . . "

I uncork a smile. "Shit?"

A laugh. ". . . Ah. . . shit. Dammit. Brain's not working. Yes. . . his name was shit. Ah. . . whatever. A Peruvian created the modern recipe in maybe the 1920s by adding Angostura bitters and egg whites."

"Bullsheet-ah." A gust of nicotine-flavored dissension when Gabi exhales. She raises an eyebrow while dangling her cigarette between her sparkly fingernails.

Marco smells at his wine with a sour look. "Eh, what?"

Gabi delivers her lines slowly for full effect. "I says that Daaaaahhhhgg-ah is going to need a broom for all that Bullsheet-ah."

There's a clash of Spanish and I dart my eyes between her brilliant fingernails and The Teeth while sipping my drink.

Marco turns to me. "Eh, both Peru and Chile claim the pisco sour as their national drink. But they are really two kinds of pisco with two different styles."

We both look down. In between all the pisco commotion, my drawing hand has been tracing Marco's face with oversized razor-wired shark's teeth on my notepad. We both look up at each other, then I scribble it out, hoping he hasn't made the connection.

Silence.

After pushing my latest pisco casualty from me, I look down at his mangled ribs. "¿Te gusta?"

"Oh yes. You will love the food here. Peru has been 'The World's Leading Culinary Destination' for six years now."

With this, Gabi's eyes fill with life. "Ohhhhh Sí. Ceviche."

Marco quips. "Lomo Saltado. The Jumping Beef."

Gabi's head sways from side to side like she's in tune with a song my gringo ears just can't hear. "Que Rico-ah. Aji de Gallina. Y Papas a la Huancaina'ah."

I have no idea what any of these words mean, but they seem to be enjoying it. Marco nods approvingly. "Y Causa, Rocoto Relleno, y Anticuchos. Grilled Heart."

Oh Christ. I knew it. He's a fucking vampire. I grab a yellow 2-liter of Inca Kola, pretending to read the Spanish words on the label as I scoot my chair further towards the exit. Gabi screams and lifts her arms like Peru's futbol team just won the World Cup. "Y Pollo a la Brasa!"

What the hell have I walked into? Some sort of anti-Weight Watchers Club? "Has Peruvian foodie culture always been this. . . spirited?"

Marco initiates me into the lore surrounding Peru's recent culinary history, simply known in Peru as 'Before Gaston' and 'After Gaston'.   "Gaston Acurio and his German-born wife, Astrid, opened up their first restaurant in Lima in nineteen-ninety. . .nineteen-nintey. . ." Marco swishes around his half-full wine glass. ". . . ah, shit. . . "

I can't help but smile. "More shit?"

A laugh. ". . . Ah. . . shit. Yes. . . nineteen-ninety-shit. Ah. . . whatever. They started as a traditional French restaurant, but since Peru has so many local ingredients from the sierra and jungle, they decided to try out more experimental plates."

A waitress drops off Gabi's iced Chilcano. She tastes it approvingly. "We have more than uh, two-thousand types of potatoes y two-hundred tipos of cheelies."

"Nice." I hold up the Inca Kola bottle. "Is this any good?"

Gabi's jaw drops. "Noooooo! Jouv never had Eenca Kooola, Daaaaahhhhgg-ah?"

I pour a glass of the golden kola and give it a go. Ahhhh. Tastes like carbonated bubblegum and looks like urine. "Nice."

It does feel good. My stress is gone. And even though I'm not doing anything important, I'm no worse off than I was before. The filthy thoughts of my potentially ex-job have finally washed away. I pour more.

Marco chimes in. "Inca Kola is the wonderful story of when a HUGE corporation didn't get to fuck over the little guy."

I sip while tilting my head. "Huh?"

The room starts spinning as The Smile chimes in. "A British guy named

Lindley moved to Rimac around 1910 and formulated Inca Kola using the Peruvian lemon. He built brand loyalty tying Inca Kola to Peru's dozens of national dishes. So, unlike other countries where Coca Cola or Pepsi prevailed, in Peru they couldn't unseat Inca Kola."

Gabi smiles smugly. "Poor Cooooca-ah Coooola-ah. HAH!"

Marco continues, "Coca Cola threw in the towel in 1999. Paying the Lindley's $300 million U.S. dollars for a minority share of the business." Gabi purses her lips like a baby and blinks her eyes, theatrically. "Pobrecitos."

I smile and look around the room. "Excuse me. Where is the bathroom?"

They both point outside the glass double doors and Gabi raises an eyebrow. "What's the matter, Daaaaahhhhgg-ah?"

I get up and frown. "What?"

Marco laughs. "You're looking a little pale, my friend."

Gabi picks a rogue piece of thread off my shirt, then smiles like an innocent little girl before blurting. "Borrrrracho!"

My cheeks warm to a pleasant smile as I start walking. "You have an interesting country, my friend."

Marco says "Gracias" as I jib towards the glass double doors, overcome by a warm, friendly glow. I slosh through a sluice of happy faces enjoying life. The sing song tempo of esoteric gibberish fills my ears, and I feel the heat of the garish, yellow lights on my sweating face. My head pulsates in four different directions as it bobs from the recoil of uneven steps towards the bathroom.

Pure bliss.

The secretary's voice jolts me awake. "You must really hate your job."

Yeah. Pretty much. And the middling management doesn't help, either.

Still in a drunken brain fog, I push myself off the bed and take groggy steps towards the toilet. "Thank God you called, Linda. I just hocked up a lung. There's no way I can make it into work, today. Shit!" Just tried cleaving my knee on the coffee table, knocking over some empty beer cans and an apple on a decorative plate. Hope she didn't hear.

"What was that?" The tone is accusatory. The chewing gum mashing intensifies.

"That? That was my cough medicine." Rubbing my knee, I limp to the bathroom. "Look, I know I forgot to call in, but I'm really sick this time." Some feeble coughs to play along. "You want me coming in and infecting everybody?"

The gummification ceases. "Doug. . . I know you're. . . unusual--"

"Thanks."

"You're welcome. But could you at least call in a half-hour before your shift starts, next time? You're getting a written warning. Next one goes to Larry at HR."

Larry means fired. Crushing. Any thoughts of retiring before I turn about one hundred and twenty-six just blew up in a shitmist of bad financial decisions.

A stern knock on my hotel door. What the hell? Did they get my GPS off this phone call? Images of my boss standing outside my hotel door, rubbing his paunch and bouncing on the balls of his feet, eager to deliver the F Bomb as soon as it opens at least a half-inch.

More bad vibes from the secretary. "Written warning. Do you hear me?"

Her tone is pissed-off, yet polite. Never heard it before, even when I totaled the work van.

So many thoughts in my head. Excuses to buy time, but my jaw's clenched so hard I feel like I'm chewing on my own teeth. What would Gus say? He's quick-witted, in a modern drunkard sort of way. I'm stuck mumbling to myself.

Her terse tone breaks up my thoughts. "I said, do you hear me?"

A Gussy answer comes to mind. Oh God, I can't say that. Something. "Yes. Listen Linda, I'm sorry, but I'll try--"

"I'm sorry, too."

CLICK.

The knocking gets louder. Impossible. Maybe I drunk-dialed room service in this morning's blackout? I wonder what the hell I even ordered? Pancakes with maple syrup would be nice. "Uh, hello?"

More knocking, then Auntie M's voice. "Dougito?"

"Uh, give me a second."

Smacking the stale taste of last night's vomit session from my lips, I rummage through the overnight kit, crammed with useless crap. No toothbrush. No toothpaste. Not even a breath mint.

She continues knocking.

Oh, shit. "Just hold on! I'm. . . getting dressed."

Dammit. Can't meet and greet with this Komodo dragon breath. More rifling yields an economy-sized bottle of 'Organic Lemongrass/Conditioning Shampoo'. Well, at least it's organic.

Down the hatch.

Ugh! Tastes like I just belted down an aromatherapeutic Jägerbomb. My body spasms. I pound my fist on the bathroom counter, willing myself not to retch.

The knocking is stronger. "Es you okay?"

I swill down water from the sink, spitting it out in a foamy spray before heading to the bedroom to toss on a decent set of clothes.

She's rattling the door hinges now. "Hello?"

"Coming." Passing by the full mirror, I give a quick cringe. Definitely not runway elegant.

Is she using a battering ram? "Dougito!"

Vaulting over, I lick off the last remnants of gargle from my goatee, but as soon as I reach for the front door handle, the knocking stops. Looking at its array of locks. How do you open this damn thing?

I brace my whole buck-fifty and give a mighty heave. The door slams against the wall, knocking off pieces of drywall. A startled Auntie M looks up from her phone in the hallway as I pose like I planned that all along. "Oh, hey. I was just. . .

With a cheerful "Hola", Auntie M barges past me. Following her, I cringe looking at the suite's transformation since I staggered in some hour beyond midnight in a drunken stupor

Bananas, placemats and cutlery have been tossed about like some blind somnambulast snuck in to play an impromptu game of disc golf. The curtains and chairs are piled up on the sofa like a play fort.

"Es you hungover?"

I outflank her, trying to block her view of the massive beeramid. "What? Me? Of course not."

She stops to stare at the opened minibar. The only items left inside are an opened Drambuie liqueur bottle and a half-eaten jar of peanut butter. Breakfast of champions.

"You look a little, uh. . . peaked."

"Well, then take a closer gander, Ma'am, 'cuz you are looking at a man who can definitely handle his alcohol."

"I see." Auntie M strolls through the bedroom, which is of particular concern. Pillows are wrapped inside sheets, raising the suspicion that during last night's blackout I had asphyxiated a small body, then left it lifeless right next to an unidentified wet spot.

"Definitely." I shut the door to the bathroom, quarantining its Guernica tableau. A sanitary disaster of Picassian proportions.

Auntie M ambles about, ignoring all signs of nocturnal distress, instead focusing on the massive TV and colourful artwork, which looks as if Leroy Neiman got a sweet commission from *Playboy* to paint fully-tatted naked immolating femlin acrobats having a pillow fight.

She smiles, "Que lindo. Ready for your Lima foodie tour?" then, abruptly heads out the front door.

Whoops. In the midst of last night's drunken time-fog, apparently we'd agreed to do check out Peru's grub scene. So, we cram into her Toyota Deathmobile and merrily merge into the marauding onslaught of honking traffic.

When she rolls into the restobar's squat parking space, my stomach's churning like a baby in a clothes dryer. Suddenly, wolfing down bunches of food doesn't seem like a great idea? But, how to get out of this artfully? Maybe, delay the inevitable and hope for the best. "How about some Italian food, instead?"

"Really?" She looks disappointed, like she'd been planning this all along.

"Yeah. Sorry. Is that okay?"

She nods, turns and huffs, backing out full-tilt into the careening flux of oncoming traffic. "¡Ya pues!"

Man those pisco sours are strong. Hope I don't ruin the upholstery. And here I thought drinking to the point of passing out was good for me. I swear Gus told me it helps him relieve his inner tension. Namaste.

I pat my tummy and frown. The mood in the Yaris has tensed. As we roll into the closest Italian restaurant's parking space, my stomach groans like a geriatric tuba. Maybe if I can stall for a bit, things will calm down. "You know, I hate to be a bother, but all of a sudden seafood sounds good to me. How about you?"

"¿En serio?"

nod, submissively. "Sí."

The sighs gets longer as we bolt off in search of seafood. Please, Auntie M, just give me a few more minutes and I'll be fine. I'm not a freak. I swear. Maybe I need some air? Rolling down the window, I stick my head out, dry heaving. Yes, that's better.

"Aye, that no es eh-safe!"

"What? I was just. . . admiring your beautiful city."

"Well, roll it up and makes eh-sure your door es locked." She glances over at my face pouring sweat, then smirks. "You es drunk, esn't you?"

I contort my face and pathetically shake my head. "No way. It's just a bit of a head cold. That's all."

Auntie M stifles a laugh, then shakes her head and accelerates, leaving my stomach jellified. Pretty soon, we're locked into a Sisyphean grub crawl from hell. After a half-hour making crop circles through Lima's sidestreets, my excuses venture to the exotic, testing Lima's prodigious fusion food scene to its absolute breaking point. "I've got the taste for some boiled head cheese goat haggis served in the stomach linings of a lamprey eel with ají dipping sauce. How about you?"

Auntie M scowls, uncomprehendingly. "¿Qué?" Then, with a sly smile. "I knows just the place."

What the hell? Is that a thing around here? "Wait! Do any of Peru's restaurants serve Frog Sashimi smothered in guinea pig paté and cilantro?"

A deep sigh, then a maniacal laugh. "Of course." The car wheels around yet again.

The tables have turned. She's getting off on this. As I search the floorboards for any containers I can throw up into, my masculine hopes spring eternal. Maybe she'll sleep with me?

She shakes her head and glances over at me, snickering.

Either that or she's setting me up to have my kidneys harvested? Things are so complicated, these days. "How about some mangled beef hearts slathered in some vegemite Eskimo ice cream with a sprig of parsley on top?"

"Es you medicated?"

"What?"

"You keep eh-saying eh-stupid eh-stuff, then change your mind. Es weird."

"Really? I'm sorry. I thought I was just daydreaming, again."

"Sí. For the last tens minutes. Es like you is. . . different."

"Uh, thanks?"

Gnashing her teeth, she grips the steering wheel like she wants to rip it off the dashboard.

A conspicuous, fuming silence.

Uh oh. I bombed big time. And all before noon. I have to do something fast. So, as we wheel past a placid-looking park, I make the call. "Here."

She stops, unfazed by the furious eruption of honking around us. "¿En serio?"

"Sure, why not? I love parks. It's be good for us. You know, stretch the legs before lunch and all that nature stuff. Especially trees. They're so awesome. Do you like trees?"

"Sí." She sighs as the Toyota's right wheels screech to a stop against the curb.

We enter the lovely Park Bosque de Olivar in the well-heeled San Isidro financial district. At first blush, I think I've finally done something right. It's a pleasant respite from the city, where lush trees line walking paths and the smell of flowering life punctures the nostrils. A perfect place to wander without care or just sit on a bench and stare at the man-made pond.

Auntie M talks herself down from DEFCON One as we saunter, side by side, listening to trilling bird songs being drowned out by the puke warning growls emanating from my stomach.

I'm not so sure things are going well. "Sorry about my weirdness back there. I've. . . I've just got a very, VERY weak Cardiac Sphincter. That's all."

"Es that. . . dangor-us? Dangerous?"

"Only if I'm throwing up on you."

"I takes it you has never been married?"

"Nah. Somehow I missed out on that boat ride. You?"

Auntie M winces and shakes her head. "No. Mi nieces and nephews es my children."

We both put our heads down and stroll. She fiddles with her well-coiffed hair and bright earrings. Silence. Say something. "And the years keep coming."

"Sí." She stops and points to some feathered creature high in the crotch of a tree plucking its armpit. "¿Qué es?"

I squint. "A bird."

She looks at me with her patented 'I know that, you idiot' look. "What type, silly?"

Okay. She asked for it. The bird looks grey so, to me, the answer is obvious. "It's a. . . Duck-Billed, Grey. . . Titted. . . bird."

Not satisfied, she immediately points over at a couple of even less identifiable creatures stuck on a branch. "¿And those?"

"Uh. . .yeah. . . that. That's a flying tree squirrel violating a chinchilla."

"¿Y esta?"

This charade goes on for some time as we stroll about, until I run out of legit-sounding names for all the flora and fauna. She turns to me. "Es my favorite park in Lima."

I look around and shake my head, pretending to admire nature. "I can see why. Very. . . green."

"Sí."

"And I especially like the flesh-eating koi."

Well, the koi aren't really flesh-eating, but whenever someone throws a slice of bread or even a bottlecap into the pond, they pile on top of each other, mouths agape, practically willing themselves en mass out of the water for a tiny morsel. It's. . . eerie. Like some post-apocalyptic painting where a colony of radioactive insectoids swarm into a giant's mouth and ravage its skull.

And with that, I am suddenly famished.

I turn to Auntie M, who's still intrigued by the koi feeding frenzy. "How about somewhere with a nice ocean breeze?"

She turns to me and starts dialing her phone. "I knows just the place."

#

We're heading south on Circuito de Playas on La Costa Verde. Traffic's lively and the sun blesses us as I stare through the window at the waves gently lolling in. I roll down my window to catch the sea breeze, turn to Auntie M and smile. "Perfect weather. I can only imagine what it's like in summer."

Auntie M never takes her eyes off the road. "It es eh-summer, Doug."

Never one to let my ignorance get the best of me, I point with the enthusiastic curiosity of a five-year-old freshly released from an underground nuclear bunker.

"What's that blueberry Whoville thing jutting out into the ocean next to all the surfers?"

"La Rosa Nautica. Best pisco sours in all of Lima."

She honks and abruptly shifts gears, jamming up a winding road along the seventy-meter cliffs of the Costa Verde.

With my stomach shoved up into my throat and a death grip on the dash, we pass high-end apartments on cliffs overlooking the Pacific Ocean and a park with a statue of some buff dude in a public grope with what looks like a young Oprah.

Auntie M pre-empts me. "Es El Parque del Amor. Young people keep making suicides by jumping off this overpass here, eh-so they fenced it off."

"How romantic." We pass a small Paddington Bear statue before burrowing into an underground parking garage at Mach 10, my head whips back as the Toyota slams to a stop with cacophony of grinding metal.

After we get out, Auntie M looks down and pinches her lips. The Toyota's back right quarter panel clipped a column, causing a big, ugly white scar on black paint. She shrugs. "One more stripe to the tiger." Then, she looks over at me and winks. "Hungry?"

The restaurant's expansive back patio is perched on the cliff with a stunning vista of the surrounding coastline festooned with color, as paragliders soar through the skies above Miraflores.

Auntie M's friend, Lara, a heavier set woman in her forties with dark eyes and an infectious smile, sits at a cozy table with an impressive spread of exotic food plates all around her. She speaks no English, so the sharp cadences of Spanish fill my ears as I sip my chilcano and scan the paragliders for any signs of distress. Good God, what if one of them fell? Maybe a rogue gust of wind or a badly buckled harness?

I'm frozen, shuddering at the thought of an aerial funride gone awry, body crashing down on the table of the family of five next to me like a gravity-fed flesh bomb, internal organs bursting like a blood-soaked piñata. Bummer for the clean up crew. Having to deal with the father, bathed in blood, waving his drink glass sporting a floating eyeball like a cocktail garnish. "Uh, excuse me, señor. . ." He twirls a long piece of intestine with his fork like some spaghetti noodles. "I found this in my ceviche. At first I thought we had ordered the octopus. . ."

Auntie M's voice. "Dougito. Fuckus!"

Lara smiles and smacks the table with her fist. "Si. Fuckus, Doog."

Fuckus? I look blankly at Lara and Auntie M. "What?"

Auntie M laughs. "I was telling Lara on how much you love nature parks." She examines the food spread, conflicted. "I eh-should eh-start my ultra-low fat, low-carb chocolate cake, baby food and chemical laxative diet today, but. . ."

The expression of longing says it all. She scoops her fork into a huge helping of potatoes. "I just try a little taste. For eh-sure I start my diet mañana."

As Auntie M carb loads her plate with more tasty morsels, Lara's smile flips to a frown when she scans the untouched beef hearts, stuffed potatoes, and sushi on my plate. "Me muero!"

"I'm sure it's just travel nerves," I say as I slam down another chilcano, hoping to oil over my social anxiety gland. Auntie M tries to explain how, even though I'm big on Lima's food, my stomach's been a little off.

Lara's shocked, explaining emphatically to Auntie M the unlimited numbers of maladies I probably have: traveler's diarrhea, Giardia, maybe even an ancient alien fetus chewing through my stomach, ready to pop its head out and projectile vomit pre-digested sushi rolls all over our adjoining tables.

A bit tipsy, I vaguely understand a couple of cognates as Auntie M mentions something about Lara being a hypochondriac.

While Auntie M talks her down, I pull out my pocket notebook and turn towards her. "Boy, if Gus could see us now."

Auntie M twists and tilts her face at me. "¿Quién?"

I smile. "Gus."

Auntie M gives me a blank look.

"The guy from Argentina?" Still nothing. "Late fifties-ish, drinks like a fish, half his teeth are rotting out?" Nada.

Auntie M finishes chewing a papa rellena. "What es you talked about?"

My English must be rusty. "The Argentinian in Oregon. He knows someone that knows someone that's related to someone that knows somebody that knows a person that you're an auntie of? Remember?"

Auntie M and Lara both look at me like I've decided to go out into the jungle and join an Ayahuasca cult.

I gesture with both hands for emphasis. "Gus. From Argentina. In Oregon. Uh?"

As Lara follows with her eyes, Auntie M dabs some food off her chin with a napkin, then mimics my hand gestures. "Dougito. I no know Gus. In Oregone. I only know a Gustavo y he has his teeth and es an architect. . . of sorts." She raises her head, thinking. "Or was that Marcello?" A confident nod. "Sí. Eh-something that ends with an O." She pauses, then shakes her head dismissively.

"That's eh-strange."

I listen to them talk in Spanish as I sip a glass of water and wipe the sweat off my brow. My brain's on fire. I've known Gus for, what, like forever? He can't even play Beer Jenga without cheating, and now he's an architect? What the hell is going on?

I'm still dumbfounded as Auntie M excuses herself for the bathroom, leaving Lara and I to awkwardly stare at each other while she gnaws on some beef hearts.

Tearing off the sheet of paper in my notebook with what I hope is Gus' real phone number, I get up, smile at Lara and mouth "I've gotta make a call" while making the international thumb and pinkie to my ear phone gesture. Lara gives a hearty wave and smiles in return.

I head across the patio away from all the tables for some privacy. Leaning against the guardrail, I admire the spectacular view of the snot-green sea while struggling to fish the phone out of my pocket.

After what seems like an eternity of ringing a familiar voice answers. "¿Hola?"

It's the man who might be formerly known as Gus and I know exactly where he's at. The sounds of video poker and '80s rock music are a dead give away.

"Hola, Duck!"

"Don't you Duck me, Gus. Or is it, Marcello?"

A pause. I can hear him rattle the ice around his drink. The Gus/Marcello voice is pure confidence. "Aye, Duck. I see you talk-ed with Auntie M's brother. No is importante, Mister Wizard." He pulls the phone away from his mouth. More ice clinking from his glass.

He's putting on a show. Stay firm. "So, what the hell do you call yourself, anyways?"

"Calls me Gus for old time's sakes."

"Why didn-"

"Aye, good news, Duck. I made the first chapter done. How thats for speed writing? A news record. Just listen."

I hear the sound of paper rustling and Gus rips out a tremendous belch as he clears his throat. "Oofah: "The Gus' Peruvian Guidebook. Chapter One: 'Peru: It was the bested of times. It was the worsted of times. It was--'"

"--it was the age of wisdom, it was the age of foolishness."

"You read it already? Imposible?"

"Yes, 'Tale of Two Cities'. Charles Dickens. Gus, that's already been done."

Gus bursts out a sloppy raspberry. "Ah, naleche. Its soundeds original when I wrotes it. I just scratch that part out."

"Gus, I'm not sure you--"

"Aye, OK. And how makes this one? Uh. Nude Chaptered One: Ahem. 'Muchos años lately-er, as he makes faces with the firing squad, Colonel Duck was rememberings that distant afternoon when his father took-ed him to discovering the lice.'"

"Gabriel García Márquez. 'One Hundred Years of Solitude.'"

"Mierda y concha su madre! This writing shit's hard!"

"Maybe Gus, but I don't--"

I hear Gus pull his phone away. "Gracias, darlin'. ...I re-worked that on the final draft." The clink of fresh ice as what's-his-face gulps down more gin. "And Duck, puts on more notes into the historia of these Sendero Luminoso."

"Sendero What-o?"

"Aye. And watch outs for them Pishtacos down there. They is a killer." He's wasted. "Pishtacos?"

"Just keeped making your e-scribblings in that notebook of yours and sexts me what you got."

Sexts him? What I've got? I think we've hit a fork in the road. I turn from the handrail and see Auntie M entering the patio area fresh from her bathroom break.

A big wave and a gesture at her to come over. "Hey Gus, I see Auntie M."

"Aye. Ain't she's a sweetie?"

"She's wonderful. Maybe you could talk to her and straighten this-"

Gus/Marcello's voice quavers. "Oh Díos Mio! No. Shit no! You're doings a goods job, Duck. Now, I gots a big conference call comings in. Is Bill Gates and his leper colony." A HUUUGE raspberry!

"Gus? Gus, what's that Pishtaco, thingee?"

CLICK.

What the fuck?

'THE GUS'S PERUVIAN GUIDEBOOK' PROUDLY PRESENTS: CHAPTER ONE: SENDERO LUMINOSO (THE SHINING PATH)

The origins of a cabrón

Once up on the times, there was a fat-joweled cabrón with a fleshy billiard ball-shaped head filled with psychotic thoughts. His name was Abimael Guzmán and he taught at the University of Huamanga in the 1960s.

Any hows, after he gets tenure, he starts to calling himself "Comrade Gonzalo" and makes Sendero Luminoso (The Shining Path). I know it sounds like the name of a Christian rock band, but they play ways more like Death Metal.

Come See!

Our stinker's career begins: time to make the jumping beef

The history of Peru is a long succession of 'Oh mierda' moments. One of her biggliest dumps happens in 1532, when Francisco Pizarro rolls into town with his conquistadors homies, captures the Inca emperor and puts they whole empire on blast.

Then things really take a crap for the worst. The natives get to enjoy the perks of slavery, by enrolling in Pizarro's worlds highest crossfit gym, digging for the gold and silver in the Andean mines. No union. No bennies. Just potatoes and coca leaves with a piece of coal to chew on as they toil away. And if they get the sniffles and wanna take the day off and maybe chill out with they llama, well, there's the whip and a miserable death waiting for them in all that thin air.

Things continue to suck after the Mestizos take over from the Spanish conquistadors, and Peru ain't lookin' so hot. So, when Abimael "Gonzo" Guzmán starts talking about some good ol' fashioned communism, people gets the fever and armed revolts start break dancing out around the country.

The Peruvian police ain't big fans of commies, so Gonzo decides to skip town and heads to the Far East for his 'Excellent Chinese Adventure'. It's a groovy time, and he eats Dim Sum while edumacating himself on the guerrilla tactics Big Mao used against the Nationalist Chinese in the 1940s.

"Serious Revolutionary Workers United, LLC."
In 1967 Guzmán returns to his beloved Peru and prepares for "serious revolutionary work". By serious he means to destroy Peru's government and start a peasant dictatorship. Aye, is nice to have career goals.

Let the revolutionary games begin!
So, you say, why don't the army come in and bitch smack The Shining Path's dick down in the dirt? Good questions. In those flucked up times Peru's military has to deal with a smorgasbord of commie parties, labor strikes, as well as some badasses named MRTA (Movimiento Revolucionario de Tupac Amaru), so they is a little preoccupated.

To tops it off, Peru's government and police is corrupt to they core and the places where the Shining Path is having their rave party keggers is brutal to infiltrate: Mountainous, high jungle passes with dirt roads in varying stages of decrapitacion.

On a happier note, that isolated jungle makes for great drug smuggling, so The Path starts wheeling and drug dealing with the Colombian cartels. The Path sets the price of raw cocaine, charging a landing fee to each Colombian plane. In exchange, the Colombians get theyselves a steadied stream of product. It's a win-win. Who says commies can't do capitalism?

About this time, Sendero and Guzmán have told any potential allies they don't need no help and to fluck right off. Even Albania. But, then again, who really needs Albania, anyhows? The Shining Path sees itself as an unstoppable juggernaut, sorta like the Macarena back in the '90s.

The deadly revolt: a shining path through a river of blood
"There is nothing more orderly than a cemetery." - Open Veins of Latin America: Five Centuries of the Pillage of a Continent - Eduardo Galeano

After pissing off all the other Communist Parties, Tupac Amaru's people, the Chinese Commie Party, and Albania, The Path decides to kick off their deadly revolt by hanging dead dogs from lampposts in every city in Peru in order to put PETA on their shit list as well.

After that, it's game on. With the discipline of a psychotic ant colony, Shining Path followers start adding to their explosives stockpile.

The Quota:
In May of 1981, Guzman goes totally emo, bringin' up "the blood quota" and talkin' about how all the Shining Path's Members should get used to dying in the most suckiest ways possible, because "crossing the river of blood" is the only way to achieve the revolutionary cause.

Nice pep talk.

Theodore Dalrymple, a doctor in Peru in those times, has a different take on the whole slaughterhouse "Quota" thingee: "the worst brutality I ever saw was that committed by Sendero Luminoso (Shining Path) in Peru, in the days when it seemed possible that it might come to power. If it had, I think its massacres would have dwarfed those of the Khmer Rouge. As a doctor, I am accustomed to unpleasant sights, but nothing prepared me for what I saw in Ayacucho, where Sendero first developed under the sway of a professor of philosophy, Abimael Guzmán."

Aye! When you is making Pol Pot look good, you got issues. By 1990, massacres, executions, and, ahem, forced disappearances turn Peru into a wasted land, with about 30,000 dead and more than 60,000 families fleeing their homes for the "misery belts" in cities like Huamanga, Ica, and Lima.

The arrest:
The police's big break comes in September 1992. A special-ed forces unit cases a ballet studio in the upper-class neighbourhood of Surco, in Lima.

But it turns out these special-ed forces dudes don't just dig Swan Lake, they also likes to dig into other people's garbage. You see, the dance instructor is supposed to be living alone, but when they search her junk, well, it turns out she's picked herself up a nasty psoriasis cream habit. And oddily enough, psoriasis is what Abimael Guzman suffers from. With that, the special-ed unit put three and two together.

On September 12, 1992, an elite unit of cops kicks the doors in and busts eight people, including Guzmán and his female companion, Elena Iparraguirre.

The trial is pure Kafka goes to clown college. The judges decides to appear in hooded robes like they is in some Hollywood Eyes Wide Shut sexy party, not just because they is kinky but to protect theyselves from the Shining Path's revenge.

And then the government gets nasty on itself. They make it a TV trial, lock Guzman up in a cage, then hire a fashion designer to dress him up like the Hamburglar and fat-shame him.

Aye. The court of fashion opinion can be so cruel, even if you is a psychotic mass murderer.

    •   But it works. Seeing their fearless leader Hamburglarized breaks the spirit of The Path, and they never commit mass genocide again.

    Guzman gets convicted of treason and sentenced to spend the rest of his life in a maximum security prison with no psoriasis cream. Aye.

    But he's got fun company, at least. Guzmán's prison buddy list includes Vladimiro Montesinos, the former top dog of Peru's Intelligencia Service. I'm guessing Vladimiro likes his prison digs, since he helped build it when he was running wild during President Alberto Fujimori's heyday, who also happens to be imprisoned.

    Today, Peru is one of the safest countries to visit in South America, with petty theft being the most common crimes—a far cripes from the violence and terrorismo of its past.

    So, why isn't Abimael Guzmán's face plastered on the t-shirts and bedroom walls of pot-smoking hippie college students who likes to brag about fighting the system in between doing keg stands and beer pong like they do for guys like Che Guevara?

    It could be 'cuz, even though Guzmán's twisted sister vision of civil war claimed thousands of lives, he never got that elusive big Win. Nobody likes a loser. Plus, it's hard to idolize some fat dude who got taken down because of a psoriasis cream addiction. I feels for him, though. We can't all be photohygenic like Che.

    In more heartburning news, in the falls of 2006, while still in prison, Guzmán proposes to his lover, Elena Iparraguirre. She probably killed Guzmán's ex-wife and is serving a life sentence, herself, but online prison dating sucks and beggars can't be choosers. So, after fighting for the right to get married with a hunger strike, the two love birds tied the knot in late August 2010.

    Who knows? Maybe Montesinos was the best man?

    Aye. El Amor.

MACHU PICCHU

Ingredients:
2 ounces of pure pisco
4 ounces of orange juice
1/4 ounces grenadine syrup
1/4 ounces creme de menthe
Ice

Preparation:
In a long glass, add about 4 ice cubes.
Pour in 1 ounce of the pisco, the orange juice
and the grenadine.
In a cocktail shaker, combine the remaining
pisco, creme de menthe and three ice cubes
and shake well (this will lighten the creme de
menthe so that it floats on the top).
Pour on top of the orange juice mixture in
the tall glass and add a straw, but don't stir or
the colours will blend together.

An early flight to Cuzco. Tethered to my seat, I sip a Cusqueña beer and scan the pages of my favourite childhood book, "Pig Pig Grows Up". Its simplicity soothes my mind from the flight jitters. My problem is the raucous high schoolers flanking me.

The banter starts out funny enough. Awkward flirting. Unexplained laughter. Silly monologues leading to nowhere. It's like eavesdropping on myself thirty-odd years ago. But when the pimply nerd brays 'Nobody puts baby in the corner' for the dumbteenth time, hoping to impress the cute faux-emo girl across the aisle, I close my book and turn to Auntie M, who is burrowed deep underneath her red jacket.

She could sleep on a bed of nails at a rock concert inside an erupting volcano. Is it narcolepsy? A Xanax addiction? So much for some light conversation on this hour-and-a-half flight.

From the first few steps off the plane and into the thin air my chest feels like it's caving in. Everything's groggy with a dull, blood-throbbing bass line bursting through my temples. Auntie M slows down in front of me. She's feeling it, too. Time to take it easy and acclimatize to the sounds of our hearts bursting through our lungs.

We slowly loll about the airport, wandering through a myriad of small shops selling travel trinkets. Dodging an endless variety of wayward travelers, I turn to a giant mural. It's a wide shot of the perfect gringa familia posing happily for that epic selfie on Machu Picchu: the daughter and father gleefully unaware as the mother stares in horror at her teenage son hunkering down in the 'I'm tossing my cuy' position.

I tug on Auntie M's jacket and point. Her placid smile blends to a frown, "Soroche."

I dip my head down. "Huh?"

"Altitude slickness." She turns and melts away to find the luggage carousel. I linger at the mural. Even with all the harried passengers darting around me, pressing to catch their late flights, I can't help but think: Yeah, it's supposed to be funny but. . . poor bastard. My trip will be better, I hope. Aside from a little breathlessness, I'm fine.

After playing baggage carousel hide and seek, we step outside the airport terminal. Auntie M slides on her sunglasses, admiring the blue skyline marbled by chalk-white clouds. "Doesn't the eh-sky looks like the ocean?"

The eh-sky looks like the ocean? Hadn't thought of that one. Then again, I live in Portland, where the clouds living above us constantly poop rain, hail, snow, sleet and ice down on us mere mortals. Say something pithy. "It certainly does."

Auntie M looks at me like she wants me to say something more pithy. . . er? All right. I'm locked and loaded. A slow, profound gaze upwards into the wild, teal yonder. "It looks like one big. . . sky. . . aquarium."

That doesn't sound right.

Squealing tires and honking.

A taxi screeches to a halt in front of us and the cabbie pokes his head out of the driver's side window, showing off his wide grin and short, spiky hair. "Heeeeey-yah!" Maxim gun style Spanish. Auntie M returns fire in kind.

After a few more short bursts, Auntie M shrugs at the metallic grey four-door Toyota. "¡Vamonos!"

We blast off in a whirl of directions, knowing immediately that this is a driver to be reckoned with. His name is Leor and he drives fast, thinks fast, and talks even faster. As we plunge uphill past signs marking Peru's political season, he and Auntie M exchange volleys of español before he looks back at me in the rearview mirror, finishing in English.

". . . Yeah, seven years here. Older brother's in Lunahuana with his wife. Just retired." He grins and pops the collar on his squash-colored shirt. "I know seven languages: Quechua, Spanish, Italiano, Ryussian, I learned Japanese in three years on the computer, Portuguese, and, uh. . . uh, dang it, there's one more. Uh. I always. . ." A millisecond later he points up. "English." He looks back at me and beams. "Hahahaha."

The roads narrow, with the distinctive Incan stone-lined water channel cutting down the middle.

"Are you sures you know where es you're going?" Auntie M looks petrified.

Leor gives a hearty thumbs up. "Don't worry, ma'am. Whoops. Wrong turn." He slows down and looks around at street signs. "Don't you worry about this little manoeuvre here. I can correct that. So, where you from?"

I point to myself. "Me?"

He tugs the wheel for a turn and honks at a tuk tuk. "The one and only."

"Portland, Oregon."

From the rearview mirror it looks like he's bit into a tart lemon. "Orygone? That sucks." Then he turns around and smiles. "Just kidding. Nice place. I kiteboarded in Hood River once. ¡Ya Pues!"

Confused, I peer over at Auntie M. "What's ¡Yah Piss! mean, again? Ah!"

The car rears to a halt, slamming my head against the passenger's seat. Leor's already gotten out, and popped open the trunk before I realize we've made it to our rustic hotel. I'm walking in molasses, spilling my heavy luggage onto the empty lobby's polished stone. Auntie M trails a few paces behind me, also breathing heavily.

The place is darkly lit and creepy, like an unused set built for a long-lost Quechuan Brothers Quay puppet film, with antiques randomly strewn about.

Auntie M scans the walls filled with pictures of Andean mountain and jungle scenes showing off all sorts of wildlife, from birds, jaguars, spectacled bears, to even a yellow-tailed furry monkey. With a conspicuous huff, she wipes her pointy finger across the lobby counter, inspects the clot of dust stuck to her finger, and opens her eyes as wide as saucers. "Oh, my!"

Leor excitedly smacks the faux gold desk bell. The sounds of honking horns proliferates outside. "¡No me jodas!"

He poses with that familiar point to the sky. "Give me a second." Before we can reply, Leor bolts past the counter and darts to a small hallway into a back room.

I sigh over at Auntie M. "How you doing?"

She manages to smile. "¿Bien, y tú?"

I grab the collar of my 'World's Okayest Peruvian' t-shirt, stretching it to and fro as fast as my beating heart while sticking my tongue out. "No problem. . . a."

She bites her lip. "No you worries. Machu Picchu is lower. Like 2,400 metres."

"What's that in feet?"

Auntie M shrugs and bats her eyelashes.

Sounds of Spanish yelling and horns honking on the street. Seconds later, Leor emerges into the vintage lobby talking to a dolled up woman with jet black hair tightly pulled back in a bun.

"Claudia will help you." Leor props himself up against the front desk and all three of them share some sort of long joke in Spanish. I ogle the artwork strewn on the walls. One of the pictures shows a close up of an crimson mask with devil horns, twisted fangs, and bulbous, hypnotic eyes that pierce right through me. A jolt shivers down my spine like I've been bitten by an electric eel.

Shuddering in disgust, I delicately step to my right. Those eyes still follow me. Very disconcerting. Bending over to pretend to tie a shoe, I stare back up at them, but the fearsome glare catches me from every angle. Leaning in, I blink and sneer with a whisper. "You're not so tough. I'll fight you with one hand tied behind my back and my eyes closed." Satisfied, I pull back. "Big pussy."

Leor's yell startles me. "It's a dancing devil mask from Puno." I gather my wits and find Claudie, Auntie M and Leor peering at me. Leor smiles, cheekily. "It's at an even higher altitude than here in Cuzco. You should go."

Auntie M frowns. "Y no mumbling."

"I don't mumble."

Leor pulls out a business card from his shirt pocket and turns to Auntie M. "And when you're ready for tomorrow, just--"

He gives her the card, then smacks the front bell desk two times and smiles. "--give me a ring. Chau chau."

We wave our goodbyes, then Auntie M and Claudia start handling the matter of the rooms. Out the window, I watch as Leor lingers to wipe a blemish off the hood of his car with a chamois while a procession of cars keep honking behind him.

Listing towards the front desk, I'm startled to find an ancient bell man, thin as a rail and with a saintly smile, standing beside me. Looks like he came with the building. He starts to grab at my heaviest luggage (Big Boy), which has been working on my scoliosis ever since I first packed it into Gus' Mini.

Guilt button activated. He's shorter than I am, built like a whippet, and should be retired by now. After we trip up on a luggage grab dance, I latch onto Big Boy. I got this. He grabs the easiers and Auntie M takes the easiests.

When we head past the elevator towards the stairs, Auntie M casually mentions some important information. "The elevator is no working. Es only two floors, though."

Blood pulsates through my temples as Big Boy's wheels bang against the steps. This could get real bad, real quick. Our ancient bell boy man vaults ahead like his muscles are made of wrought iron. What the hell? Mine feel more like hyper-atrophied Kobe beef.

Ahead of me, Auntie M's well-contoured legs stop. She sets down her bags briefly, adjusting her grip, then looks back at my crimsoned face. "Is you all right?"

Ego taking damage, I'm beyond trying to play it cool. "Fine. . . move it." When she wheels around, one of her travel bags pops me square in the puss. "Ow!

Now you're hitting me?"

"Aye, eh-sorry. Es you okay?"

"Fine!"

"You sure? Your face--"

"Is my nose bleeding?"

Her eyes take stock. "No. But your face es turning purple. Es actually a good color for you."

"--Just. . . go!"

Remember, relax and don't have a stroke. Somewhere above eleven-thousand-feet. Over one-third the way up from Everest. How do those Sherpas do it? Maybe I should acclimatize?

I gasp, imagining a smiling Sherpa telling off some rich extreme tourist swaddled in state-of-the-art climbing gear, huffing up a makeshift ladder over a crevasse. "Get up there, you big pussy!" in Nepalese. Cerebral edema. . . now, that's the way to go.

Just. . .

A. . .

Bit. . .

Fur. . .

Ther. . .

#

"Aye. There. You sees it, now. Twelve cuts."

Auntie M's pointing out the Hatun Rumiyoc, the great stone, irregularly notched in twelve-points and precisely fitted in the wall on one of the best-preserved Inca roads in Cuzco, not far from the Plaza de Armas. I push my glasses back and squint. "I don't see it."

"You es just going to have to look harder for the points, then, esn't you, Dougito?"

After some seconds, my imagination dissolves, coaxing the real image into shape. Impressive. Makes me wish I knew a thirty-third degree Freemason to explain its intricacies. But ignorance triumphs.

"Encreible." A self-conscious tongue twist between my teeth.

Auntie M cocks her head in thought. "Incredible is increíble."

"Oh, thanks."

"De nada. And the cuts of the stone is. . . very. . . delicated."

"Delicate?"

"Gracias."

Auntie M looks up while cupping her hand to catch the first droplets of rain. "Hungry?"

"Famished."

The light sprinkle grows into a steady rain as we tread towards the Plaza de Armas. Auntie M is wheezing like a pug running an ultramarathon. I stop. "You okay?"

She bends down, hands on knees. "Sí. I needs. . . to be in better shape."

I shrug casually, while rasping like my lungs are caked in motor oil. "Nah, the altitude effects everyone differently."

"Six months ago. . . I has a kickboxing class. . . I lost six kilos, but. . . then my gym membership runs out."

"You're fine."

"I'd like to train for a half-marathon. My goal is. . . eight kilos." Auntie M composes herself.

"I said, you're fine."

"Really?"

A piercing voice: "I want to die in Cuzco!"

Bewildered, we look around at the plaza's statues and architecture draped with Christmas lights before seeing the disheveled street vendor with the large, colourful umbrella.

He barks out again. "I want to die. . . in Cuzco!" Then he points to a large booklet he's cradling.

Okay. Well, I'm not gonna stop you, dude.

Auntie M and I exchange glances, then cautiously shuffle over, both to find a dry space and satisfy our curiosities. His matted hair points everywhere, jutting out under a stylized do-rag as he does his best carnival barker routine. Flipping through a laminate binder hanging from his neck by a bungee cord, he points to pictures of bright, succulent dishes while speaking conversational Spanish and pointing to the restaurant's entrance.

Watching my eyes glaze over, he switches gears, telling his young life's story in English with the faint tinge of an accent. Dropped out of university. Backpacked all around North Africa and Central and South America. Got a girlfriend in Lima.

He rattles off impeccably-sounding Italian. Auntie M laughs and nods knowingly. "Sí. Sí. Sí. Sí. Sí."

After three months, his girlfriend dumped him. But he's never, ever going back to Trieste. Not over his own dead body. "I want to die in Cuzco!"

He turns more picture pages, then gestures towards the restaurant entrance with a pleading grin.

I recognize the desperation, sensing a kindred spirit. Especially having just bent my retirement plans sideways and backwards to make this trip. Who knows, maybe this is how I'll wind up? With a glance towards Auntie M's grin, I look back at him and nod. "Okay, we'll try it." Helluva sales technique.

As we head into the darkened lobby, I turn to Auntie M. "You understand Italian?"

She adjusts her eyes and looks around. "Más o menos."

Auntie M requests a window seat so we can admire tourists on the Plaza de Armas as they get foodie mugged by our new Italian amico. The outer ring of window seats is lightly packed, but there is a larger gathering further inside, where I can just make out a stage with four Peruvians in traditional sierra garb playing folk music on zamponas, a type of high-pitched panpipe.

After ordering drinks, I take in the pungently novel food smells. The smartly-dressed waiter pours a bottle of beer into a semi-clean pint glass and nods regally.

Auntie M looks over at me. "You wants the empanada? Es like a meat turnover. Es rico."

I scoop a menu off the table, hemming and hawing as I pretend to read it. The waiter leans in between us, his stubby pencil and scratchpad at the ready.

Finally, I nod. "Sounds good."

After Auntie M orders in Spanish, the patient waiter tucks the menus under his left armpit and flees.

She curls her lips and raises her glass of Chicha Morada, an Andean purple corn drink. "Here es to eh-starting the diet. . . mañana. Salud."

I hoist my Cusqueña beer, watching the foam dissipate. "Salud."

We turn and look outside at the murky storm clouds coalescing. I swoosh my glass around and grin, admiring the beer bubbles circling. "The sky's changing, not unlike the sea."

Auntie M gurgles and Chicha Morada shoots out her nose. She quickly reaches for her napkin, re-composing herself as we giggle like nervous school children. "Claro."

Our gazes whip stage left as a sprinkling of applause breaks out from the inner sanctum. With a polite bow, the folk band's lead singer announces they are taking a short break.

Damn phone messages buzzing again. An instinctive answer, against my better judgment.

A familiar, yet sinister, voice. "Doug. This is Larry. You'd better be calling me back me toot sweet back or Human Resources is gonna can you so--"

CLICK.

I'll smooth that over later.

Auntie M's nonplussed. "What es that?"

"That?" Sloshing the beer in my glass, calmly. "That was a Nigerian prince telling me I can make ten-thousand dollars a month working from home and all I have to do is wire fifty bucks to his overseas account. Sounds like a steal. You think I should do it?"

She frowns, completely flustered. "¿No entiendo?"

"Bad joke. Sorry."

We look away from each other, pretending to admire our surroundings. A waiter walks past with a spit-roasted guinea pig splayed out on a large platter, bloodcurdling terror the final expression ingrained on its face.

What cannot be unseen. . .

She pushes her hand forward on the table, directing her eyes at mine. "Well, this es uncomfortable."

I force a grin. "Yeah, but I can get used to uncomfortable."

Auntie M takes a delicate sip of her Chicha, then smiles, staring through me. Are my palms sweating? "What are you doing?"

"I es thinking. . ."

"About what?"

"Eh, you es a shy one, isn't you?"

My eyes roll upward and turn away. A hearty exhale. "You got me." I stop myself from fidgeting with the tablecloth. "My past feels like one big crime scene of lost opportunities and every face I see is the grand jury." Raising my glass. "But thanks for taking care of me."

"My pleasure."

Clink.

Our food arrives to the patter of clapping hands as the folk band steps back onstage. I can't help but laugh. One of them is dressed like an Andean Elvis Presley. The old, peanut butter and jelly Baconator with barbiturates version, a pillow for a paunch and a chullo on his head with lambchop sideburns for earflaps.

He gyrates with hammy gusto, belting out 'Burning Love' accompanied by his zampona-playing backup band. The crowd goes wild, shouting, taking cell phone videos, and blessing the tip jar. We munch on dinner while swathed in the sounds of laughter and good cheer.

I lick the beef juice and empanada crumbs from my fingers. "Why are you doing this?"

Auntie M's eyebrows shoot up, then she glances down at her dish. "'Cuz I likes soup?"

I tilt my head. "I mean, why did you choose to show a complete stranger around your country?"

She dips her spoon back in the soup bowl. "Porque I like doing tours. . ."

She pauses, looking me square in the eyes. "and I feel. . . eh-scares for you. You seem. . ."

"Vulnerable?" I struggle to maintain a deadpan expression as I feel my teeth grinding while she reaches for a right word. "Neurotic?"

She contorts her face. "NOooooo."

I lift the glass to my lips to keep from biting my lips. "Needy?"

She sifts her spoon around her bowl. "Eh-stupid."

I choke on my beer, coughing as I shake my head and mumble under my breath.

Auntie M looks mortified. "Eh-sorry. I meant. . . naive." A prim dab of her lips. "Es actually been really fun spending your money to see my country. Water?" She reaches for her untouched glass as I continue hacking.

I can't help but think of my dwindling funds as I smack my chest to try to stop the burning. "Nah. I'm as good as I get. Have you ever heard of a Pishtaco?"

"¿Qué? Where you hear that?"

"My travel adviser told me to watch out for them. Knowing him, I figured it's some seafood dish that gives foreigners bad gas or something?"

"No. Pishtaco is an old Peruvian legend. A vampire that sucks its victim's fat out. I think someone is, uh. . . yanking your goat."

A quick mutter. "Gus, you effing asshat."

"What?"

"Nothing."

She leans over. "No hay importa. And besides, I thinks what you did makes courage."

I've never heard that word associated with me before. "What? Heading to a foreign country so I can bumble fluck around like an idiot?"

Auntie M pauses to think, then nods her head. "Sí. Most gringos only cares abouts their jobs. You don't."

"I used to, until the new mismanagement team stumbled in and started fucking everybody over like a plague of venereal-disease-ridden locusts. Now, everyone just pretends to do their job while looking over their shoulder at the clock."

"Eh-sounds like you es better off without it."

"Maybe. Yeah. I'm having trouble figuring out my next steps, though. What's that old saying? Other countries work to live. Americans live to work."

Auntie M winces just a bit, then relaxes. "We is all Americans. South Americans. Central Americans. Even you eh-strange North Americans."

I glimpse out the window and see our Italian friendito accosting another tourist couple. "So, what do you do for a living, my fellow American?"

"You means besides babysitting tourists?" She bobs her head and points to Andean Elvis and a female tourist in her sixties karaokeing to Toto's 'Africa.' Badly. "Eso."

"You're an Elvis impersonator?"

"No Dougito. I es a singer for kid's songs. I go to eh-schools all over Lima and makes eh-shows."

"Cool."

"When you es fresh out of school, maybe?" A sip of Chicha Morada through pursed lips. "But I really wants to get a Diversity Visa, to work in the United Eh-States."

I can feel my eyebrows pinch together. "Ah. The North American Dream."

She dabs her lips with her napkin. "Lots of us have two or three side jobs down here. Just to get by. It's tough." Auntie M guzzles down her drink. "I wants my shot."

I swish my beer glass, then nod over at the band. "Fair enough. Just, please, don't ask me to go up there and sing. I'd scare away every free dog in Cuzco."

"I promise."

A nod towards the band as I raise my glass. "But it does prove my theory."

Interest piqued, she watches me. "What theory is that?"

Pulling a sip of beer. "That no matter where you are in this world, somebody will be playing Toto's 'Africa'."

#

"Heeeeey-yah!" Leor the cab driver's familiar wide grin greets me as I slowly descend the stairs to the hotel lobby, sucking in air like I've got an iron lung. It's way too early for him to be so cheery.

He gives a hearty wave, blithely ignoring the cacophony of car horns while staring at the bloated bags under my eyes. "You look like shit. How'd you sleep?"

"I didn't." Groggily, I pat my stomach.

"Did you try counting sheep?"

"Not really." With a feigned smile between laboured breaths, I show off my orange pill like a carny magician casting a spell. Then, down the hatch with a green tea chaser and a hearty belch. "Feeling a bit. . . light-headed is all." That and last night's empanada sank like a beef-and-melted-cheese stone straight to the pit of my stomach.

I glance at an old Japanese man, decked out with a Hawaiian shirt and fanny pack, seated in front of a framed picture of Iquitos from the air, being swallowed up by the emerald jungle. He's sipping mate de coca in between gasps for breath and blank stares, like he needs to catch up on an afterlife's worth of sleep. The most miserable man in Cuzco.

Leor gives me a strong handshake and a pat on the back. "Up for a little dawn patrol, eh?" His smile ebbs as he inspects my face. "Go get some mate de coca."

I dart my eyes at the tourist. "Is that guy okay?"

Leor turns, then rattles off some Japanese. The man doesn't move, like he's condemned to a padded lobby electric chair. A few Japanese words finally stumble from his mouth.

"He's fine." Leor turns back to me, looks over my shoulder and grins. "Heeeeey-yah!"

Auntie M descends the stairs sucking lungfuls of air.

She and Leor speak Spanish while we head to the front desk for check out. We both lean over as he pulls out a couple of Peru Rail tickets from his front pocket and hands them to Auntie M: Ollantaytambo Estacion de Tren. Peru Rail:

'Sra. Magma Rotteri' y 'Sr. Jon Tesh.'
Auntie M mutters under her breath. "They miss es-spelled everythings."
I gaze at my ticket in disbelief. "Jon Tesh. Seriously?"
"I no es married."

We turn to each other and start giggling. Leor rushes over and tamps the desk bell twice. "¡Vámonos!"

#

"Come vanno le cose?"

I'm in the back seat, listening to Auntie M get an impromptu Italian lesson from Leor. We make the ninety-minute, two-lane jaunt arcing through lush, arcadian vistas hemmed in by an omnipresent chain of mountain peaks.

"Come vanno le cosa?" Not bad to my ears.

"Cose."

"CosE."

"Bueno. Piacere di conoscerti."

"PiaCHerE di conoSCerti." She sounds like she's re-playing an Italian movie role in her mind, like she has to sound like Giuletta Masina in 'La Strada'.

Leor's ever-present smile. "Good. Now how about a fun one. Figlio di puttana."

"Figlio di puttana."

"Eccellente."

I wonder if that's just how it goes. Does Leor speak the same way in each of his languages, or is he playing different characters? Maybe that's what accents are for?

I can't think too much about it, though, seeing's how I'm retching into a 'Mutant Ninja Turtles' lunch pail.

Leor looks back from the rearview mirror. "You know, I don't want you to get a big head or nothing, but you throw up really quiet-like."

My vomit session continues. "Thanks."

"You see?" He turns around. "It's amazing. It's like he's wearing some puke silencer or something."

Leor keeps smiling, perky as ever while I continue puking. "There's so much to see around here. Chincheros. Textiles. Moray. Incan Terraces. Maras. Salt ponds. Hey, did you know that we have over three thousand types of potatoes, Mister Jon Tesh?"

He chooses a straightaway to tilt his neck back and look at me barfing. "It's too bad we can't stop here."

Turning around, he twists his driving amulet, a picture of The Virgen de Sucorro, away from the rearview mirror and stares back at me. "Cazzo. It's a good thing my son forgot his lunch pail, heh?"

I continue going with the flow and he points his finger upwards. "You need the pasando de cuy."

Auntie M muffles laughter while shaking her head in disgust.

I cough out a fine string of spittle onto Donatello's purple mask. "What's pasado del. . ."

His smile grows. "Guinea pig x-ray. A healer, he or she, usually she, passes a live guinea pig over your stomach, soaking up all your bad spirits."

"Really? And I'm healed?"

"No. Then she has to cut open the cuy and read its innards to see what sickness you have. Hahahaha."

Auntie M looks back. "Es eh-stupid."

"You can go ahead and keep that lunch pail, Mister Jon Tesh."

The finger lifts up like an exclamation point. "Oh, there's a peanut butter and jelly sandwich and apple juice back there in case you get hungry."

Auntie M looks over her left shoulder back at me, then over at Leor. "Pobrecito. When do we gets to Olly train eh-station?"

Leor listens to me clean out my stomach and jerks his chin in my direction. "Not soon enough. Hahahahaha."

#

Ollantaytambo's train station men's restroom is a well-worn sanctuary of hygienic chaos. People of every stripe squeeze, push, plod and queue for the precious real estate that is the toilets, half of which have Out of Order signs.

After delivering my goods, I hold my breath and elbow my way to the wash basin, between a young man in a blue kurta plucking his nose hairs and a middle-aged English prof-type in a tweed sport coat weaving his hair with a multi-coloured comb the size of a small broom. Stepping out and sidling by the touristic masses milling around a small cafe, I find Auntie M blearily watching a dishevelled tourist with blond hair splayed out like a lopsided bale of hay frantically arguing with himself. I tug her elbow.

She glances at me, then back to him. "How es you feeling?"

I pat my tummy. "Like someone poisoned my empanada."

"Naw. Es the soroche. You was a eh-stupid huevón, drinking beers at altitude."

Smiling. "Hey, you watch your language."

The tourist starts screaming, cursing F-bombs at someone no one else can see while admonishing them to Get up and fight! Then, shivering, he turns mid-stride, revealing a wireless earpiece in his other ear. I nod. "All this new-fangled technology is a Godsend for the mentally ill."

She looks at me like I've crossed the mental Rubicon. "Why?"

"Because now you can talk to yourself in public and no one will think you're batshit crazy. No phone, they lock you up."

We both back up a step as the scruffy flaneur goes on an expletive-laced onslaught.

"But give the mentally ill a smartphone and 'WHOOSH!'" I wave my hand in front of Auntie M. "They're important. Wanted. Socially acceptable."

She cocks her head to one side like I've squeaked a fart.
Smiling, I scan around at all the potentially aberrant humanity schooling about. "Anyways, enough about our fine institutionalized friends. Where do we go from here?"

Auntie M swivels her head, scanning the myriad of itinerary signs. I suck in a gulp of crisp, sunny air, inhaling a tincture of Auntie M's perfume. Nice.

I step closer just as she bounds away only to stop to point at a digital wall-mounted train schedule, then twists her neck back towards me, chestnut hair flowing round her face. "Eso."

With a keen lack of guile, we move through wrong lines and dead-end queues, before embarking onto one of PeruRail's cerulean trains.

#

"We met online," the woman says with an Australian accent. Her name is Mary and she points to her beau, Louis, who's from Seattle and looks like the Monopoly Man minus the monocle. They're both in their sixties and he has a tube stuck in one nostril extending down to a wheeled oxygen tank.

The four of us share a small table in the economic expedition class, admiring the ample windows as we glide by a chocolate-brown river. A wall speaker plays Peruvian flute folk songs, making it seem like we're double-dating at a Peking opera.

"We have been to every continent together, except South America." Mary clasps Louis' hand.

"And Antarctica of course," Louis adds with a mousey squeak.

"Really," Auntie M chimes in.

Cute couple, I muse, rinsing away this morning's aftertaste with a toothbrush and a dixie cup filled with Pellegrino water.

Mary looks into Louis' eyes. "And we're not going to let a little thing like Louis having an embolism stop us from our dream vacation. After this we're going straight to Puno."

"Lake Titicaca here we come!" Louis is swept away in a coughing fit, turning his face purple and bursting a button off his casual dress shirt. Mary pats his back, then nods at me. "You're a quiet one."

Auntie M looks over. "Es his eh-stomach."

Here we go.

Nothing elicits a total stranger's opinion faster than the topic of gut health. Since the onset of my stomach problems, I've heard it all. The Flu. Altitude. Too much Pisco. Food poisoning. All well meaning-guesses by well-meaning people channelling their inner surgeon generals.

The cure theorems are even more varied: Black tea. Cocoa leaves. A local herb called Muña. Anti-diarrheal pills. Cipofloxacin. Loperamide hydrochloride. Don't eat vegetables. Only sopa de pollo. No local water or ice.

So, when Mary tilts her head, I know the name of the game. "Ah yes. The soloche. Staying hydrated is the key, so drink lots of water. What you need are chlorophyll drops and, uh. . ." She turns to Louis. "That paracetamol thingee?"

Louis doesn't skip a beat. "Tylenol."

Mary looks endearingly at her beau. "Aw. Louis is such a wiz with remembering names."

I place the toothbrush into the dixie cup and slide it to the corner of the table. "Chlorophyll? Thanks. I'll try that."

"'Course you should be fine in Aqua Calentes." Louis' eyes pan around the inside of the coach. "Do they serve lunch on here?"

"Again?" Mary looks at us with a pleased-as-punch smile. "Louis eats like a horse."

"Oh--" Auntie M squeaks while pulling out her ruby-coloured backpack. She haphazardly places our stuff on the table: Chocolates. String. Breath mints. Nail clippers. A mirror. Leors son's sack lunch.

Louis' eyes scan down, then light up as she hands him a neatly-wrapped PB&J sandwich and a cute little box of OJ.

With the face of a child at Christmas, he looks at me while greedily unwrapping the sammy. "Boy, howdie. You even got the crust cut off!"

Mary gently strokes Louis' back as he pops the plastic straw into the orange juice box and starts slurping. "How long have you two been married?"

Auntie M recoils. "Aye. We no es married. We just. . ."

She stares over at my bemused face. Could we? Is it possible to make wholesale life changes, or are we all consigned to living in the confines of our genetically-induced failures?

A thoughtful pause, then she tilts her head at Mary. ". . . Meets online as well."

We did?

Mary leans forward over the table like she has a secret for Auntie M. "Do you believe in. . . kismet?"

"¿Qué?"

Conspiratorially, Mary leans back with Louis' free arm bracing her. "The ever-shifting layers of the human aura. You know. . . destiny?"

"Yeah, destiny!" A piece of bread falls into Louis' lap as he heaves and hacks from another coughing fit.

I perk up. What's this?

Auntie M smiles. "Sí, but not for me. I believes I flipped off my soulmate in rush hour traffic years ago."

I slump back into my seat. Gut shot.

Mary nods. "Well. . . that's nice, too." Then she pats Louis' back as he blocks his mouth with his biceps and hacks away. "Don't get excited. You'll burst another button."

#

"One tuk tuk bloke is cut in half and dies on the spot. The other chap's leg is split in two pieces for his troubles."

"Mmmm. Superb. You should try them with ze garlic butter."

What?

Ever lose yourself in someone else's conversation?

Auntie M and I enjoy breakfast on the lively, sun-filled patio bar cluttered with European sports memorabilia. We arrived at Aguas Calientes, the gateway to Machu Picchu, yesterday.

After checking into our hotel, we lazily amble through the standard tourist fare: perusing the myriad eateries, shops, and crafts markets, before heading to Plaza Manco Capac and taking a shameless selfie posed next to the outstretched arms of a large statue of Pachacutec. 'Bienvenidos a Machu Picchu.'

But now I'm forcing down a spork morsel of a pork omelette while Auntie M scolds me for ordering a pisco sour for breakfast.

"Really?" Her eyes grow wide when the waitress plops the drink down.

"What?" I shrug. "It's for medicinal purposes only."

The aroma from the pizza oven distracts me. Lulled into a freshly baked torpor, I try to concentrate as Auntie M lists off a litany of flaws in my argument, but the shrill voices of an Englishman and Frenchman behind us captures my eavesdropping attention.

Over their mint-flavoured piscos and buttered bread, the topics du jour are mototaxis and stray dogs. The wreck occurred in some place called Urubamba, I believe.

The Englishman, from what I can gather, is a semi-retired engineer with multiple tourist businesses in Latin America, mostly catering to wealthy Euro types.

Christophe, the Frenchman, is the demented Hardy to the engineer's Laurel, chuckling as he tells chilling tales of culling stray dogs with rat poison.

The Englishman's face turns red at the punch line of how, if you should encounter an aggressive stray, you should lift your hand as if you're carrying a rock to bash its brains in.

Then they hold hands and kiss. Birds of a feather. . .

"Dougito! Has you been listening to what I has been saying?"

Crap. I bounce up in my seat. "Yeah."

She smiles at me like I'm some fly caught in her trap. "Then what did I say?"

I should've taken the blue pill. There must be a smooth way out. Reaching down to my backpack on the floor, I try opening one of its seventeen or so zippers.

Her voice grows more confident. "I'm waiting."

Not so fast. I pull it out. A brand-spanking new bottle of cherry-flavoured

Frutti Flex, Inkafarma's answer to Pedialyte.

"¿Qué?"

I pour some into my pisco until it makes a striking, blood-red mixture, then dramatically lift it up to my lips with a sly wink.

Auntie M stares, mouth agape. "Nooo."

A healthy mouthful. Not the worst concoction I've made. Eighty-proof cough medicine. And good for the electrolytes, too. "Ahhhhh." And a tip of the head and a toast to the lady. "Salud. You see? I told you it was for medicinal purposes."

"You're eh-sick."

The Englishman is yucking it up. Christophe probably just told a joke about a newborn pup being stoned to death.

Forcing a smile, I lift my glass for a toast, preparing for another sip. "I'm not the only sick one around here." My phone starts buzzing.

She tries hide a quick laugh by sniffing at the riot of flowers in the planter nearby, blithely ignoring the bees darting in and out.

I absent-mindedly answer my phone. "Hello?"

"Doug. This is--"

"Linda. I'm so glad you called." Crap.

Auntie M's eyes zig at me, then zag back at the flowers.

The spearmint gum-chewing stops. An incredulous voice from the phone. "And I'm so glad you answered. This is your verbal warning."

I shift my chair away from Auntie M. What did Gus say, again? Go big or go home. How about I've got the plague. That would certainly get the attention of the family of five behind me.

A little coughing fit for good measure as I get up and saunter between the tables. "Shucks, did I not call in sick this morning?"

"No, shucks, you did not. Again. And the times you have you've called in late."

Foreign faces from tables I'm passing by give me the look of the leper. Maybe I am starting to feel a little plaguey.

"But my alarm didn't go off."

"It's ten AM."

"It's this special medication my doctor's got me on. It's knocked me into another dimension." Yes it has. I take a belt from the pisco Frutti Flex elixir. "Linda, please have a heart. It's not like it's been my lifelong dream working at an extract plant with Larry and Tom and Jerry. Yeah buddy."

A whisper. "Ugh and bullcrap. Nobody hates this place more than me. But we gotta do what we gotta do. Which means I've gotta give you a written warning. Unless--"

"Unless. That means hope."

"Unless you can come up with a doctor's note."

"A doctor's note, eh?" I return to Auntie M's table and exchange smiles before scooting my chair a little further. I feign more coughing as the family of five bolts up, hand in hand. Probably won't even tip.

"Doug, I'd love to help you stick it to the system, but--" A desperate whisper. "Tom and Jerry are coming. Ugh. Good luck. Bye."

CLICK.

Crap. I'd been hoping to stave that off. Human Resources is gonna drop the hammer down. Soon. They're probably already compiling a new hire interview list. Younger and cheaper. Still, I can't give up hope. No surrender. Hell, I remember when I was that naive asshole on the other side of the equation.

Auntie M appears amused, running her fingers through the hibiscus. "That es quite a cough you has."

"Yeah. . . probably all that black smoke from the grill. Pizza smells good, though." I re-shift my seat and compose myself. "So, uh. . ."

She follows my gaze down to her plate: A cantaloupe, two sprigs of parsley, and a tiny jar of baby food. Wrinkling her nose, Auntie M pushes the it to the side. "Mañana."

". . . Uh, I've been meaning to ask you, uh, did you really flip off your soulmate in rush hour traffic?"

She lets out a quick belly laugh. "No, but I did quits looking for Mister Perfecto. There es no such thing."

Then, she frowns and tilts her head like she's nodding to herself. "Still, there es always regrets. And you?"

"Me? Regrets? Constantly."

"Really?" Plucking a bright flower, Auntie M lifts it to her nose for a whiff. Her eyes widen, then she casually holds out her hand and lets the flower drop to the floor. "I was popular in eh-school. Lots of friends." A big sigh. "I love kids, so I starts eh-singing, doing shows for them."

There's the slightest tremble in her voice. "Then, in my twenties and thirties, most of my high eh-school friends starts getting married. Having kids."

"That's the usual. Marriage. Followed by some kids." I try out a humorous tone to lighten things up. "Then, maybe a nice, refreshing divorce to top it all off?"

No dice. The tremble continues. "But, es like time stood eh-still for me. I'm not eh-sure what happened."

"If you wanted to, why didn't you get married?"

"I don't know." She bites her lip and points to herself. "It takes some of us longer to put on our game face. Sometimes es like I es still a teenager." She forces a smile and sighs. "But the regret es always there."

I purse my lips. Regret. That gnawing feeling I know all too well. "I hear ya'." A quick sip. "When you stop to think about it, everyone's dreams, ambitions, and fears, they're all absurd, really."

She takes a big breath, the tone in her voice relaxing. "I guess my nieces and nephews will always be my kids."

"It's okay. That's life. We're all fucked. Trapped between a shape-shifting past and a fading future. It's enough to unmoor anyone."

"Sí."

Listening to her, I relive my own social dumpster fires. Unrequited attractions. Horror show blind dates mainlined together. A nasty timeline of dashed hopes from the virtual meat market. Failure after soul-crushing failure, all mocking yearned for shattered futures never to be. After a while, it's tough to even care. How many times can a heart die before rigor mortis sets in?

And then I see it. The signal. Auntie M's hand sets down her glass of Chicha Morada, then furtively yet unmistakably occupies the centre of the table.

Even with a lifetime of failed attempts, should I give it a shot? I sip my drink, then sneak a glance down. Hand's still there. So far, so good.

It's go time. I slide my drink down, near the centre, then casually grasp her hand. I smile. She smiles. Her thumb playfully taps the inside of my palm. I hear the Englishman's voice, a mixture of shock and disdain. "My word."

I look over, following his horrified gaze.

A bullmastiff, so big it could have grown a six foot spread set of antlers, crouches like a double-jointed baseball catcher, back legs quavering like a crossfit body Nazi gone one air squat too far, as it humps its brindled bitch at the patio's edge. Right out in the open.

A moment of silence as all the breakfast goers lookie-loo.

A posh accent. "Get a room."

And then it happens.

I don't know whether it's motion sickness or the altitude, but the moose-dog pukes all over the back of his paramour. She sprints off.

He looks down at the puddle like he wants to lap it up, then over at this morning's soulmate scurrying away. After some seconds, the guileless brute bounds off after her. Snickers from the patio gallery.

I turn to Auntie M. Her face is frozen in disgust. Despite the obvious passion, this must be the single-handedly most unromantic thing anyone on the patio's witnessed. Ever.

I pull my hand back from the centre of the table. "Check, please."

#

Stopped again. Our bus is waiting to cross the narrow bridge over the Vilcanota River from Aguas Calientes.

On the street below us, kids with thin faces ham it up for us turistas. I can't help but wonder if this is play or work for them? It's tough to imagine having to rely on the compassion of some foreigner on vacation to eek out an extra Peruvian sol.

Auntie M's hitting it off with a young, good-looking Brazilian. He lays it on thick. Feeding orphans in Paraguay. Providing clean water in Bolivia. Now he says he wants to move to Uruguay and study architecture so he can house the poor.

What an asshole.

Our driver shifts the engine back into gear and we slowly move forward. One of the smaller waifs breaks free from the pack and gives chase. He climbs astride the flattened guardrail, balancing himself while waving and teetering alongside us, ignoring the huge, skull-cracking rocks jutting from the river below. The oblivious confidence of extreme youth.

A frumpy woman with a Kiwi accent giggles and waves at him. His little legs pump like pistons before he hops down, diminishing in the distance before our bus bends around a sharp left turn.

We bounce around like seated lemmings in a twenty minute uphill jaunt with vertiginous jungle views. The bus grinds to a halt in a dusty parking lot crammed to the gills with people milling around a set of gates under a green corrugated roof.

It is here, before even experiencing the grandeur of Machu Picchu itself, that the biological imperative of the modern day vacationist takes over. A primordial urge so powerful it has birthed an invention of almost incomprehensible importance for casual sightseeing.

The wheel. Language. Mathematics. Agriculture. Writing. The internal combustion engine. None of these inventions compares to U.S. patent #4530580A in 1985 (1983 in Japan). The creators, Hiroshi Ueda and Yujiro Mima, called it the "telescopic extender for supporting compact camera." Yes ladies and gentlemen, the selfie stick.

Word is the clerk charged with the selfie stick patent sat in awed silence for hours at his desk, uttering a variant of the Bhagavad-Gita, chapter 11 verse 32:

"Now, I am become Selfie Stick, the destroyer of vacations," unable to comprehend true nature of the pandemic he had wrought. Three days later, he selfied himself leaping to his death from the fifth floor of the United States Patent and Trademark Office. His name was Samuel L. Bronkowitz, JR.

Lots of strained faces and raised voices waiting while queuing up towards the promised land of Machu Picchu. Despite the blizzard of selfie-ing, most of the touristas are tense with anticipation.

And I'm feeling it, too. Despite the civilized veneer, there's always a potential energy lurking like a latent madness, in the chaos of crowds. Who are these people? How far would they go to get to the front of the line a few seconds sooner? Would they cutsies in front of me, ignoring my protests? Probably. Place a well-timed elbow at my floating rib when I'm not looking to get ahead? Quite possibly.

For some silly tourist sots, it's whatever it takes. Just get through that goddamned gate for that money shot: the one with the selfied, plastic smile composed in front of a backdrop ubiquitous in every every Peruvian Travel guide. The one that screams, I've made it to all your friends. I've been to Machu Picchu. One of the New Seven Wonders of the World.

The jostling grows frantic. Ouch! The peopleofwalmart.com couple behind me push their stroller ahead like a battering ram, baby howling at the top of his lungs. A short Scandinavian woman crashes into me as she's pushed forward by a behemoth rocking an braided rat tail mullet. The top of her bottle pops off, fizzing sickly sweet seltzer water all over my smiling Alpaca 'Como Te Llama?' t-shirt. She immediately apologizes, then looks down at my cherry- red bottle of Frutti Flex, and scowls.

That all started innocently enough. I tried one bottle after Empanadagate in Cuzco. Then it became my go-to thing to stay hydrated in the altitude of the Sacred Valley. But that was just a tease. Pretty soon, one bottle became two and pretty soon Auntie M's chiding "Really?" as I'd duck into yet another pharmacy. I rationalized it as a sort of undiagnosed electrolyte addiction. Some people like prescription opioids, but my hopeless habit is cherry-flavoured and way kinkier.

"Es you okay?" Auntie M startles me, gaping at me pouring sweat and cradling my Frutti Flex bottle like a wino with the shakes.

"Fine. Why?" My stomach makes noises like a constipated lion.

"Es just that you es paler than normal."

I fidget on the balls of my feet, my tummy's gurgling pyloric eructions drowned out by the baby's screams.

"No, think this is my usual pale. Boy, nothing wrong with that baby's lungs."

"Sí. Es chiquito."

"I feel for him." I wipe my brow and look her in the eye. "I'm great with children."

She smiles.

Taking a casual inventory around me. "Uh, so, where'd São Paulo's answer to Father Teresa head off to? What? No orphans to save on Machu Picchu, today?"

Auntie M scrunches her nose. "Huh?"

"Oh, nothing."

We both exchange a couple klutzy glances while shuffling forward. Finally, I rub the perspiration off my neck. "You know, maybe I'm not feeling so hot after all."

Then I hear it. A frustrated female voice answering an out-of-context conversation that pierces through the rabble. "Where are we? Jumpin' Jesus, did we come all this way for nothing?"

More screams from the baby. Where are we? What is that? Why do you think we've gathered here, forced together like gutted sardines as we smell each others' body odor? After all the effort it took to get here? Trains. Buses. Scaling Incan trails. Now we don't know where we are? It's too much.

I wanna stop myself, but I can't. Looking around, I flash a toothy grin. "I'm here to see the dogfighting!"

Their confused faces defy description. Good. I've got their attention. Locked and loaded, I'm all in. "Basic economics. The Peruvian Tourism Industry wasn't generating enough income so they killed two early birds and got them stoned. It's deceptively simple. Why not use all the stray curs around town and start a dogfighting league at the top of Machu Picchu?"

Blank stares. Too late to stop now. "They ship the dogs up from Aguas Calientes first thing each morning. It's all sanctioned with an octagon cage and everything. A little something extra to spice up that once-in-a-lifetime Sacred Valley experience. If you have a big Red 'X' on your ticket, congratulations, you go to the front row seats."

I smile at the people instinctively glancing at the lucky tickets in their hands. "They're probably washing the blood off the fighting ring right now. I heard it's up by the Sun Gate."

Nothing but puzzled and disappointed faces staring at me, but I take a deep breath and keep going. "Personally, I got 250 Peruvian soles on Snotz. He's the brindled, moose-sized bastard with the disposition of a wolverine whose had its nuts stung off by fire ants. You can't miss him. He likes to romance his bitch while throwing up on Hotel El Colibri's front porch every morning. That's what I'm talking about. There's no dog in all of Aguas Calientes who can take that big fucker."

Silence, then somewhere in the back, a faceless and misinformed voice cries out. "You're damn right!"

For the benefit of the lingering stares, I take a deep plug off the Frutti Flex like it's a J & B Whiskey. "All hail Snotz. Long live the king!"

With confused glances and concerned murmurs firing off all around me, I now have quite a bit more extra personal space.

It's amazing what batshit crazy can do.

Anyways, the voices in my head really wanted me to say all that. . . but I didn't. Too damn tame in the madness of crowds.

Auntie M's nudges my floating rib, breaking my dogfighting reverie. "What es you smirking at?"

I gaze at her and smile. "Oh, just thinking of something funny."

"Dougito." She rolls her eyes and sighs.

Taking another swig of Frutti Flex, I sheepishly move in lockstep with my fellow travellers. A hermit crab in an ocean of itinerant faces.

#

"Move forward." The slack-jawed gatekeeper sags his shoulders and yawns, then waves us through. Tourists clump together in a disorganized mass, overawed at the first sight of Machu Picchu's iconic dry-stone walls. Auntie M inhales a gasp of pristine mountain air and stops to open her backpack.

"¿En serio?" She gingerly pulls out a full bottle of Frutti Flex like she's handling a death adder on fire. "Does all Americanos acts like you?"

I pause, ruminating. "I don't think so? Why?"

Forgot about sneaking in that little beauty while she was in the bathroom. No cherry this time. This one was yellow and tasted like licorice, but addicts can't be choosers. I shrug. What could I do? I was caught Anise-handed.

Auntie M slams the yellow bottle back inside and zips the backpack shut tight. "¡Carajo!"

"Hey, be careful with that."

All us vacationeers are rounded up in groups of twenty, separated according to whatever languages we pretend to comprehend. Our inglés group's guide is a squat Andino with an Indiana Jones hat, polarized sunglasses, a windbreaker, hiking shoes and grey tube socks that come up to his knees like lederhosen. With the lush, green mountains feathered with cloud wisps, I half-expect him to start yodeling 'The hills are alive with the sound of music' any second now.

He calls himself Papa Juan, and we're his adopted familia for this tour. His powerful memory rattles off arcane minutiae about Machu Picchu in a nonchalant cadence every few seconds, but there's a slight whinge in his voice. It's like his brain's locked on autopilot from retelling the same old spiel.

A phlegmatic voice wafts from the back of the group. "We can't hear you!"

Papa Juan turns up the volume. "And in case anyone gets lost. . ."
He hoists his fiery red flag slung from a walking cane-sized pole.

Auntie M and I stare dumbfounded as he fields questions in French and other languages in an effortless, Leorlike fashion.

Then, he belts out, "You will all have plenty of time to explore after the tour. There will be plenty of time for pictures." With that, he walks off.

Everyone pauses, looking at each other, not quite sure if the tour has officially started or not. Finally, we fold into a line behind Papa Juan.

"Most archaeologists believe Machu Picchu was constructed as an estate for the great Inca emperor Pachacuti. . ."

Some anonymous, raspy voice from the back. "Whoah!"

Auntie M giggles, then looks around trying to find the source as she whispers, "Gringos."

I lean toward her while we plod forward. "Hey, you wanted to get your visa, remember? To join in on our happy melting pot?"

"Oh, es melted, all right."

Papa Juan's flag becomes a walking stick as he ascends a slope.

"Even though it's located only 80 kilometers from Cuzco, the Spanish never found Machu Picchu, and so it was not plundered, like so many other sites. . ."

The Voice. "These clouds are just. . . wrapping around. . . like I can swallow them!"

Everyone looks around, stifling laughter at the anonymous voice's enthusiasm. To my left a Japanese mom shushes her two teenage boys, who giggle up a storm.

I have to admit, though, those are picturesque, billowing clouds.

Papa Juan cranes his neck and balefully scans towards the back of the group. "It remained unknown to the outside world until Hiram brought it to international attention in 1911. . ."

Wait. Who's Hiram?

'GUS' PERUVIAN GUIDEBOOK'
PROUDLY PRESENTS:
Chapter Eight: Hiram Bingham and the Re-Uncovering of Machu Picchu.

Hola and felicitaciones. I wrote this on some napkins after I pissed on myself at the Dark Bar. Hope you enjoy my nude and improved fit-shaced writing style. ¡Vamos!

Hiram Bingham is a tall, pencil-neck geek who becomes assistant professor at Yale, then a senator. But when he marries his Tiffany heiress and her fluck you money he finds his life's true calling: farting around in jungles playing Indiana Jones, pissing off his Yalie buddies and getting censured from the Senate. Aye, we all has dreams.

His first expedition to Peru in 1909 ends in flailure. So, Hiram does what Ivy leaguers do: hits up his rich classmates for more dinero. He returns in 1911 in search for the Inca capital, the lost city of Vitcos.

Pffffffththththththah!

Bingham and his expedition leaves Cuzco in July 1911. A few days later, his mule train makes camp betweens the road and the Urubamba Rio, near some dude in a hut named Melchor Arteaga. Ol' Melchor's probablemente thinking 'Why is these guys crashing on my lawn?', but he's a chill dude and mentions he's seen some ruins up on the hill acrossed the river.

So, Bingham sets out the morning of July 24, 1911 with Arteaga, his new BFF.

They did all the cool comic book archeology stuff—crossing rapid rivers, hacking through hot, sticky jungles, even taking lunch with two farm Indians on some ancient terraces two thousand feet up.

Bingham probably leaves these farm dude's hut thinking 'More horseshit about Incan ruins. This sucks.', but he takes off anyways. And in the deep jungle above, Bingham makes his breathstinking un-recovery: buildings after buildings of Inca Ruins, a holy cave, and a three-sided temple with granite ashlars cut just like them buildings in Cuzco.

On his first attempt, without any of that dumbass formal archeological training, Hiram Bingham finds Machu Picchu, the most famous ruins in South America. It was loco!

Durings his exploititions, Bingham removes thousands of artifacts from Machu Picchu—ceramics, silver statues, jewelry and human bones—

and takes them to good ol' Yalie University, supposedly for only 18 months. However, citing the federal case law of Peruvian antiquities, otherwise known as the 'Finders keepers, losers weepers' clause, the last of the artifacts didn't make it back into Peru's hands until 2012, where they is exhibitated at the Museo Machu Picchu, La Casa Concha ("The Shell House"), close to Cuzco's colonial center.

With the clink clank of our collective high-tech hiking junk echoing throughout the Sacred Valley, la familia gathers round Papa Juan. Wiping sweat off his brow, he looks like he could faint from boredom, but manages to point his chubby finger down at a willowy green plant with striking red shoots.

"Among the first things Hiram noticed was the vegetation. . ." The honorable Papa Juan pauses and raises his head, like he's reading from an invisible cue card up in the sky. ". . . This is Heliconia subulata. Most of the species are native to the tropical Americas, but a few are indigenous to certain islands of the western Pacific."

He takes a step back and points to a wilting seedling. "And this is-"

The Voice from the back. "Ayahuasca!"

Mumbling in the front to my right, the young Japanese mother looks on impassively as her two teenage sons snicker to themselves.

The younger son gives a surprised, "Oh!" and steps forward, clicking pictures of the pathetic-looking plant as we all watch uncomfortably.

Papa Juan rolls his eyes in resignation. "No. It's not Ayahuasca. This is a shrub."

The scrawny youngster looks crestfallen as his older brother translates that there's no Ayahuasca in them thar hills.

It's the same for every monument Papa Juan attempts to show us.

The Sacred Plaza:

Papa Juan pontificates, "The Principal Temple is an example of excellent Inca stonemasonry, with its large stone blocks polished smooth with the look of fine-cut ashlar."

The Voice. "Whoa!"

The Inti Mach'ay and the Royal Feast of the Sun:

Papa Juan intones, "Architecturally, Inti Mach'ay is the most significant structure at Machu Picchu."

The same Voice. "Like the ashes over a blood-red corpse!"

The Temple of the Condor:

Papa Juan soliloquies, "Here is a breathtaking example of Inca stonemasonry. A natural rock formation began to take shape millions of years ago and the Inca skilfully shaped the rock into the outspread wings of a condor in flight."

The Voice. "Looks like a chicken froze in midair that's melted into the sun!"

As Papa Juan heads off to our next destination, Auntie M nudges my ribs and whispers. "Mira."

I turn to see some weird fucker, high as a kite in the Andes, fondling the Intiwana Stone like he's trying to cop a feel. Wait a minute? Is that the foodie guy who said he wanted to die back in Cuzco? Can't tell. I'm always bad with faces. I turn to Auntie M. "Is that--"

She doesn't miss a beat. "Sí. Dios Mío."

Everyone gives him plenty of space to finish whatever he's doing while they try to forget what they've just witnessed. Except for the younger Japanese boy, who stops and snaps a picture of him. It's gonna make one helluva Instagram post.

As we lean upwards on the earthen trail, Auntie M falls behind with the rest

of the tourists, who are focused on selfie-ing amidst all the grandeur.

When I catch up to next to Papa Juan's firm strides toward the next monument he shows me a dour expression. Then, with a furtive glance and a whisper, he tells me the reason. His name is "That asshole 'Troy' who got deported from Italy or wherever." Well, none of the guides knows his actual name, but 'Troy' is what they all start calling him when he shows up, practically weekly, a few months ago.

At first blush, 'Troy' seems normal enough. A tad burnt out, perhaps, like any college student whose willpower crashes like a flaming zeppelin after finding out his college loans can't be written off and his PhD dissertation, a one-point-two million word Magnum Opus entitled 'Investigation of Sperm Number and Motility in Reproductively Active and Socially Suppressed Male Naked Mole Rats', complete with hand drawn pictures of rodents in all sixty-four Kama Sutra positions and written in Pig Latin, won't land him a job that pays better than a grade school janitor.

So, 'Troy' spends his post-grad years lost in a technicolour DMT haze, talking to the ghosts of dead relatives with mechanical clown faces when he's not hawking glass blown artwork at the local county fair.

Papa Juan eyes grow wide as an owl's as he flashes me a sinister grin. "After smelling 'Troy's' body wash for two months straight, we're all starting to think the Incas built Sacsayhuaman to protect Cuzco from a patchouli contact high. Everyone hopes 'Troy' gets re-deported soon to whatever fancy European shithole he comes from, but no one across the pond wants to take the blame, either."

He abruptly stops and stares at me, solemnly. "Remember, it takes an entire idiot-filled village to raise one village idiot."

Nevertheless, there's a sense of awe as Papa Juan leads our group to the familiar perch seen in every picture of Machu Picchu. He turns around where a large sugarloaf-shaped mountain is perfectly composed in the background. It's the holy grail, that money shot in the travel porn of every vacationeer's sweetest wet dreams.

'Troy' snakes his way to the front, using his hemp oil musk to nasally bludgeon unsuspecting tourists out of his way. He sidles in front of Papa Juan and stands there, eyes closed and arms crossed.

Papa Juan shakes his head, then sidesteps 'Troy' before facing the rest of the group. He points at the mountain behind.

"This peak behind me is called Huayna Picchu, which means--"

"Aliens!" 'Troy's' eyes bulge as he suddenly bursts out of his psilocybin coma.

There's an evil twinkle in Papa Juan's eyes as his lips curl into a Grinchy smile. "He's absolutely right."

We all stare as 'Troy' closes his eyes and nods, obviously pleased with himself.

Papa Juan looks tempted to push 'Troy' over the ledge, but there's just too many witnesses. "It's true. The aliens travelled halfway across the universe to admire our pretty rock collection. You see, all ancient aliens have such incredibly advanced technology that we humans can't even begin to fathom, but. . ."

Our Papa sweeps his hands, slowly pointing at all of the ashlar masonry around us. ". . . their rock technology absolutely sucks. So they had to create a ripple in the fabric of space-time to come to this exact point and study how the Incas put together their stonework. Over here. . ."

Papa sternly jabs his pointy finger towards Hyana Picchu. ". . . on the top of Hyana Picchu is the secret stargate. You see that line of tourists climbing up it? They are life's winners because they paid the extra twenty bucks to visit the mother ship."

I fold my arms, then hear a nondescript voice from the back. "You mean like 'Close Encounters?'"

My God. Another one. Papa Juan nods soberly. "Yes. Just like 'Close Encounters'. Once inside, they'll be blasted off to the other end of the universe in less than twelve parsecs."

It's theatrical bullshit, of course. And everybody in our group knows better. I hope. Except 'Troy', who lets out a overwhelming "Wowwwwww" as he drops to the ground in a badly-formed lotus position while locking eyes with the sacred alien landing spot.

With that our fearless Papa shows a self-satisfied grin. "All right, la familia, class dismissed. Feel free to look around at your leisure, take all your pictures, but remember, if you decide to go to the Sun Gate, it takes about forty-five minutes to an hour each way. Thank you all for visiting Machu Picchu and enjoy your time in Peru. Thank you."

With a light chorus of thank-yous from the crowd, Papa Juan glances over at 'Troy', shakes his head in disgust, and walks off. Shortly thereafter, people wander off in varying directions, others selfie themselves where they stand, but the majority stay to get that posed postcard shot.

The only problem is 'Troy' is right smack dab in the way with his back to us, facing Huayna Picchu, rocking to and fro in a seated Namaste position.

Everybody's silent, not really sure what to do. Auntie M looks at me, like I'm obviously the useful idiot that's been assigned the small task of sweeping away this fiasco.

Damn it.

Cautiously, I walk over, giving 'Troy' his space. He's crying, softly chanting as tears stream down his face. "I do believe. . . I do believe. . ."

Who knows where his headspace is at? Probably channeling all the Sacred Valley's positive energy towards some higher power. Anything to guide his strange life's journey. Something to build his soul's strength so he can slip away into the Condor Temple undetected, roast a bowl, and ponder how to come up with that precious extra twenty bucks for a ride to the end of the universe.

I gawk at 'Troy' chanting in his own lost little world, then back at my fellow vacationeers, and grimly nod. "I'd head to the Sun Gate if I were you. It's gonna be a long wait."

#

It's the edge of midnight on a funride tour from Aguas Calientes to Cuzco. The thick, flesh-filled folds twitch on the back of our bus driver's neck as he fidgets with his Panama hat. He wipes the pouring sweat from his forehead and peers past the fog roiling around the bus, out into the gloom.

And here I am, my thoughts skipping beats like a Ritalin-addicted ferret. "Not again!"

He chuckles and we're instantly slaloming into the oncoming lane for a better angle of attack on the next S curve.

I close my eyes, pressing my head against the seat in front of me and praying my traveler's diarrhea doesn't kick back in. The Peruvian soles my Handler and I saved by choosing the bus tour instead of the train now seem like a sick joke. I'm the lone gringo on a bus crammed beyond capacity, creasing mile after stomach-churning mile through the Andes. With each soul-crippling curve the bus lurches violently, provoking an outburst of frenzied Spanish from the tortured voices quailing from the back.

But hey, the train would've cost twice as much.

The mind's constantly screaming, "Do something!"

But the body's glued here, trapped to this seat, basking in the hellish joys of travel.

What is travel, if not fleeing from life's normalcies? Why does my electric razor start smoking when I plug it in? What's a Delta-Wye transformer? For that matter, what is the proper etiquette for hailing a cab in Mongolia? How did my luggage make it to the other side of the Earth without me? And why am I straddling a freshly-dug pit swatting away tropical sand fleas when I could be seated on a post 1851-style toilet with all its newfangled technologies, like rolled toilet paper?   WHY?

And what's this oversized ladle for?

Where am I?

My stomach tightens. Bodies twist from the torque of another S curve.

What's that smell?

I tuck in my arms and do the calculations. Five hours walking at altitude, bookended by a full day's worth of jitney shuffles on planes, trains, and now what technically counts as an automobile. The tourist trifecta. Did I shower today?

None of this fazes Auntie M, Peru's sleeping beauty, draped on the seat to my left, head burrowed deep in her red traveling jacket. A strand of spittle vibrates on her tucked chin as she snores, blissfully unaware of the psychotic breakdown afflicting anyone awake.

Up front, the driver exchanges glances with his thick-jowled wingman, who plays whatever strikes his fancy from the comfort of the boombox perched on his lap. The DJ wannabe flashes a devious smile. Suddenly, ear-splitting Andean flute opera cranks up from the battered boombox perched lazily on his lap.

High-pitched screams from the back.

Now what?

The playlist instantly shuffles to fare from ABBA, Journey, The Beatles, and some Phil Collins thrown in for good measure.

I'm in hell, bound to this seat, heart thundering through my sternum. What's going on?

I look back just in time to see an old lady slap some young guy so hard his chullo flies off.

Was he too handsy?

The brim of a cowboy hat pokes the back of my head, and a wrinkled face juts past me, mottled lines creased with age. A spastic finger shakes circular jabs at the driver's back, drilling home some urgent point.

Is this normal?

Wait! Calm down. This is my fault. I should have known better than to wake up one morning, take a hard look in the mirror, then head to the first place picked at random by a drunk at my favourite dive bar.

Never mind that dead-end job I ghosted. That's so last week. Now I'm a world traveller, an expat. Sounds so exotic. Worldly. Cultured. Broke. No house. No pension. No future.

When the adrenaline's pumping you come to realize that life is nothing but a series of happenings on a blade's edge, and the nitty can turn gritty before the whiplash sinks in. It's times like these a man and his bus full of closest compadres can easily get themselves killed while listening to 'Sussidio' way up here in the fine Andean air.

Everybody hates travel stories. Especially the insipid details and insignificant incidents, such as, for instance, falling off a precipice sometime after midnight from a mile up in the Andes.

Our driver could take us straight off this cliff yawning out beyond his windshield, and he might not even care. Anything to quell this Quechan version of 'Mutiny on the Bounty' wailing from behind him. A little zigging when he should have been zagging, then a fleeting, final nanosecond of wide-eyed, doomed clarity. The wheezing sound of thirty sphincters puckering in unison as we crash against the escarpment, churning into an eggbeater of dashed dreams, bashed brains, crunched bones, and ripped arteries. Then, a final banshee's shriek in our collective psyches as our bodies break apart all set to the beat of 'Dancing Queen'.

But death is the ultimate once-in-a-lifetime opportunity, where all things conspire against immortality. And the locals have a saying when riding buses up here: it's better to arrive a little late in this world, than early in the next. We arrive in Cuzco more than a little late, but still early enough for our flight out. . .

. . . and I saved 200 Peruvian Soles. About sixty U.S. Dollars.

'THE GUS'S PERUVIAN GUIDEBOOK' PROUDLY PRESENTS:
CHAPTER EIGHT: THE CONQUEST OF THE INCAS, PT. 1

It's a Pizarro World.

They hads a statue of Francisco Pizarro in Lima's Plaza Mayor, all buffed out like a roided-up superhero in full body armor and posing on his warhorsie. It was a rionic tribute, 'cuz if Pizarro really sucked at something, it was horsiebackriding.

The statue gots moved, because, well, Ol' Francisco's Inca skullflucking invasion reminds Peru's peeps of they not-so-happier-times. But Pizarro gots his not-so-happier-come uppance as well, when rival psychopaths chops Frankie into itty bitty bloody Marquis bits a few yards from the plaza one fine Sunday morning in 1541, just in time for mass.

Lighten up, Francis.

The story of the conquest of Peru has enough theft, murder and rape to make even Stalin puke. Just for sheered ballsiness, Pizarro's South American Bang Bus Joyride of Ultimate Conquest is right up there with Ghengis Khan's Harvey Weinsteining massed rape-a-thon of Eurasia, Alexander the Great Sociopath's Theban Holocaust, Tecumseh Sherman's scorched-earth disco party march to Savannah, or even Elon Musk's unleashing of that crappy Model X unto our world.

If Frankie hadn't gotten himself Julius Caesared that fine Sunday morning he coulda been a corporate criminal contenda. A little sprinkle of PR fairy fart dust from K Street here and some re-branding bullshit there, just the way our beloved media jackal-offs likes to play with theyselves, and Pizarro might be re-knowned today as the George Washington of the Andes, instead of a berserking psychobot with a giant halberd shoved up his fat ass, sideways.

After alls, what is more heartwarming than this Dr. Cop A Feelgood story of an illiterate pig-farming bastard from the shathole of Extremadura makin' whoopee on himself through the conquistador's 'slaughter on the job' vocational assistance pogrom?

Cool Story, Bro!

How did Peru get to be called Peru? The Gus will tells you. Is 1522 and Pascual de Andagoya is sailing, Piña Colada in hand, along the coast of

Colombia, looking for a tribe called Virú or Birú; and when you is fitshaced and can't say Birú, why not say 'Perú'? So, a mish-pronounced name of a tribe in Colombia becomes the name of an entire country. ¡Increíble!

A Mafia Family for the New World.

Is 1524 and Pizarro and his brony, Diego de Almagro, is hanging out in Panama, smokin' blunts and talking up Hernan Cortes' epic Aztec Empire buttkicking adventure, when theys catch that conquistador fever like a bad case of the clap.

They decides to head out on two exploiditions along the west coast of South America, but after a four year tour of farting around all they accomplish is getting most they crew killed in new and exciting ways. Howevers, on that fateful second trip, they hear wonderful third-hand news about a great city in the mountains, just begging to be looted. . . uh, converted.

When Pizarro heads back to Spain, King Charles is so impressed that Francisco's still breathin' he awards him governorship of any cool new lands he finds. Diego de Almagro, remember that name, can't stick his nose up the king's ass like Frankie does and gets to rule any territories that Frankie thinks sucks.

Now Pizarro's ready to kick ass in earnest. He brings his boy band of brothers back with him to Panama, forming The New Kids on the Block of Shathole World Conquest: Francisco is the leader one; Hernando is the charming one; Juan is the tough guy warrior one; Francisco Martin de Alcantara, the donkey-flucking, half-bastard one; and Gonzalo, the homicidal berserker one.

The Gus's Guide To New World Conquest.
New World Conquest Rules Number One: Gets lucky.

When Pizarro first sets sail, the Inca empire is ruled by Inca Optimus Prime, Huayna-Capac. His badassery stretches almost three thousand miles, from central Chile to modern day Colombia.

While fighting the tribes in the great green North in Colombia, Huayna-Capac hears about the tall, fartknocking foreigners from the sea. But, sadly for him, he never gets to see the fun of mass genocide unfold in person. He croaks from some shitty disease around 1527. Coulda been smallpox. Coulda been a bad case of gingivitis.

New World Conquest Rules Number Two: Take Advantage of Chaos.

Inca Huayna-Capac's death forces the Inca empire in a mutual nutchopping contest, like something out of the BME Pain Olympics. The Inca's son, Huascar, makes himself ruler of the capital city Cuzco. Atahualpa, the younger brother, becomes the northern city of Quito's leader. After a couple years of brooding quietude, is time for Huascar and Atahualpa to make they best Cain and Abel impersonation and go after it.

When uncivil war breaks out, Atahualpa has the badass generals, making him the designated asskicker. Huascar has no badass generals, making him the designated fleeing bee-atch. After Huascar gets his shit pushed in at the Battle of Quipaipan, Atahualpa marches southwards like a degenerate Santa Clause in a Macy's Thanksgiving Day Parade float filled with reprobate elves.

When Pizarro hears about the civil war, they is a raging boner of new world conquest schwinging deep in the loins of his chainmail. After alls, that same divide and fluck off model was how his second cousin, Hernan Cortés, got over on the Aztecs twelve years earlier.

New World Conquest Rules Number Three: Play Opponents Against Each Other.

Provings the case of rule #1, Pizarro rolls into the mountainside campground of Cajamarca at the samed time and place when Atahualpa just happens to be hosting a rave party celebrationating his badass victory in Cuzco. After taking away his glow sticks, Atahualpa's messengers tell him all about the conquistadors doing what conquistadors likes to do: abusing natives. But he's too busy enjoying his little uncivil war party to worry about some bearded pissants. Whoops.

Carajo-marca!

"Prepare your hearts as a fortress, for there will be no other." - Francisco Pizarro

When the Spanish force reaches the flat, green valley of Cajamarca, Pizarro realizes he and his 160 peeps have marched into an '¡Oh mierda!' moment. They is in the shitmidst of an army in prime butt-kicking form, which Hernando Pizarro guesstimates at forty-thousand, but most likely is over eighty-thousand. No sense getting your fellow conquestadors all depressed and stuff.

But Cajamarca square is perfecto for the Spaniards' planned surprise attack to capture Atahualpa. When morning goes by and there's no sign from the natives, the conquistadors starts getting the super jitters until one of Atahualpa's pleb messengers arrives, saying that the Incas is gonna arrive fitshaced and unarmed. Shwing. Music to a conquistador's ears.

After a late night of jello shots, Atahualpa's army walks off they hangovers and by midday fills the entire plain with men. Is a bummer for them Spaniards, who is staring out from they ambush spaces in the town square, all sneaky like. Pedro Pizarro recalls: 'I saw many Spaniards urinate without noticing it out of pure terror.' Aye, I'll take the two-ply chainmail, por favor.

So, Atahualpa smells the plains full of piss but sees no Spaniards, so he calls out "Where is these bearded dickwads at?" or something to that effects.

Time to fire the cannons. The Spaniards charge straight into the unarmed natives. Trumpets blare as the Spanish troops give they battle cry 'Remember the Ala. . . uh, 'Santiago!' The conquistadors are decked out like 2Pac in 'California Love', placing rattles on they horses and with big boomboxes playing Iron Maiden's 'Run to the Hills' to terrify the Indians.

With the noise of the cannon shots and the trumpets and the horsies and the epic rap battles, the Incas panic. And that's when Francisco 'The Governator' Pizarro flexes his grapefruit-sized biceps and grabs his magical flaming sword Justice to enters the thickets of the battle. Once he reaches

Atahualpa's litter, he snatches the Inca's left arm and shouts "Remember The Alamo, uh. . . Santiago!"

Each Spaniard gets they butchering on, slaughterhousing an average of fourteen or fifteen defenseless natives apieces. The only wound them Spaniards sustains is Pizarro, who chafes his self from overflogging his Boner of Ultimate Conquest.

Phew. Rough day to be an Incan.

The Ransom.

Atahualpa . . . 'asked whether the Spaniards were going to kill him. They told him no, for Christians killed with impetuosity but not afterwards.'

Anyways, the Inca offers his famous ransom, 'a room measured 22 feet long by 17 feet wide, and filled to a white line half way up its height' full of gold. He would also give the entire hut filled twice over with silver.

So, the conquistador's gold booty train starts chooh choohing into the city. 'On some days twenty thousand, on other days thirty thousand, fifty, or sixty thousand pesos de oro would arrive.'

If Atahualpa's thinking, "Is been fun, guys, now time to takes your gold-plated party gifts and go home" then he didn't gets the flucking memo. Captain Almagro, staying true to form, comes up with a long list of reasons why they should kill Atahualpa, the first ten beings that Almagro thinks murder is fun. . .

---

* "You can't help but compare yourself against the old-timers. Can't help but wonder how they'd have operated in these times." - No Country for Old Men

GOOD NIGHT, SWEET CACIQUE.

. . .So, Atahualpa gets condemned to die, causalings an argument 'bout whether he should be strangled or stabbed and burned. Both is nice, but personally, I'd prefers death by 'Carpophorus' rape giraffes', . Although I is sure that overseas shipping and training a large male giraffe to burgle a noncompliant bunghole to its death at 9,000 feet in the Andes would proves damn near impossible in those barbaric, pre-internet times*.

Aye, sadly, the pissed-off conquistadors has to settle for stranglulating him on a bright, sunny day on July 26th, 1533. The followed up morning, his body is brought to the church with neat-looking crosses and all decked out in that fancy religious stuff. While all the Inca chiefs is bummed out about they leader getting snuffed, they is pleased by all the poop and circumstances that went into it, thanking the Spaniards for going to all the trouble of murdering their Inca Lord with such great fanfare.

Aye, it is the little things in this life, uh, death.

"You can't help but compare yourself against the old-timers. Can't help but wonder how they'd have operated in these times." - No Country for Old Men

83

AREQUIPA

Chilcano de Pisco:

Ingredients:

2 ounces Pisco
1/4 ounces Lime Juice
5 drops Angostura Bitters
Ginger Ale

Preparation: Add all ingredients save for the garnish to a Collins glass and fill with ice. Stir until chilled. Garnish with a lime twist.

Alcohol can save your commute.

What? Can't be right. Must've missed a conjugation somewhere. What are we talking about, again?

The debate roils over a patio table's worth of beers and pisco sours in Lorena's well-manicured backyard. I cock my head to the side for any familiar Spanish words and saunter in and out of the silvery glow of a dozen Chinese lanterns festooned above the raucous New Year's Eve revelers.

Shark-faced Marco, drunk as a Patagonian skunk and wearing a kitchen towel for a bib, gnaws his four rows of teeth on a pickled pig's foot while seated between the barbecue grill and a decorative Pagoda water fountain.

After a huge belch, he yells above the Morrissey playlist, at everyone in particular, followed by a full Lima minute of unintelligible, free-for-all rantings.

You have to respect Limeños' capacity for fun when they make a point of getting their entire neighborhood crocked at least once a year, filling up their Plaza Mayor fountain with 1,300 litres of pure pisco and then stepping back and letting nature take its course.

I cast a keen glimpse at Auntie M jeering in the middle of this soused mess.

This could get nasty. Everyone's drunk. Even Lorena's Chihuahua, Tippy, feels the vibe. He's hunkered down on the patio floor, ripping a decorative Christmas tree sock to shreds and growling like he's some bigshot mastiff in the Colosseum gnawing on freshly-rent blood and excrement-soaked gladiator intestine.

Any more pisco-enhanced jocularity and a sierran religious ceremony might break out. I down another pisco shot while my mind's eye darts to the fighting festival of Takanajy in the tiny town of Santo Tomas, 12,000 feet above sea level. It starts out innocent enough, with a weeklong parade of drinking and dancing. Pretty basic stuff. But the final day is the real kicker when everyone gussies up in cowboy chaps, multi-colored ski masks, each with a dead bird or a deer skull hat for good measure, then settles their small town grievances with a mass brawl on Christmas Day.

Gus' vulgar whiskey breathe taints my nose and tickles between the ears. *Aye, Duck, you is a gringo here. Never forgets that.*

At the apex of 'Bigmouth Strikes Again', I take a large step back to the relative safety of the kegerator.

"Hiiiiyaaah!" Marco struggles to lift himself up, then strikes a karate pose and blurts out how his father taught him to drive in Lima with the expression, "You must bend the traffic to your will."

After a boisterous chorus line of 'Bullshit!' and 'Cut the crap' in Spanish slang, the conversation turns to the lamentable subject of Lima's soul-crippling traffic.

With a small frat house party's worth of empty pisco glasses in front of her, Auntie M leans way back in her white plastic chair and belts out, "You just has to drive when there is no cars."

A thunderstorm of protests. Lima is over 10 million people and counting. There's always cars.

Clutching a brand new pisco glass, Auntie M sticks to her sloshed rhetorical guns like she's some hectoring barrister at a failed Alcoholics Anonymous intervention. *Just drink you pussy!*

And that's when she espouses The Drinking Saves Time theory. Like all great drunken master works throughout history, its moving parts can all be boiled down to one sacred truth, or in this case the elegant equation of demographics plus habits.

And somehow, someway, maybe Gus' smartass immersion program clicks in for a fleeting second, or maybe everyone is so shitfaced that their conversation slows down, but I actually understand Auntie M as she screams, "Like tomorrow morning. No one will be on the streets. They're too hungover."

Marco ruptures a puny pig's foot between his razor wire teeth. "Prove it." *Oh shit. I don't like where this is going.*

All eyes fall to Auntie M as she takes another pisco shot, then points at me like I'm the hunchbacked embodiment of a two-legged chancre. "Oh yeah, I es going to let the gringo drive."

There's a drunken silence. Then, astonished laughter. *I'm gonna what? In Lima?*

The murmuring dies down and they point their glasses towards me. Marco toasts. "Good luck dying, my friend."

More guffaws. I scan the merry, besotted faced. *I'm not ready for this.* But, after downing another pisco, I have a revelation: I have used a variant of this tactic back home in Oregon.

While the more spiritually enlightened spend their precious Sundays speaking in tongues to The Great Pumpkin, I, pagan that I am, burn rubber, morally bankrupt but giddily free before Portland's unfettered highways turn back into a glorified parking lot. The start of the Super Bowl is another time to put this theorem into practice, maybe even tackle the weeks grocery shopping before the drunken slob mob takes a halftime break from their Athlete-Privilege-Industrial-Complex worship.

Sure, you can get whipsawed if enough people are jibing with your logic and take to the streets en masse, but, in the case of Lima's love affair with pisco, if you can't count on the sanctity of a holiday hangover, what in the world can you trust?

So, on New Year's Eve, Auntie M and I have it all planned out. Satisfied and piss drunk, I turn in early. Keeping to Peruvian tradition, she stays up into the wee hours chatting with family and friends, keeping a nervous eye peeled towards the window as her neighbors try blowing up their barrio with an impressive arsenal of illegal fireworks.

#

Even as I'm buckling up and adjusting the driver's seat of the Yaris, what I'm going to attempt barely seems real. Painfully stupid, yes. Tantalizingly fun, definitely. But not really real. It feels akin to a potentially fatal passage rite of manhood, like spearing a lion or sticking my hand into a dirty mitt filled with stinging bullet ants. Something to bring back that eye of the tiger. (Wait a minute, forget about the bullet ants)

After familiarizing myself with the dashboard controls, I inspect the car's cramped quarters as Auntie M sits in the suicide seat, fielding text messages.

My nostrils fill with the fresh scent of spearmint from the 'Little Tree' air freshener as I nod to myself in the rearview mirror. No matter what happens, act cool. "Nice car."

"Gracias." She pauses, then puts down her phone and shoots me a concerned look. "Has you ever driven outside of the United Eh-States before?"

A big breath. "Not really."

Auntie M tightens up her seatbelt and straightens up in her seat. "Just take it real eh-slow."

"No problem."

And. . . we're off. With the *Slow and steady wins the race* mantra screaming through my head, we launch out the garage like a turtle on thorazine. Time for that dreaded first point of contact. As I'm executing my first right turn, my mantra's been replaced by *Oh, fuck!*

Auntie M yells out, "¡Oh mierda!" as I stomp on the gas and veer into the fray. Lashing my hopes onto false confidence, I start whistling show tunes, but my right foot just keeps pounding the gas pedal. I've driven only two blocks and I've been honked at once and flipped off twice. Well, thrice if you count the pedestrian, which most Limeños don't. Seems like a moral victory.

"Eh-Stop!" Auntie M screams.

The tires squeal like a pig being spitroasted as I lock up the brakes at a stop sign-looking thing next to a Wong superstore. She stares at me like I've already committed multiple felonies. "What es you doing?"

The ol' bod is contortioned upright forward with a ten-and-two death grip on the steering wheel. In my mind I was doing quite well, but maybe not? I blurt out with false bravado, "I'm bending the traffic to my will!" not looking her in the eye.

"Is you okay?"

"Fine!"

More honking from the pandemonium behind us. We both peer out at the traffic ripping through the two-way street.

With eyes as big as saucers, I glare at Auntie M. "We fucked up!"

She tilts her head. "We?"

"How was I supposed to know there were so many teetotalers in this city?"

Auntie M glares at me like I've finally driven her insane. "Teak toileters?"

"Nevermind."

"Tranqui--."

"Hold On!"

Aaaaaahhhhht. Aaaaahhhht. Aaaaaaaahhhhhhht.

Her head whips back as I hunch over, steering the Yaris through what I hope is a moving safe space through the jankiest of left turns.

At some point I re-open my eyes, just in time to see Auntie M point at a big Carretera Panamericana Sur turn off sign staring me in the face.

"¡Doble derecha!"

"Eh?"

"Turns right! Now!"

Shit. My one and only hope out of this godforsaken traffic.

I'm not really sure what happened next. My best guess is that the Yaris, sensing it was being driven by a complete idiot, goes into full-blown automotive survival mode, willing itself to jump back and to the right, like a surprised alley cat.

Before I can even soil my underwear, we've already crossed three lanes and darted between two speeding cargo trucks. Just the type that shark-faced Marco likes to play suicidal games of chicken with while winding down from a stressful day.

I've been in Lima long enough to ignore the honking. Truth be told, I'm so busy waiting for the doomsday shudder of final impact.

Fortunately, I've prepared ahead, steeling my nerves by engaging in several practice wrecks in my youth. Surely, the piddly little dent on my '82 Honda Civic's right quarter panel from careening into a stop sign at college counts as something. Sort of.

One other time, I was calmly stopped at a red light when I was swiped by a semi truck, an adrenaline spike for sure. The semi's ass end picked up my work van's frontside like one of those porcelain tea cups little psychotic girls like to play house with before they kill and bury their whole family using rat poison and a hatchet. Car wrecks are like that

But it's the first good, solid wreck in high school that was the bees' knees for me. Jamming out to AC/DC's 'Highway to Hell', I floored my parents' banana -coloured 79 Impala down a short side street, slick from Portland's interminable rains. Probably hit the vicinity of seventy when we passed my friend's house.

My friend yelled, "Stop!"

Oh, I stopped. As soon as my right foot pawed the brake, the yellow submarine lurched right, barreling into a ditch, blasting through a fence, catching air off a small boulder and skewering the top of a mailbox, running over a small forest of ferns, then carving a deep gouge in an ancient tree before bouncing back out onto the road and coming to a dead stop like a deer strafed crossing a freeway.

Pure adrenaline. Glasses knocked askew, I was bumped onto the passenger seat, dumped on my friend's lap, still clutching the steering wheel with a death grip.

After changing my underwear, I managed to get out and circle round the dead beast. The prognosis was grim: the front end was completely smashed. Radiator fluid and some greenish sludge bled out of the large gashes on its lacerated underbelly. Pieces of the car were later found in faraway neighbor's back yards like they had been shot out of a trebuchet. A beached narwhal's twisted mass of mangled metal.

Totalled.

Almost.

The radio worked, and 'Highway to Hell' was still jamming on strong.

#

Stuck in Lima's interminable traffic, Auntie M's giving me the Evil Eye. Somewhere around the Pan-Americano exit, I had drastically overestimated my driving ability. All seemed kosher at the time.

Now, we're trapped in a long line of cars, sitting ducks held captive by one of the billion-odd construction sites that pockmark the city.

After sneaking glances at Auntie M's forehead vein twitching on her reddening face, I finally give in. "Would you care to drive?"

She bolts out of the car, slamming the door in a fury. "Gets out!"

Fine. As we switch sides doing the walk of shame, Auntie M points at me and snarls, "You es cute when you es eh-scared, but you must be the eh-stupido-est gringo in the whole world!"

Did she just call me cute? Cool. "I am not!"

"Eh-scaredy cat."

Honking and the sounds of a small dog yipping seize my brain. Time for a witty comeback. "I know you are but what am I?" There. I nod, satisfied I have made some sort of a point, however stupid.

Swinging around, I spy an old lady behind the wheel of a late model SUV. Both her and her little brindle Cairn Terrier are dressed like chiffon princesses. Taking advantage of my distraction, Auntie M snatches the keys from me just as the elderly princess honks her horn and flips me the bird.

I shuffle around like a chastened pet ferret that's relieved itself on the family heirloom throw rug, before piling inside the Yaris.

Auntie M re-adjusts the rearview mirror. I shake my head, pleading my case. "I was just testing your car's performance characteristics, that's all. I wasn't trying to drive batshit crazy."

Back in the benign control of the driver's seat, Auntie M multi-tasks by adjusting her seat for leg room while yelling at me. "Carajo y concha su madre! You never drives my car! Never again!"

Sitting there, staring straight ahead at the traffic, I feel the raw nerve endings in my fingers vibrate, as Auntie M launches into a diatribe in Spanish.

Come to think of it, that was a pretty bad performance, by anyone's standards. Tilting my head down, I let out a faint chuckle. Christ, what have I gotten myself into? What if there is no job back in the states? How the hell will I get by down here, bills piling up but no money? "I'm so beyond fucked." It's all I can think of. I explode in laughter.

Auntie M locks eyes at me chuckling with a thousand-yard grin on my face like she's a bull and I'm wearing a red cape. Her voice ratchets up, washing out the car horns and that damn dog's yapping, piercing through my skull. I can't take it. "Okay, I get it! I'm grounded, all right!"

A soft, deflating sigh. I peer away. Maybe I didn't really want to learn to drive down here, after all. A sudden tsunami wave of relief washes over me as I pivot to face her. "May I do one last thing, please?"

Before she can reply, I wheel around in my seat and flip off the old lady and the dog. "There you go, lady!"

Auntie M tilts her neck back in surprise, and I nod at her with a pleasant smile. "There! Happy now? Let's go!"

"Helado? Dougito? Earth to Dougito!"

Auntie M's tone jars me from my Guinness Book of Stupid Fails and Daydreams reverie.

"What?"

I arise from my ride-along doldrums, staring in disbelief at a rash of disturbingly happy life-sized alien cardboard cut-outs holding up ice cream cones and giving the thumbs-up along Panamericana Sur.

Otherworldly.

They're the first thing you see as you pass sleepy coastal towns like Punta Hermosa and Punta Negra, "El Sur Chico", heading towards Peru's South Beach scene.

The glint in Auntie M's eyes says that this is a must-do. "Do you want an ice cream?"

Before I can say *Yes* she's cut the steering wheel and we're fishtailing through the dusty parking lot.

For research purposes, she's stopped us at Helados OVNI (UFO), which, according to local lore, is superior to its dreaded ice cream rivals, Helados E.T.

She marches right up to the counter and before my legs can fully stretch out, the grim-looking man behind the counter has scooped up two cones with the Tang-colored lucuma ice cream.

We plop down on a bench as my taste buds explode beneath supersweetened butterscotch and pumpkin.

Auntie M is in heaven, dabbing bits of helado from the corners of her mouth. "I'm not sharing mine."

I pause my scarfing and scowl. "You should. I paid for it."

"Mister Moneybags."

"Hardly," I guffaw, thinking of the daily sacrilege damning my bank account.

She looks at me and stiffens her posture. "What es the matter?"

My eyes dart away, but then meet her gaze. "Nothing."

We suffer a brief coughing fit as a huge, grey pickup filled with lucuma-loving kids kicks up the dust around us. Auntie M leans over. "If it's your driving, no worries, Lima's traffic es insane."

"So am I. That's why I thought I'd be a good match for it. But I fucked that up, too." The cone slips between my fingers and drops on the ground. "Fuck!"

Auntie M glares like I just committed sins one through eight on the Ten Commandments bucket list. "Hey!"

Pacing around the small bench, I can't stop babbling. "I can't believe I've pissed away my job, my retirement. What was I thinking?"

She glowers at the cone on the ground. Her face is like a little girl's after finding her favorite toy broken on the floor. Then, she snatches up the cone, wipes off the dirt, and starts licking.

"That's disgusting."

Auntie M licks at the cones in her hands, without a care in the world. "Five-second rule."

"Ugghh." I pinch my lips. "I can't believe how everything's turned out." I stop and reach for my cone. "Can I have that back?"

"No." She pulls back both her cones like they're made out of frozen gold. "What was you expecting?"

"Uh, I honestly thought coming down here might do some good."

"How?"

"I dunno. Make me worldly. Cultured. Are you gonna finish that?"

"Sí. So you es hoping for some kind of magic lifestyle change?"

What the hell is in those cones, crack cocaine? "Exactly. I pictured. . a not -quite-so-me type of me.."

"¿Que?"

I raise my hands. "A comfortable-in-his-skin, life-of-the-party-type posing in a blazer and khakis at far-flung cocktail parties and drinking wine spritzers. You know, delighting all my extremely important friends with my 'most interesting man in the world' travel snob stories."   Raising my hands in a Ta-da posture.

"Not this."

"I see." Auntie M wolfs down the last of her cones, licking the remnants of melted ice cream from her fingers.

"Fuck it. If I'm gonna die broke, I should enjoy what's left."

"You es being mel'an'chol'ic, Dougito."

My pacing slows to a stop, admiring her pronunction. "Good word. That's it! I'll become a hobo in Spain. I've always wanted to run with the bulls. Might as well do it now, before I'll need that artificial hip?"

"Gracias and you es the same age as me. Mas o menos. Finished with the pity party?"

I stop, hang my head and let out a deep sigh. "Yeah."

A faint chuckle. "Bien."

She gets up and throws the napkins in the garbage. "Then vamonos."

So, sated with a healthy sugar buzz, we hit full-tilt Manic Mode, streaming down the desert coast to our next adventure.

Bienvenidos to The Big South.

Peru's familiar fog kicks in, smudging out the coastal blue sky like we're driving through a photoshop filter. Parts of the South run are beautiful, but there are stretches of desert down here so forsaken they'd make Cormac McCarthy go 'F- no! Not that bleak!' Just kilometers and kilometers of dunnish brown with barrels of trash strewn along the side of the Pan American Highway, all encased in a choking, murky haze.

Auntie M's feeling carefree, though, singing along to the Beach Boys' 'Surfing Safari' as she checks out the gas gauge. "We needs more gasolina." A quick glance over at me. "This tour of yours could get eh-spensive. You sure you want to go on?"

My eyes gleam, matching my devious grin. "Visa/Mastercard. It's what shitty financial decisions are made with."

We stop off in Cerro Azul to fuel up. We catch a quick stretch of the legs on the sidewalk, watching vendors selling snacks and knicknacks to families fogbathing under bright umbrellas while perfectly-arched waves cascade at a long pier in the background.

"Es you ready for the next beach. . . Aosis?"

"Oasis?"

"Asu mierda. O-A-ses. O-A-sis. . . oasis. Sí."

I can almost hear her thinking as she collects her novel word sounds, stacking them like seashells on the beachfront property of her mind.

It's back on the road. I've managed to tie a small Ekeko Smoking God of Prosperity figurine to the rear view mirror, hoping to ward off any evil spirits and Pishtaco hitchhikers heading down the Pan-American.

Most Peruvian drivers have some totem for road protection stuck on their windshields and we were sorely lacking. Amuletless. Driving while spiritually naked. But now, thanks to this shrewd $1.50 investment, all is right with the world. The fog has blown off, and life's positivity is shining through.

Auntie M keeps the Yaris' accelerator pegged as we take in the debris-strewn town of Pisco. She runs her fingers through her chestnut hair. "A eh-size eight earthquake here eh-short while back." We glace around at the damaged houses and buildings. Auntie M lets out a soft whistle as we pass a big lot filled with dust and rubble. "The ground eh-shooks for two minutes. Lots of deaths. Over a hundred dies attending mass at the San Clemente Cathedral."

My precious. I rub the Ekeko Smoking God while watching townspeople sporadically mill about, living whatever constitutes a normal life for themselves.

No earthquakes, please.

#

"All the infinities of this world are swept up in the winds of Paracas."

Where did that come from? Sounds almost deep and kick-ass.

Auntie M adjusts her life preserver, running her fingers through her chestnut hair as the forty-two person speedboat plunges out of Pisco Bay, into gale-swept waves. "Es eh-sounds nice. Who says that?"

"Me."

"You?"

She shakes her head, vehemently. "NOOooooo. Dougito, you es un goofball. Now you es a writer, too?"

"Yes. . . well, no. Just a writer's apprentice."

The boat tour's a father-son team and they've synchronized their apparel for the benefit of us all: blue-and-white striped shirts, weather-beaten captain's hats, aviator sunglasses. The young man of the sea abruptly kills the engine.

The old man sneaks a puff off his hand-rolled cigarette, then points to a giant three-pronged dildo sketched on the hillocks to our left. "Da Candelabro dates back ta an estimated 200 BC, do' some estimates es much older."

A Rubenesque Peruvian mother, adorned with a red and tan poncho, stands up rigidly to take pictures, practically knocking over her thin, stern-faced teenage son overboard. A small price to pay for the perfectly composed shot she'll get. He looks like he's recovering from some sort of bizarre hairstyling accident, sporting a cotton gauze headwrap over his curly, black hair and an eye patch. No fresh blood, though. He'll survive.

Our co-capitan smirks. "Da geoglyph is sis hundred feet tall and was created by makin' two feet deep cuts in da petrified sand. No one knows what da Candelabra of da Andes is fer. Could be fer sailors at sea. Could be da trident of da Incan god Vircocha." He sneaks a puff from his ciggy before cupping it in his hands. "Personally, I think it looks like God's Jimson weed. Any questions?"

Before anyone can respond he nods to his son. "Good."

Junior pinches his sunglasses to his face, then guns it, knocking everyone back.

"Aye." Auntie M slams into me, squishing me against the side of the boat. I catch my breath as she peels a glaring eye my way. "Dougito?"

"Yeah."

"Where es your hands?"

"Oh! Sorry."

Everybody holds on for dear life while we blast off further into mother ocean, towards Las Islas Ballestas, competing with a small handful of other touring boats for ocean space.

At first, "The Poor Man′s Galapagos" look like a pissed-off ant colony swarming over white termite mounds. Upon closer circumspection, though, the randomized masses of gyring movement turn out to be thousands upon thousands of Humboldt penguins, sea lions, Inca terns, pelicans, cormorants, Peruvian boobies and crabs overwhelming every square inch of pewter-stained, craggy rock.

About thirty feet away from the menagerie the smell hits us like an olfactory force field and Capitan the Younger cuts the engine. We bob like a disarrayed armada of corks shoved through the bunghole of a wine cask while everyone distracts themselves taking pictures. Capitan the Elder tosses his cigarillo in the ocean. "Da Islas Ballestas is protected, so don't even think of going fer a walk."

Staring over at the assemblage of yelping seals and screeching birds and crawling crabs fighting over razor-sharp rookery space, I'm quite sure no one in our group thought about jumping overboard and taking a casual stroll, but it's good to know there that rules are rules.

The Rubenesque mother blurts out. "Why are all the rocks colored white?"

Capitan the Elder beams with pride, raising his voice above the howls of sea lions as they sun bathe. "That's shit. A round-da-clock factory drippin' tons of phosphates and nitrates. Peru's da world's top producer, far ahead of other pretenders to da throne like Chile and Namibia. We'll collect some 23,000 tons of shit dis year. As good as gold."

It turns out Peru is a bonafide birdshit superpower. Who knew?

Without warning, Capitan the Younger kicks up the engine, jerking us around the other side of the islet, which forms a small beach head bombarded by gnarly surf. Our boat rocks and rolls in the swells, while touristas take pictures of an alpha sea lion using his sledgehammer noggin to bludgeon a rival into submission.

Capitan the Elder braces his legs against the rolling waves while lighting another fag. "It's a combination of cold water, warm air currents and no rain. Da nitrates don't evaporate. Instead da guano leaches into da rock and dries in da sunshine. It's a national treasure. Peru has literally got da best shit in da whole damn world."

This arouses chuckles, but my God. Our future. I see it. Cheap oil will peak. Nuclear power will give way to wind and solar. But bird shit is forever.

"Under a constant drizzle of bird droppings, generations of hardy farmers do back-breaking seasonal work, scaling the islands narrow pathways before dawn."

The ramifications are clear to me. A pigeonshit specialist from Lima talks to a biochemist savant from Huancayo who takes a Snapchat with a leading Bolivian metallurgist who just happens to share her notes with a cutting-edge propulsion physicist from Asunción. . .

"After eight months on da islands, most workers pack up and head home for a break. Leaving behind a lone guard to protect da birds from shit poachers."

. . . And I can see it now. I was here, at sea level zero, when the nitrate-rich Peruvian booby-powered revolución formed, finally cracked the U.S. hegemony. An entire division of 500 ton Peruvian pelican dung-fueled main battle tanks tearing up the New Mexico steppes at 75 km/h, outflanking the hopelessly outmatched 1st Armored Division in the Battle of the Albuquerque salient.

"It's a lonely bidness." El Capitain the Elder. "But it is kinda nice workin' with da birds."

Panic at the Pentagon. Aircraft carriers in fearful retreat. Over 800 overseas U.S. bases, all abruptly abandoned like the fall of Saigan, under immediate threat from hypersonic Bolivian shit missiles raining down like Mach 30 comets. No defense. And coming from La Paz no less. The ultimate sneak attack.

"Da Incas were da first to collect guano, what dey called *wanu,* and anyone caught disturbing the birds was punished with death." El Capitan the Elder smiles while lighting another cig. "Now it's making a comeback. Shit has a great future."

Of world domination. I stare at the hordes of birds excreting. Constantly. Twenty-four hours a day. Every day. A clockwork colonic. A truly awesome sight to behold, like staring straight into the targeting lasers of a guano-filled Death Star that's set its sights on a defenseless solar system.

#

Back on dry land, Paracas' salty air swirls with aromas of fresh seafood being cooked nearby, so we wander from the beach area along a dirt road lined with stores.

Auntie M beams, "Eso is mi real Peru."

We step carefully to avoid the lanky naked dogs with punk rock mohawks lounging on the street.

I struggle to keep up as she pumps her legs faster, sniffing the air while her purple beret bobs along the rows of rustic cantinas and shops. "Ceviche. You want some ceviche?"

"Sure do. It smells like. . . shit!"

I delicately raise my right Brooks running shoe, inspecting the flattened dog dung.

Auntie M snickers. "Uh. . . congratulations. That es good luck."

She breaks into laughter as I start pawing my foot along the ground like a horse trying to count. "I don't believe in that stuff."

"And where has that got you?" Auntie M darts her eyes, then pirouettes, listening to a female voice belt a pop song in Spanish from the cantina up ahead. A worker in jeans and a white shirt drenched in sweat tack-welds the gaudy entrance sign while reaching up on a ladder, exposing his butt crack.

"Karaoke!" Auntie M beams.

Scrubbing my right shoe on the dirt, I walk like I've pulled a hamstring, following her towards the noise.

She stops and grimaces as I duck under the ladder. "That es bad luck."

"Then it evens out." I straighten up, expecting to find a healthy crowd belting out off-key show tunes. My bad. Only a boombox playing on the counter.

This place is in the throes of rejuvenation, with another contractor, pants mottled in drywall mud and with a bushy mustache splayed like caterpillar's legs, spackling the wall to our left.

"Hola!" Almost hidden behind the counter, a green-haired Asian girl with an hourglass figure smiles while her vape cigarette billows immense blueberry-flavored clouds towards the ceiling fan.

When Auntie M orders a ceviche and Inca Kolas, our hostess lifts her lithe arm and points to a couple of semi-clean tables.

I can feel Auntie M thinking, *Maybe let's pass,* but then she sees a dingy foosball table plunked down all by its lonesome in the corner. "¡Eso!"

She races over, prodding me to indulge in a game. "I used to beat the pants off my brothers when we was younger. Except my older brother, Juan. Ready?"

As soon as the foosball drops into play, Auntie M deftly spins her wrist, knocking it hard into my goal with a loud Thwack!

"Is he the one who knows Gus? I'd like to meet him."

"That Gus again? Just because my brother knows a Gus does no mean he knows your Gus. And we're not going to meet my brother. He lives in the jungle. In Iquitos and I hate bugs."

"And what if I beat you? Ready?"

The ball drops. With a simple flick of her wrist while biting her lip, Auntie M performs another powerful slap shot goal. "Qua-Qua-Qua-Qua."

Auntie M nods with a chuckle as our hostess drops off a couple of cans of Inca Kola, then slinks back behind the moat of a counter to vape to her heart's content. A queen in her castle.

With the sweet, refreshing Pshshshshsh! of carbonated air escaping from the can, I relax, lean back, and do a little budgeting math. If I don't get too crazy. . . about three months savings left. Three months for twenty years in the shitshow, stunned into a defunct state of half-brain death watching humanoid chancres, nepotists, and brown-nosed asskissatchiks soil themselves for a slot at middling managment. Bite my tongue. Do what I'm told. All for three months of freedom, fading fast. A lump-of-coal.

"Dougito."

What the hell is wrong with me? I've ditched everything on the career advice of a drunk at my local dive bar who believes in dolphin telepathy.

"Dougito?"

Jesus, I was in my twenties when I started. Back then I was the star in my own universe.   But life hits back. Hard.

"Dougito!"

Lockjawed and bewildered, I rubberneck around, then at Auntie M's friendly smile, revealing cute dimples. "You es mumbling again."

"No I'm not."

"You es mumbling." She raps her magenta fingernails on the table like a marching centipede.

"I don't mumble."

"You mumble all the time."

As the hostess arrives with the ceviche, we both sit upright in our chairs, realizing we've been leaning forward at each other.

"Gracias."

"Thank you."

Our hostess dips her head quickly, then about-faces wearing a pursed smile like she's thinking *Whatever.*

Auntie M stabs a fork at the shrimp and sweet potatoes. "So, how long es you planning on staying en Peru?"

I suck in a lungful of air for a long thought. "Maybe forever, if I can't come up with a good excuse or get a note from at least a semi-legitimate doctor, soon. Do you have Lyme disease down here?"

"Eh, what's that?"

"Nothing."

She opens her mouth, then pauses to daintily pick off a piece of lint from her blue blouse. "I just don't get you gringos wanting to moves down here."

"And you want to move to L.A. with that visa of yours? Live in a postage stamp studio in Pico Rivera so you can fight through shitty traffic for two hours on the way to a cattle call audition as an extra in a rectal ulcer cream infomercial?" I snap my fingers. "Is that the way to the American Dream, becoming an actress?"

Auntie M looks around, then locks eyes with me. "Voice actress. Nobody wants me in front of the camera. I no es twenty-one, anymore."

"Ah, the American Dream. Good luck on all that."

"Es better than ditching hope with no dream at all. Plenty of people go to L.A. and makes a success. Look at Ar-nold Schwarz-E-negger."

I laugh. "Okay, Terminator. You've got a lot of moxie."

Auntie M grins. "Y besides, I es used to shitty traffic. I live in Lima, remember?" She lifts her can. "Here's to our futures. Salud."

"Salud."

After a sip of Inca Kola, I try out my best Arnold Schwarzenegger impersonation while getting up. "I'll be back."

"Faxing a Fujimori?"

I stop in my tracks. "Huh?"

"When our ex-presidente, Alberto Fujimori, fled Peru to Japan, he sent his resignation with a 'FujiFax'. It's slang for taking a shit. He is back in prison en Peru now."

"How enlightening."

She waves me towards the restroom. "Enjoy."

I'm in the bathroom stall, still registering the Peruvian colloquial potty humor I've gleaned when another telemarketer call comes in, trying to sell me a surefire bitcoin trading system.

CLICK.

And then I see it. On the wall, under the sign pleading with the foreign tourists to not flush the toilet paper and plug up the sewer. Magic marker doodles on a handmade linoleum tile placed with crack-filling compound. Leaning forward, I squint for a closer look:

'TOYNBEE IDEA
  IN MOVIE `2001
  RESURRECT DEAD
  ON PLANET JUPITER
  REMEMBER HIM—BEFORE THE SILVER CORD IS SEVERED
  AND THE GOLDEN BOWL IS BROKEN'

                        WTF?

The same, damn lettering. To a tee. Jesus. Fuck! Is that my handwriting?

When Auntie M sees me barge out of the bathroom, she stops with her fork full of camote dangling in the air. "Es you okay?"

Are my hands trembling? "You know when I said I don't believe in ghosts?"

"Sí."

"I do."

                        #

Tired from the day's journey, we bolt for a quick bite and a Cusqueña beer before checking into our hotel.

That evening, I fry my brain cells figuring out the Jenga puzzle of track sliding glass terrace doors as mosquitoes buzz about me. It seems easy, but these damn doors come in three sections each with two layers, and I can't remember the common denominator. What starts out as an annoyance quickly devolves into an orgy of stupidity, like watching a zoo monkey trying to fuck a football for a half-hour.

I fall asleep slapping at imaginary bloodsucking bugs while listening to Auntie M record cartoon voices next door, ranging from a cheerful grandma to a sultry mid-forties vixen to a playful talking kitten.

Oh, well, sometimes the fancier hotels aren't necessarily the best, but at least I'm not alone.

I know why the caged bird sings karaoke.

This place is like a comfy, windswept tomb. Zombie tourists slog, cram a chicharron with sweet potato fries and salsa criolla down their gullets, then stumble off to kitesurf, fish, and dune-buggy before a decadent night of tasting piscos.

Auntie M puts in her hair barrette very casually. "So, es you ready for your blind date?"

"What?" I bash my knee into a chair, coming back from the hotel's

breakfast buffet counter with a Greek yogurt and a coffee.

"I set you up. In Arequipa." Auntie M laughs, then starts humming along to the instrumental theme song from 'Charlie Brown' playing in the background.

I carefully sit down on the steel trap chair and exhale. Well, there went breakfast. My stomach puckers at the social threat of dating, like a hemorrhoid drowning in a giant vat of Preparation H. "Why would you do that? You know I don't make good first impressions." Or second or third impressions for that matter.

"It will be fun. Es part of your tour. And besides, I hears she gets dressed up and kinky for gringos." Auntie M holds up her glass of orange juice and nods at the full cup on my placemat. "Jugo de naranja with un poco de poop. Just the way you likes it."

She twirls her head around to the beat as I dig out the crusted yellow gunk that's sealed over the corner of my eyelid. "Uh. . . we're drinking orange juice with some freshly-squeezed poop?"

She stops twirling long enough to pause in thought, then nod. "Yeah."

Is this a riddle? I lean in. "You mean pulp?"

"Síííííí." If she could boogie any more she'd be dancing on her chair.

I pause, admiring the flock of fishing boats bobbing in the bay, then pull out the Cusqueña beer can from the inside pocket of my windbreaker. "No thanks. I'll stick with beer."

Is this the last Cusqueña? Cripes, supply lines are being stretched perilously thin.

Auntie M stares into her cell phone screen, pressing buttons. "I wants to do kara-oke."

"Karaoke? Now?" I look around at the hotel's buffet/TV room, a piecemeal grouping of and hungover late-night partiers and stoic pre-dawn early risers. "It's a little early, don't you think? Besides, I haven't even finished my. . . postprandial."

I pop open the beer can, preparing for a deep, refreshing sip.

"Ooh-Wah-Ah-Ah-Ah!"

Beer foam explodes and I jump three feet in the air. "Shit." After blowing out my colon hole, I land back on tierra firma wide-eyed like a barn owl caught masturbating. "What the Jesus fucking Christ was that?"

Auntie M shrugs, then points and laughs. "Your crotch!"

"Fucking cripes!" I grab a handful of paper napkins and dab at my soaked shorts, trying to be pissed off, but her laugh is infectious. "It's not funny." Dammit. Don't laugh. "And no blind dates!"

"But she es just your type."

"Ughh." I sit back down, shivering like I've been dunked in castor oil. "That's even worse. What asylum did you pull her out of?"

Auntie M sets her phone on the table and starts putting on her red windbreaker as she sings.

"You better be ready. And don't be. . . mel'an'chol'ic."

"What?"

"Mel'an'chol'ic. You es being mel'an'chol'ic. You wants me to eh-spell it for you?"

Where is she pulling these big words from? Slamming down my orange juice, I slowly uncork myself from the chair. Auntie M freezes, locking in a stare that seems to envelop me.

"What? I'm heading to the pool."

"Are you wearing those eh-shoes?"

Black tube socks with white sneakers. They're clean. What's the problem? "They. . . Don't. . . go with these socks?"

She raises her arms like her favorite team just scored a goal. "Dios mio. He is learning. He is learning!"

"See? You can teach an old dog to turn tricks."

A titter before I can correct myself.

"You know what I mean."

Lifting up her orange juice, she smiles. "The pool it es. . ."

. . . Not. It's full of seagulls. About fifty of the suckers are bobbing up and down like feathered corks, preening themselves. A plastic scarecrow kite of a bird of prey, tethered to a pole, flails helplessly above, ignored by all.

"Ooh-Wah-Ah-Ah-Ah!"

Auntie M and I look up at the speaker perched on the patio ceiling behind us. It blares out supposed seagull predator sounds like the lead singer of a hard rock band.

The gulls couldn't be calmer, ignoring the screeches and shrieks while floating serenely, bobbing their heads up and down. Very Metal. So much for the pool.

Before leaving Paracas, we pay a visit to The Museo de Sitio Julio C. Tello. It's built like an intellectual bomb shelter, a rustbelt red reconstruction necessity from the aforementioned earthquake, housing the most famous discovery of the 'Father of Peruvian Archeology': a set of cemeteries connected to Paracas culture.

"Mira." Auntie M tugs my shoulder and points at the elongated skull ensconced in a glass case. Looks like you could fit two brains inside, one stacked on top of the other.

Shaking my head. "Talk about a split personality."

Our tour guide, who looks like Peru's answer to Ichabod Crane, blathers out in a stiff monotone.

"A very young child's skull is pliant at birth, and remains in this way for months. It is therefore possible, by lashing a rope around the head, with a board placed at the back of the skull, and perhaps the front as well, to alter the shape of the head over time."

Some of the remains date back at least 5,000 BC.

Back on the Yellow Sand Road. .

Our mind's bursting with head elongation knowledge, we leave Paracas, heading due South like a barrel's worth of flying monkeys. My tour guide's happy and carefree, tapping the steering wheel while jammin' out to Los Prisioneros' 'We are Sudamerican Rockers'.

After the deja vu nightmare in the bathroom, I'm happy to be gone, with a manic urge to break away. Now. Scamper through this barren desert of unyielding sand before whatever malignant force plotting against me comes full circle.

Auntie M's enjoying herself, singing as she tousles her hair. She pats the Ekeko figurine, smiling. "First you don't believes in anything, now you believes in eh-spirits?" I lean back, soaking in the sun. "Getting there."

I rub my fingers on the amulet. How to explain the bathroom graffiti? I wouldn't put it past Gus to fly down here just to fluck with me. All these years and how well do I actually know him? We both go to the same bar and we both drink way too much. It's like we're congenitally joined at the liver to see who can fuck up their life the fastest. No more playing fast and loose. I've got to keep my wits down here. Smiling, I think about how any curses coming our way are weakening at the square root of the distance of every click on the odometer.

A furtive glance over at my puzzled look and she grabs the iPhone. The playlist changes to Duncan Dhu's soothing 'Te Quiero'. "There. You like that?"

I nod. "Yeah. Sounds nice." Leaning over the dashboard, I squint and peel my ears. "No. Wait a minute. That's fucked."

She stiffens. "Fucked. I thinks es. . . tranquil."

"It's not the song."

A foreign, rhythmic sound, emanating from someplace in the engine block, pulsating in menace.

Oh eee oh. Oh eee oh. Oh eee oh.

Impossible to ignore, even with the music.

"You hear that?"

"What?" Auntie M responds like I'm socially tone-deaf for interrupting her well-crafted musical interlude.

"Could you turn that down?"

"Es my favorite song."

Seizing her iPhone, I frantically push buttons until the music ceases.

"Aye!"

An extra, very rhythmic, squeaking. What the hell could that be? "Hear it?"

Her placid smile gives way to a frown. "Sí."

El Tigre couldn't have picked a worse place to get funky. We're running roughshod through *THE* desert. I thought yesterday's desert was The Desert, but it turns out it was just an amateur. This is the real deal. But, unless you're a lizard or a scrub bush, you're not interested in the desert per se, only the undeserted parts of it.

"What es it?"

"Oh, that's easy, it's the Tri-shaft exhaust flange."

"Really? Es that easy to fix?"

"I wish I knew. I just made that up."

"Should we goes back to Huacachina?"

She's talking about the aosis. . . uh, oasis we passed by heading through Ica. It's a tiny townlet encircling a tree-lined lagoon flanked by sand dunes. Massive ones. The desert on the up and up. A postcard from the set of 'Lawrence of Arabia' with 'Mad Max' dune buggies going off in every direction in search of vehicular mayhem.

"Nah, the closest thing I saw to a mechanic back there was a guy juggling machetes in traffic for spare change."

Right on cue, the Ekeko figurine falls to the floorboard near my feet. I try showing off a confident grin, but I'm freaking out inside, imagining being stranded here. The rattle noise slices through the silence. My right eye twitches. "I hope you brought good walking shoes."

Auntie M pats the dashboard above the steering wheel and coos like she's soothing a crying baby. "Pobrecita. Maybe she just needs some rest."

Auntie M's four-wheeled camel rolls into the town of Nazca, the only conspicuous dot on the map between Ica and Arequipa. As soon as El Tigre totters to a halt, Auntie M and I bail out like its an unwanted hitchhiker with herpes and a panty-sniffing fetish. We stand in the fresh air with the sun beaming warmth on our faces at the outskirts of the delightfully green plaza mayor.

Closing my eyes and stretching upwards like a yogi, I intone "I'll try to find a mechanic. . . you hearing me?"

"¡Eso!" Auntie M has run over and started photo-bombing the Nazca Line -inspired figures cut into the grass in the park with her Canon EOS. They all warrant a peek-see, but the monkey figure is her big shooting star.

Shaking my head, I barely start ambling across the narrow street lined with brightly-colored tiendas when my phone rings with a familiar number. Time to face the music.

A well-placed coughing fit. "Hu. . . hey. How's it going?"

"Better than you sound. Larry wants to know why he hasn't seen you at work for two weeks."

"I'm so glad you asked."

"I bet. And make it good."

"Fecal transplant surgery." Dead silence on the other end. "Uh, hello?"

"Fecal transplant surgery?"

"For sure. It turns out the "good" bacteria in my colon are feeling kinda wimpy. Even Vic Atiyeh's grandson says the surgery is absolutely, super necessary. It's a real game-changer."

Spearmint-flavored godsmacking like it's going through the roof of her mouth.

Not good. "You think he'll buy it?"

"Doug, that is the single, lamest excuse since Jerry took the company truck for steak bites at the strip club. They don't pay me enough for this shit! I mean shoot."

"Yes, shoot. . . but just don't fire. Hahaha. You see, we're all in this together."

"Just be prepared to have this discussion with Larry when you get back."

CLICK.

"Linda? Hello? Hello?"

Shit. I'm doomed. Pacing in front of a green mom-and-pop fruteria while smacking my cursed phone against my thigh. Fuck! Think for a second. Yes.

I've got the number on speed dial. "Time for a little pow wow."

Four rings already. Answer the damn phone, Gus. Five rings usually does it, but that's assuming he's sober. So, here I am, waiting. A telephone tale told by an idiot, full of blank, monotone pulses, signifying nothing.

I about-face, watching Auntie M compose shots around the monkey like she's Anselette Adams.

Eight rings. Guess not.

I pull the phone away from my ear just in time to hear a faint ". . . Aye. . ."

"Gus?"

A pause. "Duck?"

"Are you passed out, again?"

The voice springs to life. "Pissed out? Pffffhhhththhthaahhh! Of course not! I is just re-working myself into a writer's trance. Like Coleridge."

"Gus, I don't--"

"Aye, Duck. What is your thoughts on who could win in a fair fight between a lowerland mountain gorilla with brass knuckles and a broadsword against a pack of honey badgers?"

"What? What the hell are you blabbering about?"

"Is a bet."

"A bet?"

"Aye. A bar bet, Duck. Tim, Java, Jon, y me came up with it after we all got fitshaced last night. I gots fifty smackeroonies on the gorilla, but only if he gets to use nunchucks and a chain saw. You want in on some of that action, Duck?"

"Gus, this really isn't the--"

"Pffffhhhththththaahhh!"

I quickly pull back to make sure Gus' spittle isn't spraying into my phone. "Trick question. Honey badgers don't travel in packs. I thoughts you is smarter than that, Duck. ¿Qué pasa?"

"Don't '¿qué pasa?' me. You lied to me. My Es-pan-ol still sucks."

"Is español, Duck."

"Shit. See? It's getting worse. This is a disaster. I lost my shit at the airport. The traffic is kamikaze, and now I'm seeing things."

A pause. "¿Que?"

"There's batshit-crazy things written on the walls down here. Mega batshit. Tiles talking about '2001' and 'Resurrecting the dead on Jupiter'. I swear to Buddha I thought I saw the same message in the Dark Bar."

"Pffffhhhththththaahhh! Those is Toynebee tiles, Duck. They is nothing special. . . except that they shows up in every city I shows up to."

An evil laugh at the other end.

"Gus, my cargo cult excuse didn't work. The secretary's pissed and HR is ready to drop the F bomb on me."

A belly laugh at the other end. "A cargo cult? Aye, Duck. You really is flucked. Well, at least I has my writing job."

"You mean waking up dead drunk next to a notepad every day?"

"That's the secret to my kluge writing styles! I is going to be the next Roberto Bolaño, somedays."

"Who? Listen Gus, society doesn't need guys like us anymore. You and I, we're. . . replaceable."

The clink of ice mixed with a deep, raw chortle. "Duck, you is a janitor at an extract plant. They will find someones else."

Impossible. Has Gus not seen how I use a squeegee? Surely, that counts for something in this crazy, mixed-up world.

"Is about that times we has the talk, Duck. Now, this is really important so you listens up good."

I gulp. "Okay."

He belches. "I once knows a hooker in Honduras who could type over one hundred words per minute while calculating the daily fluctuations in the LIBOR rate, all in her head."

Bigger belch. "She can instantly tells you any foreign exchange value, from Japanese Yens to Swiss Francs to the cross currency exchange rate between the moose jaw centennial and a rai stone from the island of Yap."

"Damn."

"Aye. Then, she'd recite her John's fake names in alphabetical order, backwards and forewards in seven different languages, including Esperanto. She did all this all the while she would ass-fuck a lime-green dildo the size of Dizzie Gillespie's trumpet."

Gus slams down his drink glass. "I'm telling you, Duck, with your disorganized thinking, there's no way you can compete with a brain like that. So don't even try."

"Oh, I won't."

"You is nothing special, Duck. And you never was. But misremembers, Duck, time has a brilliant ways of dealing with all our best-laid plans. It just doesn't give a fluck. Understands?"

"I guess so."

"Duck. Don't gets the paranoids. You is one lucky son of a bastard, today. I has just founded your calling."

"What? Just like that?"

"Sí."

"What is it?"

"Aye. You will know when the time comes, Duck. You will hear the call of the electroshock boogaloo."

I pull the piece of scrap paper out of my wallet. "Gus, I have this piece of paper."

"Oopah." The clink of ice cubes. "That's amazing, Duck."

"That's not the part that cracks me up. You see, I'm staring at it and I can't remember if you wrote it or I wrote it or she wrote it. Looks like her handwriting, though."

"Why don't you asks Auntie M? She would know."

"Nah. I don't want to explain about us. It might--" I read from the note. "Freak her out." A shrug. "You know?"

I spot Auntie M crossing the street towards me. Silence on the other side of the line.

"Gus? Gus, are you there?"

"Phphphphphphphphph! Now figure that one out."

CLICK.

Enshrouded in darkness, pleasant and restful. Faint, random popping noises counter notes of Beethoven's 'Moonlight Sonata' off in a vague distance. Was it coming from inside the room with the piano? No. Was it a recording. . . probably. . . not? There's an unsteadiness to the notes. No. Definitely outside.

The same passage over and over and over.

Awake! A thunderous heartbeat! A vivid dream bleeds away quickly, mummifying into inscrutable unconsciousness. Quick blinking and a gaze out the window. A beautiful, cobalt blue.

A worker in all white is perched on a small ladder, scraping paint from the side of a house. He's tethered a large yellow, green, and pink-banded umbrella to the nearby wall, shielding himself from the sun. The sounds of fireworks and music float through the air. A birthday party?

Arequipa. 'The White City.' Auntie M's mechanical chariot limped in late in the day, the victim of some ravenous rodent with a hankering for soy-based wire coating. At least we made it. Auntie M's friend, Carolina, a divorcee with an over-expansive house, is our gracious hostess.

'THE GUS'S PERUVIAN GUIDEBOOK' (not so) PROUDLY PRESENTS: WHAT'S IN A NAMES?'

Hitler returns to power in an historic showdown against his long-time pain-in-the-commie-ass, Lennin.

It sounds loco but is true. In a chicha beerhall putsch, Hitler Guesclin Alba Sánchez out-llama- krieged his bitter rival Lennin Vladimir Rodríguez Valverde in the race for mayor in the small Peruvian town of Yungar.

Hitler-mania has felt up the Andes, with campaign slogans reading "Hitler returns" and "Hitler with the people" being heard among Alba's fanatic followers in this sleepy, post-weirmacht pueblo of eight-thousand eager voters. "I'm the good Hitler," Alba said.

Aye. It always starts out like that. But, promises is made to be broken.

To be fair, Hitler Alba Sánchez does seem like a decent enough dude. He says he rejects alles that Nazi dictator stuff Adolf Hitler stood for. Alba said he wants to oversees a fair and honest government in Yungar, a farming town in Peru's central Andes.

But Alba's triumph of the will campaign had to bunker down this year, after it cames under attack by Lennin Rodríguez Valverde, a resident of a neighboring district who tried to block Alba's registration as a candidate on the grounds that it's not the votes that counts, it's who counts the votes.

Electoral authorities rejected the request last week, allowing Hitler to appear on voting cards for the October elections, and possibly averting World War III.

Alba says his father didn't know who Adolf Hitler was when he named him, he just thought it sounded cool. After learning the history behind it, Alba said he considered changing his name but eventually got around to accepting it. Good call. After alles, the original Hitler is the one who sucks, not Alba.

This "pick any name that don't even fits stuff" ain't just a Peru thing, either. All over Latin America, parents often choose exotic-sounding first names for they children despite negative meanings abroad.

In another tear-jerking story about never givings up on your dream, Osama Vinladen was named to Peru's national juvenile football team last year.

'THE GUS'S PERUVIAN GUIDEBOOK' PROUDLY PRESENTS:

Chapter Eight: The Lines of Nazca.

In 1927 Peruvian Archaeologist Toribio Mejia Xesspe was chillin' out all villain-like on some Nazca river basin hills bout 250 miles South of Lima when he sees some odd shit:

Massive Etch A Sketchings of humans, insects, birds, fishies, spiders with trippy designs, all carved into the earth. For miles. It was fluckin' awesome.

After Toribio's amigos tells him to quit sniffing glue, the lines is kept a secret until the 1930s, when pilots start buzzing around them Nazca skies.

From there on it was a conspiracy theorist's wet dream.

Some of the first scientists of the Nazca Basin, like Paul Kosok and Maria Reiche, has theories about how all them those crazy lines marked where the sun and moon would rise on important holidays, like some giant 2,000-year-old Google Calendar.

These theories has one important setback, however: they suck. Up into this day, all the world's most egg-headed scientists can't agree on exactly what the fluck these lines mean.

But no worries, when logic and science falls flat on its ass, greed and stupidity is more than happy to step into the mierda.

So, in 1968, Swiss author Erich von Däniken fills in the blanks when he writes that the Nazca Lines is some half-assed runway for alien spaceships in his book 'Chariots of the Gods.' It's a best-seller, putting the lines on the interstellar map as E.T's favorite place to phone home in the minds of ancient alien fans.

The alien theory goes like this: 2,000 years ago, ancient people was too shat-all stupid to create anything as awesome as the Nazca Lines. How could they? Only people with big brains to make gnarly flying machines could have made them. After all, some of them designs is only visible from the air. And we know they didn't have cool stuff like airplanes back then.

Other dingbats say the Nazca built the lines themselves but with E.T.'s help, sorta like little green permatemps. Fans of this theory point to the Nazca Line drawing called "the astronaut," a human figure with a lightbulb-shaped head like a flying dork in a space suit. Or a dude wearing a KFC family bucket meal on his noggin? Or a cyclops? Or heavens forbid, the ancient people of Nazca, which started chilling out in civilized numbers around 100 B.C., were a bunch of flucking slackers and never got around to taking community college art classes?

So did our alien friends play a role in the creation of the Nazca lines?

Most likely, flucking no.

While it's super-exciting to check out the lines from out of the window of a UFO or even a crashing airplane, they is all visible from the nearby foothills. You know, like the one Peruvian archaeologist Xesspe was hiking up when he spotted them in the first place.

And besides, everybody knows that them lines was made by the underwear gnomes. Thinks about it, why couldn't a race of super gnomes pop up from the molted pressures of Middle Earth and starts doing some landscape calligraphy?

So, why would them gnomes go to all that trouble of pickaxing through thousands of miles of magma and stuff, you might ask The Gus?

Easy peasy. With them poor Nazcas distracted checking out all the cool artwork, the gnomes can sneak up from behind, then give them wedgies as they steals they underwear.

Is so logical. . .

Or maybe our ancient incestors weren't as shat-all stupid as we thinks they was, back in those simpler, pre-nimrod days?

Any hows, if you want to visit the Nazca Lines, do it soon. In 2009, they got their first recorded damage when a heavy rainstorm dumped sand and clay onto three fingers of the hand-shaped drawing. Saddingly, The Gus can't report on if the middle one is still there or not.

Five years later, and The Gus ain't making this up, the environmentality group Greenpeace flucked up an area near the hummingbird drawing when they trampled through the desert to lay down a large huge sign promoting renewable energy.

So, who is the stupid ones, again?

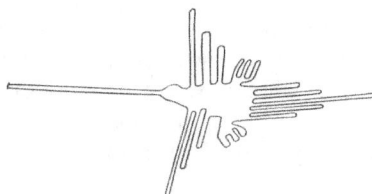

I'm nervous. I hate blind dates.

It's a breezy, sun-filled day in the altitude of Arequipa and Auntie M and I are slowly huffing along the main square.

Auntie M lets out a belly laugh, her eyes glued to my future date's profile page on her iPhone. "Awww. You two es so much alike. She doesn't talk, y you es the not-so-strong and mumbling type."

"Very funny. So, let's see her photo."

I reach for her phone, but she teases "Ah, ah, ah" before pivoting past an iron gate and into an open courtyard of a one-story, raspberry-hued building contoured with large, white doorways. Handfuls of tourists amble around the scrub trees and benches.

"What? Is this part of the tour?"

"Sí."

Why not? I'm feeling cultural. Auntie M and I head inside, shepherded into the cool, dark room by a friendly usherette. The small front rows of cafeteria chairs facing a film screen are taken, so we glom onto a pair of back seats. Auntie M immerses herself in her phone, while I watch the stragglers stumble about as their eyes adjust to the darkness.

"You has to pay to see her."

"Who?"

She winks, shielding her phone's screen. "Your date."

"What the hell does she do for a living?"

"No hay importa."

"Not important? That's one helluva red flag where I come from. Is prostitution not illegal in your country?"

"Oh, no!"

"Not that I'm judging, mind you."

"No, she es just a little high maintenance. That's all. Y quit mumbling."

"I don't mumble."

"Yes. You es mumble core."

"I'm not mumble core, dammit, and what do you mean high maintenance?"

The Andean answer to Vincent Price steps to the fore, informing us all that we will be watching a thirty-minute film about the discovery of a frozen 'mummy', a 12-year-old Inca girl sacrificed to the gods in the 1450s.

Dramatic music booms from the wall speakers, swelling the room with raspy feedback before whomever in charge of the audio lowers the volume.

The Story of The Ice Maiden Mummy!

Cue the narrator in feigned gravitas. "It's 1995 and Björn Vänsterätt, extreme archaeologist and all-around daredevil, is hunting chupacabra while mogul-skiing down an erupting volcano when he happens upon the mummified remains of a young girl sacrificed to the Inca Gods."

Holy shit. Sounds like my cup of morbid tea. "Awesome. I love zombie flicks."

"Shhhh." Some of the seated silhouettes sway their necks, scanning the room in disapproval.

The narrator hams it up. "Call it just another day in the life of Björn, a man who has skydived with great white sharks, bungee-jumped from the summit of Everest with a yeti tied to his back, founded his own Atlantis at the bottom of the Mariana Trench, won the world's largest Easter egg hunt in the Bermuda Triangle, and has personally found out, beyond a shadow of a doubt, just where, exactly, the fuck is Waldo. . . and then Björn hit puberty."

My God. I'm gonna need some Thorazine to wrap my mind around this cinematic trip. I turn to Auntie M. "Is this shit for real?"

Auntie M whispers, "She eh-sleeps in a hyperbarium chamber?"

"Hyperbaric. Who?"

"Your date, Dougito."

"She sounds like a real freak!"

"I guess eh-so?"

Auntie M cradles her iPhone against her forest-green shirt, as I grasp for it. "Shhhhhh."

I am whispering! Geez, I wish I was more like Gus. Just tell them all to fluck off.

"No more of a freak than you." She smacks my arm away from her precious phone.

"Nope!"

I stare in silence, amazed at the audience glued to the onscreen exploits. "And so, after another amazing discovery, Björn loads the Ice Maiden Mummy onto his trusty pet llama, Taffy, and together they luge all the way to Arequipa, where the Ice Maiden is preserved to this very day."

The words 'THE END' form in bold script before there is a final hiss and the film screen turns black and the lights turn on. Then, we are chaperoned into the antechamber, to see the Ice Maiden.

I walk up to the glass enclosure. Serenely swaddled in an ancient shawl, bony face is an expressionless death mask. The Ice Maiden.

The usherette lays out the grim details. "The Ice Maiden was sacrificed as part of a rite known as Capacocha. Apart from the young girl's remains, archaeologists also found offerings to the gods to ensure a good harvest or prevent a natural disaster: numerous miniature clay statues, shells, and gold objects." .

Auntie M taps my shoulder. "So, what do you think of your date. Es it a deal breaker?" Auntie M smiles, whispering next to me amongst the room full of onlookers.

"Very funny."

The usherette raises her voice without looking at us. "These objects, along with food, coca leaves, and chicha, an alcoholic drink made from corn, would have been brought by the priests as they led the girl up Mount Ampoto." She pauses, waiting for the murmurs to silence. "The latter would have been used to sedate the child. Once she was in this intoxicated state, the priests would carry out the sacrifice. It was revealed with radiology, that a club blow to the head caused massive hemorrhaging, resulting in her death."

Auntie M inspects the mummy. "You should keep an open mind, Dougito. She could be your perfect match."

Except she has been dead for over 500 years.

"Very funny." And sad. There's always that catch, being on the living side of things for a bit. Life's vanity stokes the ego, but death delimits the ground rule: choose wisely while you can.   We're all gonna die of something, sometime.

#

"A little to the left," Auntie M commands.

A sun-filled, chilly day in the Colca Canyons. The caravan of tour buses parks on the side of the road after dropping us travel geeks off at the Cruz del Condor. It's an astounding viewpoint, compelling each tourist to ignore the handful of local women in traditional dresses hoping to sell bright textiles, trinkets, and bottled water on the way to the canyon's lip.

It's cramped quarters, with huddled tourists snaking a long line about the edge, braving wind gusts to snap pictures of Colca's profundity. The wheezing breaths and loping movements don't lie. We're definitely high up here. At 3,270 meters deep, the Colca Canyon is twice the depth of the Grand Canyon, one of the deepest gorges in the world.

Everyone pans their cameras at nature's real superstars: the condors. Today's a banner day. More than seven are circling above us, their ginormous wingspans performing lazy spirals amidst the updrafts.

Auntie M elbows her way past the flesh fence for some space, then points at a jagged rock jutting in front of a steep precipice. "Aquí."

"What? More pictures?"

"Sí."

"And what if I don't want to?"

She tilts her head. "What was that?"

I said, 'What if I don't want to?"

"Just do it."

"But you've been chiding me all along about taking control of my destiny. You know, being my own boss?"

"Sí. You do need to be your own man." She frowns and points at the ground. "Now stand over there because I tells you to, Fuckercito."

With a slow shuffle to my marker, the division of labor is complete. She is the maestra taking the pictures. I'm her obedient guinea pig filling the frame.

"No. Moves to your right just a bit. No. More. . ."

"Escuse me." I smile, hoping to ingratiate myself to the Colossus of Rhodes in the stars 'n' bars pinstriped shirt and Stetson cowboy hat next to me who smells like he's been dunked in a vat of Old Spice. "Um, excuse me?"

He puts down his fancy camera with a telephoto lens that stretches halfway across the canyon, sneers down at me as he tousles his Salvador Dali mustache, then grunts a deep "Ugghh" and goes back to his photo fun without so much as ceding me an inch of space.

I turn to face Auntie M's Canon EOS with a fake, cheesy smile.

"Aye carajo! Un poquito más a la izquierda."

"Huh?"

"To your left. Más. . . más. Eso. Smile!"

Just shoot me, already. My empty stomach grumbles as I shift to my left next to a pig-tailed Pippy Longstockings art teacher-type clicking away on her tiny, flamingo-pink camera. Oh, Great Fireball in the Sky, give me strength. I've run out of my medicine, but I am not going to have any altitude issues compared to Cuzco. For once, I've played it smart this time. No booze. No food this morning. Just lifegiving water.

This all started when the tour bus picked us up at 3 AM.

Not far into our drive, the amiable Peruvian guide handed out coca leaves for soroche. I grabbed a softball-sized wad and stuff it into my left cheek like smokeless tobacco chaw. Auntie M showed me two huge containers filled with water in her backpack. Yes. We got this.

All cameras veer my way when a condor glides right over my head. Part turkey vulture. Part pterodactyl.

"Back. Back and derecha, uh, right."

"Again?"

"Sí. I needs the condors in the shot, but they keeps flying."

My skin turns clammy. I'm gonna lose my shit if she doesn't hurry up.

"Yes. It's kinda what they do. They have wings."

Auntie M lowers her camera and locks her lower lip over the top and shakes her fist. With her bright yellow sun hat, heavy, blue coat, and thick boots, she looks like a pissed-off Paddington Bear. I better play along.

Smiling, I remember how groggy I was at 6 AM when our bus stopped at Mirador de Los Volcanes, the trek's highest point at 4,910 meters above sea level. I know it's 4,910 meters because every time she sees an altitude marker, Auntie M immediately turns to me, announces the number, then pretends to throw up.

"Eh, cuatro mil, novecientos y diez metros. Blaaaaaaahhh!"

Lovely.

By mid-morning bus stopped at the highest point in our trip. The busload of tourists zombie-walked for some searing lungfuls of thin air, a shake of the legs and, of course, a snapshot. I stayed inside to gasp for air in the luxury of my comfy seat while gulping down more water. Why waste the energy walking? At this altitude, everything's about maintaining a proper lack of effort. With the oxygen deprivation kicking in, the view from the bus was like a Salvador Dali moonscape, dreamlike and alien. Peaks of volcanoes encircled us, standing guard at over 6,000 meters. After ten minutes, the panting began as tourists filed back in, overwhelming the bus in their collective BO. And that's when the buzzing in my ears starts.

Back at Colca's edge, Auntie M just can't quite line up that money shot.

"No. Izquierda."

"Izquierda? You mean my left?"

"Sí. To the left and back."

Just take the picture, already! I swear, if she doesn't take this picture I'm gonna blow up.

Gingerly, I inch towards Pippy Longstockings, tapping her gently on the shoulder. "Sorry."

At noon, the bus descended, carrying on to Chivay, where we had a breakfast buffet. I'm ravenous, but not stupid. The Doug abides to the rule of the land on high: What goes in, must come out. I carefully studied the breakfast spread like it was the lead suspect in a dimestore crime novel. Something light. Only fill the void. After I nitpicked half the allotted time away, I return to the lunch table to find Auntie M scraping her spoon at the bottom of her yogurt.

She looks up at me. "Peaches?"

Meanwhile, back at the firing squad on the Cruz del Condor, I'm awaiting my cigarette and blindfold. My tinnitus is growing worse, like some cursed fruitfly running a NASCAR race between my ears. Can insects live up here? What if something weird has laid its eggs in my ear canal?

Auntie M huffs. "Backs!"

"Backs?" I tilt my head around. "There is no backs."

The lady in pigtails frenetically clicks pics next to me stops. She take a long, wide-eyed look at the lack of real estate behind me and scowls. I move one angstrom back and smile at the camera. "Do you want me to pull a Ciro?"

Auntie M's camera goes down again. She is definitely not amused.

My Handler told me about that tidbit on the way up here.

In 2011, during a field trip to the Colca Canyons, Ciro Castillo Rojo and his girlfriend became lost. She was found alive nine days later. After an intensive search, Ciro's body was eventually found in a deep ravine. The forensic opinion is that Ciro must have fallen on his own. If Ciro had been pushed, the lesions would have been more traumatic. "From such a height, one literally bursts," the report indicated.

"Backs." Auntie M balances her camera for a shot while waving me away with her hand.

Balling up my fists, I press my knuckles into my ears, frantically trying to rub the buzzing away.   "Are you serious?"

"Sí. Backs just a little more. And put your arms down."

"A little more?" Is all this sweat from the altitude or delirium?

At this point the lady in pigtails is more interested in watching me than Colca Canyon's natural beauty. A voice screams inside my head, "From such a height, one literally bursts."

I pick up up my feet and place them down in exactly the same spot. "Bien. Say cheese!"

I still remember it, in slow motion, the look of absolute horror on the pigtailed lady's face, as I spew undigested peaches everywhere.

CLICK.

Now that's an action photo.

'THE GUS'S PERUVIAN GUIDEBOOK' PROUDLY PRESENTS:

Chapter Eight: The Conquest of the Incas, Pt. 2

The flies ain't even done puking up they digestive juices over Atahualpa's dead corpse when Pizarro picks some poor geek named Tupac Huallpa to be the new, official puppet-in-chief. But Tupac can't even makes it through his 90 days probationated period before the biggie smallpox disease decides he's a bad fit for the job of life, and he croaks so he can pays a visit to his ancestors. Aye, but the shit show must goes on. . .

Enter the Manco Inca Era.

So Pizarro finds Manco, yet another son of the ever-fertile Huayna-Capac, and sticks him on the hot throne. With this new excuse for a king decided, the conquistadors gets back to the bidness of looting the fluck out of Cuzco.

Falling-out with Almagro.

After beating the piss out of them Incas, the conquistadors has lots of free time on they hands. Being an ocean away from the royal shmancy pants in Spain, Pizarro and his peeps starts to picking up some bad habits, like genocide, mass rape, and setting theyselves up to be worshipped as a living sun gods. Aye, who is we to judge? They probably just has a tough childhood? Any hows, mistakes is made; so the conquistadors decides to offload some of that pent up testicularosterone by kicking the shit out of theyselves. Is like working on Wall Street, but with arquebuses instead of them gaydar-loving men's pinch penny loafers.

Through the out of all this, Almagro can't shakes the feels that the Brothers Pizarro are flucking him out of his unfair share of the Cuzco rape and pillage booty, the gold-plated cherry on top of the Incan empire sundae. Of course they is, but this is abouts four-hundred flucking years before collective bargaining y the conquistadors sure as hell never got around to settin' up a complaints department.

So, Pizarro tells Almagro to take a long, forced walk into an unknown territory way down into what we likes to call Chile. It gets Almagro outta Pizarro's boogered-up nose hairs for a while, and if Almagro's exploidition finds gold, hey, fluckin' awesome. If he winds up getting his self killed, oh well, even better. Karma's a bitch and more Cuzco gold for the Pizarros.

Inca Revolts.
Somewheres between 1535 and 1537, Manco Inca finally gets tired of Francisco Pizarro playing Balinese shadow puppet theater games up his ass, and heads to the hills with a gallon of K-Y Jelly to start a full-on rebellion in Cuzco.

The Spaniards gets all surprised when they see Manco's big ass army at they gates, all natty and charging through the streets and lighting the buildings on fire.

Is a bummer of an ending for the Inca capital: stripped for Atahualpa's ransom, looted by the Spanish, and burned to the ground by its own people. Reading the past of inhumanity is like a series of neverending donkey punches to the pills. Just ask The Gus.

Aye.

The Battle Over 'Saxy Woman'

"(Ruminavi) extracted all the bones through a certain part leaving the skin intact, and made him into a drum. The shoulders formed one end of the drum and the abdomen the other, so that, with the head, feet, and hands embalmed, he was preserved intact like an executed criminal—but transformed into a kettledrum."

-Historian Gonzalo Fernandez de Oviedo, on after Inca general Ruminavi captured a noble accused of collaborating with the Spaniards.

Surrounded and constipated, the Spaniards gets all desperate-like. Most the Incan attacks is coming from Sacsahuaman, a brontosauras burger-sized-boulder fortress just above Cuzco that local guides call 'saxy woman' to gets bigger tips from dipshit turistas. One of Saxy's biggest gallstones is twenty-eight feets tall and weighs more than 361 metric shit tons (MSTs), makings it one of the largest LegoLand pieces ever devised.

But, the Spaniards gets all sneaky and pull out some of they ol' European warfare tricks to get medieval on the Inca's asses: scaling ladders.

The defense of Saxy is left to a badass Inca noble, who vows to fight to the shitty death, and the conquistadors is happy to oblige. When the Spaniards start they attack, the noble fights like a wild warthog outta hell, bashing Spaniard skulls with vengeful glee.

But, the poor bastard winds up taking a couple arrows for his troubles and the rest of his Inca peeps fold faster than a drive-through laundromat. Still, with true natty badassery, the Inca noble rips the flaming arrows sticking out of his crotch, throws his down his weapons, stuffs a handful of dirt into his mouth as sort of a last-resort happy meal with no toy surprise, then vaults to his death from the top of the fortress. Sore loser.

With the super badass outta the way, Hernando Pizarro and his maniacs enter Saxy and start playing hacky sack with rest of the Inca's vital organs, leaving huge heaps of stinking, unburied corpses as party snacks for the vultures and giant condors. Ugghh.

Things suck even worse for the Incas back in Lima. Manco's numero uno generalissimo, Quizo, decides to go for the gusto and runs a blitz on the city of kings.

Quizo's Lombardi Trophy speech to his troops sets the tone for the shitfest to come: "I intend to enter the town today and kill all the Spaniards in it. . . . if I die all will die, and if I flee all will flee."

He died. The Spaniards charge they cavalry out on the flat ground and bash the Inca's brains in before they can even shit theyselves properly. After that little stinker of a slaughter is over, the fight goes out of the rest of them Incas.

Remember Me?

Meanwhile, back in Chile, Diego de Almagro can't find any gold, only crotch rot and pissed-off natives. So, when he finally says 'Screw this' and returns to Peru, he ain't exactly in a happy homicidal camper kind of mood.

In 1537, he leads a uncivil war between the conquistadors, but Francisco's surfin' Bra Boy Hernando stomps a mudhole in his chainmail at the Battle of Salinas and executes the BLEEP outta him. One would thinks that they all woulda had they fill of violence by now, but nah, fluck that. New conquistadors rally around Diego de Almagro the younger, son of Diego de Almagro. Aye, those wacky pre, pre, pre, pre, pre, pre, pre, pre, pre, pre and pre Gen-xers and they new ideas.

All Bad Things Must Come to an End: The Death of Francisco Pizarro.

For the next three years, Francisco Pizarro chills out in Lima, trying not to get the syphilis. But on the morning of Sunday, 26 June 1541, a group of about twenty pissed-off and armed Almagrists force they way into his palace. Most of Pizarro's companions wuss out and flee, which sucks, because cowards die a thousand deaths. But it sucks even worse for Pizarro, who gets the shit beaten out of him worse than a birthday piñata when all the parents hand they kids dynamite and pick axes and tells them to get to work. Still, before the block party music starts kickin' in, the seventy-year-old codger whips out his flaming sword Justice and slices and dices up three of his attackers before the rest take turns filleting him like sushi.

Even in this flucked up, bitter beer-face ending, Pizarro keeps faith in the religion in whose name he'd slaughtered millions, finger painting the sign of the cross with his own blood like he's Picasso and crying out "Jesus!" before joining the vast majority and biting the big, stanky one.

A violent and dramatic end for a man whose name, like his asshole cousin Hernan Cortés, is known for greed, treachery, and bad table manners.

Aye, human folly.

MEANWHILE, BACK IN LIMA. . .

PADDINGTON BEAR MARTINI

Ingredients:
2 spoons English orange marmalade
1 3/4 ounces Rutte Dry Gin
3/4 ounce BarSol Mosto Verde Italia Pisco
1/2 ounce Martini Bianco Vermouth

Preparation:
Shake all ingredients with ice and fine strain into a
chilled glass. Add an orange zest twist for garnish.

Ahhhhhhhh.

This is it. High up. Floating in the traffic-light cloudcover while perched on a double-decker tour bus built like a giant red tank. The semi-sane way to deal with Lima's gridlock. The first dozen or so rides here are like being stuck in an absurd virtual reality game, where 'Frogger' meets 'Grand Theft Auto', except you only get one life with no power-ups and the video game's boss comes at you from every direction, even falling from the sky.

But, in a few days, the mind acclimates. Pretty soon, even bloodcurdling visions of your vital organs smeared on the back bumper of a water truck start to seem blasé. And after a few weeks in Lima traffic, forget about it. Something you first dreaded--say being impaled by a school bus crammed with kids after forcibly merging across three lanes in front of a traffic cop is child's play. Whew. Stay relaxed and tuck 'n' roll. What the fuck? Recent brushes with death aside, Auntie M and I are actually enjoying this particular jaunt. The tour bus lumbers through lane changes like an elephant on four wheels, ready to punish any motorist foolish enough to hold its ground.

The bus is filled with loud tourists enjoying the three-hundred-sixty degree spectacle of watching the world's largest demolition derby competition from the safety of a comfy seat slicing through the playing field.

Our tour guide, Julio, is a slight, taciturn young Peruvian whose ponytail juts from his baseball cap. We recoil at the feedback hiss as he taps the microphone and begins narrating our ride from tonier places like Miraflores and San Isidro juxtaposed with barrios of striking poverty on the way to the city center, the 'City of Kings.'

All gazes veer left as Julio points at a large stagger-stepped adobe structure seemingly plunked down at random, out of place in Lima's cityscape. Technical difficulties. "This is Huaca Pucllana. It served as an important. . . Asu.."

The guide tries his best to fix the situation by jabbing the head of the microphone into his open palm, recreating the concussive sounds of mini-shotguns blasting out our eardrums.

That's too much for my cringy tourist brethren. Yells and murmurs. A spastic shout of "Oh my God! Make it stop!"

Julio sheepishly whistles into the mic, then laughs, satisfied the problem is behind him.

"It (inaudible)rved as an impor(inaudible) ceremonial (inaudible) advancement. . ."

"Dios mio." Auntie M holds back a chuckle.

Not an entirely bad act. He strains a smile, pushing through his doomed performance like a deflated ventriloquist ready to bolt the stage. ". . . of the Li (inaudible) Culture, a soc(inaudible) which (inaudible) in the (inaudible) Coast between (inaudible) 700 (inaudible) D."

A voice screeches. "Could you repeat all that?"

Dark humor. More laughing.

Julio turns away from us and looks down. "(inaudible)aca Pucl(inaudible). Mierda."

He slumps into his seat, frustrated in defeat as the tourists start blathering back and forth.

"Acapulco? Where the hell is that?"

"Is he talking about that, uh, pyramid-looking thing behind us?"

"That's Mexico, darling."

"But we passed that five minutes ago. I think he's talking about that Chifa restaurant over here."

"Well I can't see anything, anyway, with this fog."

"Yeah, what's it called again?"

"I wonder if the people riding downstairs can hear any better. Maybe we could switch seats?"

"What's a Chifa? Looks Chinese to me."

"Ah, dammit. I just googled it, yesterday. I know what it is."

"I thought this was summer?"

"The locals call it, uh, gout or something. Something with a G?"

Tough crowd. Especially the loud couple seated kitty-corner from us from Las Vegas with their baby, Lil' Ray Ray, Jr. They seem friendly enough, at first. With the audio production thrown into chaos, however, Ray Ray Sr. has taken it upon himself to try his hand at stand-up comedy. Some things are best left to the professionals.

I turn to Auntie M as she looks up from her phone. "What do you call the fog down here?"

"Garua."

That was fast. "Guaru-ah?"

She goes full turtle mode. "Ga-ru-a. Es because the ocean is cold. You knows Herman Melville?"

I blink.

She smiles. "He calls Lima the strangest and saddest city no one can see." Then, with a firm nod, she stares back at her phone.

"Where do you *get* all this stuff?"

"Oh, silly Dougito. There is still a lots you don't know about me. I es an international woman of mystery."

#

It was bound to happen.

After our tour guide surrendered to his audio problems, everyone eventually settles down to enjoy the refreshing breeze on our faces and a low murmur of polite conversation. I watch five cars up ahead all turn left, blatantly ignoring a red light. Normal stuff.

We're passing by a lush green park when Ray Ray, Jr. lets loose his flat-out, hypersonic assault on the ears, informing every living soul within a moving five-block radius exactly what he thinks of this bus ride.

As his screaming bursts eardrums, he looks up at me, a face of total, pissed-off innocence. All I can do is smile, and look over at his proud parents. "Precious."

Little Ray Ray's mom smiles, pleased her fleshy little gem has sparkled for yet another soul. Yes, so precious.

#

'Oohs' and 'ahhhs' as tourists jostle over to our side of the bus, and I'm up close and personal with a gringa grandma's armpit folds. She's taking pictures, oblivious to my plight, and all I can think of is some bizarre live-action, geriatric armpit-licking fetish that's so kinky it's not even covered in the entire canon of internet porn. Pushing Grandma aside, I uncoil out of my seat and look around. Auntie M jabs at my shoulder, pointing down at the commotion on the street. A guy in a homemade superhero outfit the color of a ripened key lime somersaults between rows of cars at the stop light.

It's an impromptu Cirque du Soleil street show. A surreal venue to see a skillfully-trained performer risk a snapped ankle from a failed pratfall or a gashed face from a side view mirror, and all for spare change.

The light turns green. Sprinkled applause as the masked man stashes his tip money into an old tin can. Our bus pulls away and I ponder how many other surprises await us in a city teeming with the creative working-class hustles.

"This is it!" Julio has ditched the microphone, preferring to scream through cupped hands. He admonishes us fifteen times that we're getting off now and not to stray too far away, waving his yellow flag on a twig for emphasis.

The tour guide's lecture ends with Ray Ray, Sr. yelling out, "Could you repeat all that?", then cackling like he's just finished up his sold-out South American comedy tour.

He beams at his wife. She hands him a stroller as the other tourists leave the bus in a disorganized clot.

Stepping off the bus, I peer along a long street filled with vendors, then over at Julio. He's itching his back with his yellow flag while flirting with a young lass working at a booth hawking Moche erotic art.

Great. He could drop us off at a city dump and say it's an Incan shrine to Atahualpa and we'd be none the wiser. Looking down at my 'World's Okayest Peruvian' T-shirt. Ah, yes, the tourist life.

I watch as Auntie M takes a long, catlike stretch and yawns without opening her eyes. "Where are we?"

"No sé." She stops, looking around. "You been here long enoughs. Español, por favor."

I feel the words wedge uncomfortably between my teeth. Shit. She's called my shitty Spanish bluff. "¿Qué. . . hacemos, uh, ahora?"

"¿Ahora? Caminamos. ¿Por qué?"

"Uh. . ." Whatever comes out. Comes out.

"Go ahead."

"¿Nadachante?" Cringe worthy.

"¿Nadachante? You is makings up words?"

Guilty as charged.

Auntie M puts her phone in her pocket and unfurls her arm in an affected manner, pointing down the street where our tourist group clamors and shops. "Just follows the jello brick road."

A sharp slap to his face signifies that all is not well with Julio's flirtship. Primal Directive frustrated, Julio breaks free, cat-herding his gringo charges around his yellow banner and leading us into the courtyard maw of the Plaza de Armas' amazing architecture:

The Neo-Baroque Government Palace, with Pizarro's coat of arms displayed on the main portico; the Baroque Archbishop's Palace, with its facade of reintigrated rock and ornate cedar balconies; the Lima Cathedral and its neoclassical slate towers; and the Municipal Palace with its mustard-colored facade and influences from the French Renaissance.

Auntie M and I follow closely as our guide walks towards the center of the Plaza, keeping his head down and speaking in hushed tones like an actor badly reciting rehearsed lines.

"The historic center was founded by Pizarro in 1535. The Plaza was heavily damaged during an earthquake in 1746. Almost all the churches, convents, monasteries, chapels, and hospitals were flattened. The Cathedral of Lima began its reconstruction in 1752. . ."

I smile, hearing Ray Ray, Sr., somewhere in the back, spout off "Could you repeat all that," followed by his own smug laughter. The joke that never dies.

We admire the Central Fountain. Beautifully-carved mastiffs dry-hump gargoyles who projectile-vomit streams of water at a three-disked obelisk surmounted by a bust of a fairy king playing the trumpet. As a confirmed non-expert on just about everything, I'm at a loss, but it looks important.

More "Oohs" and "Aahs" as everyone selfies themselves into a smart phone oblivion while Julio narrates.

"In 1651 this bronze fountain was erected. It was here on July 28th, 1821, when the Fiestas Patrias or Independence Day of Peru was proclaimed. Lima also celebrates Pisco Day on the 4th Sunday of July. They replace the water and fill up this fountain with 2,000 liters of Pisco, and when Pisco Day falls on Independence Day. . . "

He frowns and places his thumb and index finger in his mouth and screeches a coarse whistle. Heads snap around.

Then, back to his shy, deadpan self. ". . . watch out."

'THE GUS'S PERUVIAN GUIDEBOOK' PROUDLY PRESENTS:

Chapter Eleven: Peruvians Independence Day!

One fined-ass day on 9, Dec. 1824, Simón Bolívar's awesome lieutenant, Antonio José de Sucre, beat the piss out of the Spanish. The locals thought this was neat, so they decided to throw a party, and Peruvian Independence Day was born.

It takes place every July 28th and 29th, and is called Las Fiestas Patrias.

What can you expect if you is in Peru during Las Fiestas Patrias?

Most government offices and all banks will be closed, so grab a fist-full of drinking dinero early. The Plaza de Armas in every city around Peru will be in full party mode, with a gi-huge-ic number of Peruvian music and dances, from traditional folkloricos and Afro-Peruvian songs to modern rock and reggaeton will be played. Official fireworks begins at midnight, and there is an crackin' 3-D light show at the Fantasia Fountain in Centro De Lima.

All week there will be even more food carts and vendors on the streets than usual, so chow down 'til your knees bend and your belt buckles on anticucho, papas rellenas, chicharrón and ceviche.

The skulls in the well were artistically placed in a concentric circle.

The curator's voice drones, "The Franciscans took a vow of celibacy and obedience. . ."

My God. Sounds like my high school years.

After walking around the ancient library of the Convento de San Francisco and its thousands of antique texts, some of them predating the conquest, our tour group gapes at the fine artwork, then descends to the catacombs. The crypts of built of brick and mortar, and have stood up well to earthquakes. They're also expansive, with an estimated 25,000 bodies laid to rest there. Everyone's respectfully quiet in the crypt, except for little Ray Ray, Jr., who's screaming like a cherubic air raid siren. His mother pulls him from the stroller that Ray Ray, Sr. has been lugging down the steps. Ray Ray, Jr.'s cries grow louder as she bounces him on her shoulder. . .

. . . Can nobody else hear that?

The Monastery guide's voice intones:

"It was customary to bury people under the church here up until 1808, when the cemetery of Lima opened. At that time, the catacombs were closed off, after accepting somewhere close to 25,000 bodies, where they stayed undisturbed until they were rediscovered in 1943."

That faint sound again, like threading needle scratching a warped vinyl record. It just won't leave my ears alone. I can barely make it out over Ray Ray, Jr's. shenanigans and the guide's learned babbling, but there's something there droning. A faint buzz. I wipe the sweat from my brow.

"As'sid'u'ous'ly."

I turn. Auntie M looks up from her phone and continues zombie-walking.

Finally, a voice of reason. "Hey, do you hear th-"

She ignores me, blithely pacing while peering into her phone and whispering a soft chant: "Pro'pi'tious'ly. . . Me'tic'u'lous'ly."

The guide keeps reciting, ignoring the child's bawling.

"Archaeologists decided to sort through the skeletons. Instead of keeping the bodies semi-intact, they put all the skulls together, all the femurs together, all the tibias together, and so on."

"Pfffffhhhththththaahhh!"

What the hell? I look over at the guide.

No way. Can't be.

It's Gus. He's dressed in a powerfully weird getup: felt hat, leather jacket over a Franciscan robe partially covering a canary yellow khaki shirt and matching pants, high boots and wielding a curved knife.

What the fuck? He looks at me and laughs. "Pfffffhhhththththaahhh!"

#

We're back on the double-decker bus. I thought the fresh air might do me some good, but that buzzing noise in my ears is getting louder.

Auntie M sits next to me, a life-sized voodoo doll tethered to her phone. "Con'spic'u'ous'ly. . . Trem'u'lous'ly. . ."

The filter and the noise. Swear I've heard this before.

To my left, Ray Ray, Jr. is safely tucked between his mother's arms. She looks down at him, then over at me and smiles. "Precious."

Ray Ray, Jr. and I lock eyes. He squints and shakes his little fist at me, then lets out a unholy shriek as his head twists completely, all 360 degrees, around his neck.

I don't know whether to faint or shit my pants. Quick glances around the bus. No one else seems to mind the fact we've got a lil' Lucifer in our midst.

"Hey, you!" A deep, raspy voice that could boil nails.

I peer around, frantically. Did no one else hear that?

The Voice. "Yeah, you buddy."

I look down. Ray Ray, Jr. has horizontal goat eyes. He raises his little hand and flips me off with his stubby middle digit with a gravelly baritone "Fuck you!" and a serpent's forked tongue flicks from out his mouth.

What. The. Fuck?

An aneurysm of psychosis. I jump up and point. "Devil baby!"

Snatching the little bundle of hell from his shocked mother, and, before anyone can do anything, I boot that bald Beelzebub-looking bastard right off the bus.

I punt that little fucker straight through the uprights of the park's two biggest trees. Hundred-to-one shot. Easy. I'm telling you, that little spawn of Satan caught some serious hang time. Pausing, I admire what I have accomplished in my short time in Peru.

Now, before you get the wrong idea, I want to set the record straight. I'm not much of an athlete. Never claimed to be. And it's not like I've had a lot of practice kicking devil babies, before. This is a first for me. But, God as my witness, when it comes to kicking them babies, I'm a one-hundred-percent, genuine, Goddamn All-Star.

A tug on my shoulder. And that's when all hell and Ray Ray, Sr's. fists-- break loose on my face. Lusty cheers as my body flies backward. Before I know what hit me, I'm falling down the bus steps and landing hard.

For a split second I think my neck's broken, but as Ray Ray, Sr. picks me up to knock me back down again, I realize I do have some basic motor skills left. Reminds me of kindergarten, when a couple of behemoth first graders threw me off the monkey bars. Just for the hell of it.

It's a strange sensation swallowing your own teeth. A bloody, plaque-and-broken-enamel-filled mess as Ray Ray, Jr. curb-stomps me, grinding my molars down my throat. I wouldn't recommend it. Somewhere in the ass-kicking time fog, he's knocked me off the bus. I think it was a knee, although I'd have to check with the replay booth to be sure.

There's a clamor of throaty shrieks and curdling cries ranging from 'That's right! Kick the shit out of him!' to 'Fuck you, baby kicker!' to the instant classic 'Rip off his fucking balls!' Anything to satiate the Just Bleed God as the tour bus crowd selfies and applauds from the benign sanctity of the moral majority.

My inert body lands on the park grass. His weight's on my chest as he towers over me. Breath smells like ceviche. Even through all this bloody mess I can't help but think we're gonna be instant Youtube sensations soon. A dynamic slapstick duo. Hell, Ray Ray, Sr. will probably get a 'Father of the Year' award back in Sin City for this righteous little knuckle-dusting. A bonafide international super hero for the dad bod set.

As he rains down hellbows, I gasp for precious last breaths. I'm in no shape to defend myself. All my effort is going into counting which shot to the temple is gonna rip away dear consciousness. Just do it. Finish me, you big pussy.

That's it!

Jesus Christ! That's the sound that's been rattling in my head this whole time. 'Islands in the Stream.' Is it the same for everyone in these crucial, shedding off the mortal coil moments? Tongue's numb. Breathing's labored. Heart's thudding through the cracked sternum. A sickly, metallic taste in my mouth. Blurred vision and ears ringing. . .

. . . And now the Bee Gees are serenading my big send-off into an afterworld party. . .

"Pffffhhhthththaahhh!"

With the one eye that hasn't been bashed in, I look over at the bus. Gus has stolen the tour guide's microphone and is leading all the tourists into some sort of frenzied karaoke dance-off. And Pishtaco 'Troy' and an enano gimp are serving drinks to these fuckers. What the hell? Gus stops dancing with Auntie M and locks eyes with me.

Peering down with a grin, he presents the back of his hand, holding it high in the air, then stretches his fingers out, and they fall off, one by one.

I look at them all piled up next to me and they start wriggling like worms in the dirt.

You know, all in all, it's been a bad day.

"AAaaaaaaaaggghhhhhaaaahhh!!!"

#

I'm stuck, shifting in this plastic chair in the doctor's waiting room, listening to a muzak version of the Bee Gees serenading me. Auntie M stares at my bony knees in loose-fitting jeans, then up at my disheveled hair. "Es you okay? You looks like a homeless pirate."

I shrug. "I'm fine."

Lara confers with her in Spanish, then Auntie M nods at me sympathetically. "Es it your eh-stomach?"

"It's not that bad. . ."

"You knows, I've been talkings to Lara. . ."

Oh Christ. Each time Auntie M starts that sentence I find myself cast in a conspiracy theory that would rival an epic Alex Jones rant about unseen Zapruder footage of JFK and Elvis flying suicide planes into the Twin Towers on 9/11 narrated by the lost eighteen-minutes of the Nixon Tapes found floating in the Gulf of Tonkin.

In the elevator up to the doctor's office, Lara confesses to Auntie M about the good seventy-plus deadly diseases she thinks I just might have: IBS, all flavors of colon cancer, GERD, Cystic fibrosis, the onset of Cantu Syndrome, Chiggers, a Peptic Ulcer, Hantavirus, Jejunal Atresia, Whipple Disease, Hairy Black Tongue, Intestinal Pseudo-Obstruction. And so on. Finally, Lara convinces Auntie M that I need to see Lara's doctor, whom she visits at least twice a week to stave off her bouts of hypochondria.

Once we hit seventh-floor waiting room, Lara plunks down onto the faux-leather couch and tells Auntie M I look tense and to relax. This is her best doctor, whom she visits at least twice a week to stave off her unrelenting bouts of hypochondria.

Then she starts into a diatribe worthy of the Wailing Wall about her ultimate nightmare: being trapped in a high-rise building during a major earthquake.

I saunter over to inspect a window to jump out of just as a lanky nurse with a clipboard appears. "¿Uh. . . Senor Dung?"

Snickers from Auntie M and Lara.

"Dung is my. . . Doug is my first name."

She snatches the ball-point pen nestled behind her ear, scratches out a line in the paperwork, then gestures towards the open office door.

"Buena suerte." Lara and Auntie M give two big, cheery thumbs up for the moment of truth.

The doctor is a short, balding, affable man who immediately puts me at ease. "So, Auntie M says you've lost some weight and you mumble to yourself? Is this true?"

Should I spill the beans? "Yeah."

Chuckling, he pulls out a clipboard while flicking his pen. "What was that?"

I sigh. "Ahem, I said that sounds about right."

He shakes his head, smile evaporating. "Well, do you answer yourself back?"

"No." I tap at the tile floor with my feet. "Not usually."

"Ah, then there's nothing to worry about." He takes one peep at my 'Wooden Spoon Survivor' T-shirt and khaki boonie hat, asks my age, then politely broaches whether I'm aware of any undiagnosed severe retardation in my family history.

"I don't think so."

His concerned look warms to a pleasant smile. "Just thought I'd ask. No offense."

"None taken. And the buzzing."

"Buzzing?"

"In my ears. I've always had it, but it seems to be getting louder. Sometimes it's all I can hear at night."

"Really?" He pulls a water pistol-shaped flashlight with a tapered barrel. "Turn your head to the side, please."

I do and he shoves it into my ear for a good look. "So, your tinnitus keeps you up at night, eh?"

"Yeah."

"Other side. Well, that could explain a lot right there. Lack of sleep."

"Weird dreams."

"Wet dreams?"

"I said weird dreams."

"Ah. See, you are mumbling. Raise your shirt, please."

"Oh!"

My belly skins forms goosebumps as he slides the ice-cold stethoscope around while my innards moan like an ill-tempered howler monkey.

He gives me a thumbs up. "Besides, it's amazing what a positive attitude can do. My gardener's quite slow thinker, but I'd bet a million Turkish Lira he trims hedges better than you."

"What makes you say that?"

"You don't look very handy. That's all." He leans in and scowls. "Oh!"

"What?"

"Shhhhhhh. Boy, you're really missing out on some gastronautical awesomeness, my friend. Madam Tusan, an impeccable chifa owned by Gaston Acurio; Bistecca, a buffet-style pasta grill--"

"Am I okay?"

"Shhhhhhh! Cala, oceanside fine dining, listening to the waves suck back through the rocks; Central, a Michelin-rated restaurant that's like eating through a 16-course Chihuly exhibit."

"Sounds nice, but what's the diagnosis, Doc?"

With an accommodating smile he rips off a paper sheet from his clipboard and hands it to me. "The verdict is that you're hungry." He sneaks a glance at his watch. "Come to think of it, I'm hungry, too."

The paper seems official, typed in both Spanish and English:

'HURT FEELINGS REPORT'

After reading through a few sections about my personal history and injury data, there's a list of unchecked boxes:

PART IV - REASON FOR FILING THIS REPORT (Mark all the apply):

> **I am thin skinned**
> **I am a wimp**
> **I am a crybaby**
> **I want my mommy**
> **Someone needs to fix my problems**
> **My feelings are easily hurt**
> **I didn't sign on for this**
> **I was told that I am not competent**
> **the weather is too cold**
> **the weather is too hot**
> **the weather is too dry**
> **the weather is too wet**
> **ALL OF THE ABOVE AND MORE**

My doctor's tone is pleasant, yet firm. "You gotta get out there and enjoy life, son. Take some risks. And if you wind up blowing out your O ring. . ." he grabs a bottle of knock-off Pepto-Bismol, passes it to me and shrugs. "Maybe try some chicken soup for a few days."

He orders a pizza on his cell phone, then listens patiently as Lara launches into an hour-and-a-half long seance over her litany of ailments. To this day, Lara still thinks I'm in denial about suffering from Munchausen Syndrome.

#

Auntie M leaves her Hobbit House, plopping down at the glass living room table to edit an ad jingle she's voiced.

I'm stuck to the faux leather couch, basking in a Pepto Bismol brain fog. A big yawn. "I'm bored."

She puts on her reading glasses and stares into her laptop screen. "Tranquilo, Dougito. The answer to all your problems is in the back of your eyes."

"What?"

"In the nook in the bookcase behind you."

I rummage while listening to her cut and loop a happy little ditty that sounds like an old ad jingle. "Nothing."

"The other drawer."

She glances over to see me pull out a TV remote. "Aye. Eso."

It's a complicated-looking sucker. Where's the damn power button?

"It es not going to bite you."

OK. I haphazardly press buttons.

It's a local news report, *Las Millionarias "Palpas" Del Amor*. The well-to-do in Huancayo, *The happiest place in South America*, are going crazy, over-the-top themselves for bragging rights on who can wield the most fuck-you bling for wedding gifts.

"I think some bride in Huancayo just got twelve-hundred cases of cerveza and a condo in Lima as a wedding gift."

"Aye. Try the news."

"I thought that was the news."

CLICK.

I alight on a goofy guy in a tweed suit, day-glow white teeth, and a felony of a haircut seated behind a naugahyde news desk.

"You mean the one that looks like a capybara shit on his head?"

"Sí. You might learns eh-something."

He grins a big gap-toothed smile, talking to the camera in Spanish while the camera angle changes. The news geek turns awkwardly before cutting to a busty Latina reporter dressed to the nines and holding a microphone infront of three women in shapely green and red costumes. They are being cheered lustily by a festive crowd while they take bites out of large pieces of watermelon.

"You're right. I did learn something. I now know Miss Watermelon has been crowned in the middle of the Amazon?"

CLICK.

Time to take the channels for a spin. Terrible choices. I settle on 'Night at the Roxbury', but it's so badly dubbed it feels like watching 'Turkish Star Wars' on acid.

"Nothing but crap." Chucking the remote to the side, I sink into the couch and rub my tummy.

She looks my way. A hearty guffaw.

"What?"

"Your hair." Stifled giggling. "You looks like a payaso. A clown."

It's true. Despite Gus' promises, my immersion hasn't improved my Spanish one iota and I still haven't mustered the courage to ask for a haircut. My last failed foray into BilingualLand, I tried ordering a coffee at the local Starbucks. All seemed well, until the friendly barista misunderstood my name, writing 'Dung' on the side of my coffee cup. Then, somehow 'Dung's' Vanilla Latte order morphed into a weird Frapucchino mixed with Lucuma. A tasty upgrade, but one I barely had the Soles to cover.

I'm not taking those kind of gambles with my hair, so I just let it grow. And grow. In the place where my imagination never meets reality, I thought I'd look cool in my new, long-maned style, kinda like Jesus or maybe even the lead guitarist of Tool. You know, somebody with a life plan.

But as the days stack up, one thing is certain: I am right-haired. Who knew? The starboard side has branched out, from tiny acorn follicle to pre-mullet sequoia, able to defy both gravity and moisturizing conditioners until the end of times. The left side, on the other hand, looks like the pathetic patchy pubic hairs on a mange-infected female hyena's spotted clitoris. A bit of a train wreck.

It's gotten so bad that every time I put my trusty emerald Mark Twain 'Territory Ahead' ball cap on without caking on the styling gel, my hair flares out, earning stares and making me look like a four-eyed circus clown.

I clutch my belly and moan.

Auntie M snaps her laptop shut. "Let's try a. . . different cure."

"Oh, please, not that doctor, again. I can't go back."

She rises to grab her red jacket from the coat rack. "Tranquilo. Western medicine es only been around for 2,500 years or eh-so. This es debased on mythology."

Did I hear that right? "Debased on mythology?" I struggle to my feet.

"Sí. And besides, how can you knows the "real" Lima hanging out in Miraflores or San Isidro?"

I want to file a protest, but she's already passed my rhetorical Maginot Line. "I'm game. What do you have in mind?"

She looks me dead in the eyes and grins. "I am taked you to the Witches Market in Gamarra."

"Gamarra?" Sounds like some giant, radioactive flying turtle that gets its jollies off fighting Godzilla and ripping up downtown Tokyo. "What's a Gamarra?"

Auntie M picks up her laptop and brushes past me. "And the first rule. No bringing any valuables."

Huh?

#

Question: What's red and green and goes 175 miles an hour?

Answer: The cure for my stomach problems.

Auntie M and I are riding around with her friend Merlina, an unrepentant shopaholic, who's driving with the hair-pinned aggression of a fighter pilot. I mean aggressive by even Peruvian standards. Vehicular rampage. Lima's fearless Blue Angel of the highways and byways.

Merlina's Toyota Tercel speeds toward a place I have been warned, repeatedly, to avoid: the district of La Victoria.

I guess it's all relative. The TV news in Lima is not unlike the U.S: If it bleeds, it leads. But the constant hum of dramatic crimes and tragedies makes parsing what's merely dangerous from what's completely fucking dangerous surprisingly difficult. Walking around middle-class neighborhoods like Surco and San Borja, I've yet to encounter my worst street fears. But I feel prepared.

Not with any sort of fancy martial arts training mind you. No Rex kwon do. No boxing. No Aikido. No Karate. No Brazilian Jiu Jitsu. Not even Roshambo. Nada.

But I have the right mentality for violence.

Most people take being mugged at gunpoint personally. This is wrong. Even the phrase 'armed robbery' starts the whole venture off on the wrong foot. Bad language. Bad vibes. It's no wonder so many hard-working, honest-to-goodness street thugs get such a nasty rap. Where is the justice in this world?

A lot of unenlightened people have been brainwashed into viewing the barrel of a fully-loaded .357 pointed smack-dab between their eyes as a disaster. But not me. I like to think of it as opportunity for spontaneous charity. A 6-inch serrated blade placed a whisker's breadth from your carotid artery will make you a giver as well. Gives you confidence in your fellow man. And all you needed was that little extra-caliber push to overcome your inner Scroogie. Hallelujah!

After all, only in these precious, powerful moments will you come to realize that all the disposable wealth stored in your greedy pockets is a mere pittance compared to your newfound generosity. It is only then, with nerve endings raw and the brain squealing in stuck-pig survival mode, that one can honestly say, "Hey, everybody! Look at me! I am a giver!"

I came to Gamarra's twenty-four square blocks of the hardest of hardcore swap meet for two things for my sensitive stomach. After a failed fling with the pills-and-diet approach of western medicine, it was time to give folklore and superstition a crack at it. So, I'm off to the Mercado de Los Brujos.

There's one slight problem. Merlina seems to have forgotten where the Witches' Market is. Was this her plan all along? Less Brujos means more time idling along in the throng of people, enjoying the lure of deeply-discounted prices and the fever of haggling for your prize. So, Merlina and Auntie M amble into the small city of clothing stalls and tiendas, on guard but chatting happily.

I bring up the rear, a disowned pet, trying to make some semblance of order out of Gamarra's writhing, undifferentiated mass fading into the clouded haze. We weave through an ever-tightening chessboard of storefronts stuffed with every stripe of garment imaginable, all overflowing beneath garish umbrellas and nylon awnings onto the street.

Passersby glare at me as if I'm suspect. Is this the gringo novelty factor or just me? There's a sense that the day's safe pleasantries can change on a dime amidst the crushing chaos. Maybe I picked the wrong day to wear my 'Be Ready For The Alpacalypse' T-shirt?

Dipping into a side store, I catch Auntie M patiently waiting as Merlina equivocates for an eternity about which blue blouse to buy from the high stacks of boxes and crates.

Auntie M gives me a withering scowl. "Dougito! Don't you eh-stray so far or you might get robbed."

"How? I'm piss broke."

"¿Que?"

"Well, damn near piss broke."

"Y then what?"

Oh, boy. Good question.

Merlina whistles as she approaches us, showing off a darling blue 'No Drama Llama' T-shirt.

"Chevere." Auntie M gives her a plucky thumbs-up.

"Ready?" Satisfied, Merlina perks up in front of us, both hands grasping plastic bags full of sartorial gems.

Pointing towards the exit door, I give my most respectful bow.

"Après vous, Madame."

Merlina surges ahead like an icebreaker, wriggling through the fissures in the fleshstream as Auntie M and I tow along like dinghies.

While keeping a carefully-peeled eye out for signs of shamans, I break the silence. "When I was a young lad, I was so sure that one day, I'd grow up to do something amazing. . ."

A look, like I've asked her to sew my eyeballs into the palms of my hands. ". . . or at least competent. Yeah, let's go with competent, shall we? But now that's never going to happen."

"Why not?" Auntie M stops and studies Merlina bobbing around lost until she backtracks, heading off on a different tangent.

Keep going. "Doesn't matter. I came down here. Nothing goes right. Can't read the signs. Can't decipher the language. Ya'll need to speak slower, by the way."

A quiet giggle. "We can work on that. Being fair, English es not an easy piece of postre, either."

"Point taken. Now I'm stuck. I can't go back and live out the rest of my days as a guppy in the Estatos Unitos economic shark tank blender. I just can't do it."

"Es Estados Unidos, Dougito."

"Shit."

A sharp dog whistle trains our eyes ahead. It's Merlina waving back at us, the trace of an impish smile on her face.

Aha! We're getting close. I can feel it.

When we walk under the Gamarra tram station, on Aviacion, Auntie M points to two large crocodile heads splayed on a plastic tote along with a gargantuan boa constrictor carcass. A tall, sturdy man in a colorful chullo sidles up to Merlina with a big jar of snake fat, claiming it's a cure for arthritis. Yep. We've arrived.

We venture down the maze of everything dead, stuffed, and weird. It's a street of crocodiles, snakes, frogs, quail eggs, strangely-scented fruits, dried llama fetuses, slimy mixtures, incense, amulets, and monkey skulls. To the right, one stand overflows with multi-hued beakers filled with potions, each with labels listing what a witch in Peru might need to concoct an elixir for those suffering from asthma, impotence, anemia, parasitic growths and possibly even Mad Cow Hairy Black Tongue.

To the left it's a cram-packed macabre menagerie, from the whimsically quaint to the quite odd to entire displays that look like the Halloween party decor underneath a serial killer's trap door basement.

Auntie M and I join Merlina, who's busy staring at a multi-colored candle shrine.

Merlina presents a dried llama fetus in a glass jar filled with liquid gunk. "This is for you."

"Uh, no thanks."

A playful grin. "Oh! And if I see a guy with a little monkey in a box, look away."

What? Why?

A tall salesgirl with dark pigment spots on her face and a receding chin, approaches us with a crooked squint and gesticulates at the candles like she's casting a spell.

The salesgirl demonstrates every eccentric candle at Merlina's beck and whim while I walk up to Auntie M, who sees my approach and puts down her phone. "So, what es you going to do, Dougito?"

"The truth?"

We nonchalantly drift about like corks in an ocean of relics that look like something out of a psychopathic clown's primordial wet dream.

"Sí. Why not?"

"Oh, I don't know. . ." *Wow! Whatever the fuck we just passed will NEVER be unseen. Ugggh.* "No, you know what? Fuck it. You wanna know?"

Auntie takes one step back. "Uh, I guess so."

"Fine I'm gonna piss away the rest of my cash on a fucking trebuchet, fucking lighter fluid, five fucking metric shit tons of alcohol and a kick ass, righteous sound system. Then, after a final flight check, I'm gonna blast music thundering 'til it shreds my eardrums, take an absolutely heroic dose of LSD, pull my nutsack over my head with both hands for good luck and launch myself into a fuck-this-stinking-flesh-and-searing-lungs-end-of-my-existence. Then, with flames burning the skin off my face, I'll toast myself with a big fucking farewell jägerbomb as my consciousness hurtles my fucked-up soul towards oblivion at nature-raping speeds, pointing at a black hole somewhere in the vicinity of Bulgaria. God willing."

She stops. I think that got her attention, but she's stuck for something to say.

My big, warm, happy Bogart smile. "How about you? What would you like to do for fun?"

"Feeling better?"

I look around, self-evaluating, then bob my head up and down. "Yeah, I think so."

"Es you. . . eh-serious?"

"Let's just say it's something I've been thinking about from time to time."

"Why Bulgaria?"

I pause, searching for a thought. "Why not?"

"Dougito, that es no option."

"Oh, Bulgaria is always an option. It's just not a particularly fun one for most people to think about."

"You just gotta has faith."

"Easy for you to say. You're going to be a big-time voice actress, remember?"

She places her hand on my shoulder, carefully. "I knows my odds. . . I just accepts them."

"Well, then we're in the same boat. A special friend of mine once said, *Time has a brilliant way of dealing with all our best-laid plans. . . it just doesn't give a fuck.*

"Eh-special friend?"

"Gus."

"Oh, he's eh-special, now."

I look into her eyes, coldly. "Yes."

She winces, then smiles. "Then gives me your credit card."

"My credit card?"

She leans in, her stare overpowering mine. "I wants to help you."

"Magdita. Magdita! Eso." We both gawk as the salesgirl hands Merlina a candle molded into a pornographic wax sculpture. Merlina grabs it with gusto, eyebrows raised.

"Chevere." Auntie M nods. Merlina purchases the erotic waxwork, mentioning something to Auntie M about her husband.

I delicately tap Auntie M's shoulder. "What about that thing?"

"Aye." She barks in Spanish over at Merlina, who speaks with the salesgirl. The girl nods, her dark eyes shooting zigzag looks, before pointing directions further down the way.

We wander from shop sign to shop sign until we finally arrive at the moment of truth and time-space: a small booth with a tank full of live frogs on the counter.

Auntie M summons the young man with a black T-shirt and closely cropped hair behind the counter. As soon as she points at me he grins. With nimble fingers, a specimen is plucked from the tank.

Like an lithe automaton, he rips apart the writhing frog in front of us, throwing body bits into a boiling pot. As Auntie M and Merlina murmur behind me, he adds ingredients from a nearby row of plastic buckets.

I stare with morbid curiosity. *Eye of newt, and toe of frog, Wool of bat, and tongue of dog, Adder's fork, and blind-worm's sting, Lizard's leg, and owlet's wing.*

Then, he takes the potion and throws it in a blender. BZZZZZZZZZZZZZZZ! The ladies laugh nervously while watching my face pucker. I'm trapped, my stomach sinks watching the ground-up body parts spinning at dazzling speed. Frog Smoothie. Gamarra's answer to the Bass-o-Matic.

Finished. He pours the slurry into an espresso-sized coffee cup and reaches over the fish tank without a hint of emotion. "Eso."

I cradle the cup, still warm with gizzards. All eyes stare at the orange-ish, filmy contents. The point of no return is at hand.

I wanna flee this crime scene, like a disgusted blackjack player going bust after he's bet his wife's wedding ring, but the guts of no return are literally at hand. No matter what, poor Kermit doesn't die in vain. Waste not, want not.

One last look around at the small mob of gawkers.

How do I always manage to set myself up, again and again

Shooing flies, I squint, releasing one last sigh. Then, with a deep breath and a bit of fear, I dump the contents down my gullet. Voices squeal.

Auntie M takes a pic. "How does it tastes?"

"It's warm. Pretty good, though." Pretty good is quite the stretch. "Wanna try some?"

Reaching out, I extend the cup towards her, but she backs away and raises her hands like a judo player. "Aye. No gracias. That es desgusting."

A contained burp dredges up a gnarly aftertaste. *Yes, desgusting it is.*

MANCORA

El Capitán:

Ingredients:
2 ounces pisco
1 ounce sweet vermouth
2 dashes Angostura bitters

Preparation:
Add all ingredient to mixing glass with ice.
Stir for 20 seconds.
Strain into a coupe glass and garnish with a lemon twist.

Assiduously. That's how the mother with the pixie face and pipecleaner fingers wipes down the retractable tray and plastic cutlery in front of her toddler.

Even on this short flight, her little lass is lost in a video game trance. The mom's elvish, almond-colored eyes gaze over at her as she grabs another handiwipe from her travel bag. "Peanut allergy."

To my left, Auntie M's purple beret pins down her brown locks as she swishes her head to the beat in her earbuds next to an unflappable elderly Peruvian man sporting a peppercorn mustache. Mancora is her prescription after my trial by ring of fire in the Andes. Mancora means lounging on the beach at a nice, safe sea level. None of that high-altitude madness.

Just. . . boring tranquility.

I lean back in my seat, conjuring up visions of a lush tropical jungle adventure, but Mancora is way up north, in the desert just south of Ecuador.

Our plane touches down mid-morning in Talara. Waiting at the luggage turnstile, Auntie M and I divy up a small bag of banana chips while waiting at the luggage turnstile with the handful of bored itinerants blithely ignoring each other.

Auntie M taps her fingers while bopping her head, lost in her own musical world. Out pops the earbud. A sigh. "What now, Toadie King?"

After my frog smoothie stunt in Gamarra, word got out and I got pinned with the nickname. Definitely not hipster cool like The Lizard King, but still a conversation starter.

"You mentioned your brother's in Iquitos? Can we--"

She stares me down like I'm a pubic hair in her ceviche. "No. Too many bugs and es dangerous." Then she pushes the earbud back in, leaving me scratching away at the tinnitus in my ears. *That went well.*

After corraling our gear, she takes off for the exit, but my feet stay glued. Something's tugging on my backpack. I scan around, then down.

A glinty-eyed dwarf, in a blue uniform, smiles and pulls the pack off my shoulders. He snatches my lighter piece of rolling luggage and nods for me to go ahead.

My new compadre and I forge our path through the airport. Once outside, I shield my eyes from the sun and find Auntie M standing next to a gleaming black Toyota Hilux.

Quickening my stride. "Hey, I've made a new friend."

She cocks her head warily as the luggage wrangler chugs to keep up. The young Hilux driver steps out. He is dressed like a Johnny Cash impersonator, wearing all black, from the bottom of his brand spankin' new Converse hightops to his huge wraparound sunglasses that make him look like a film noir praying mantis with a ponytail.

As Auntie M steps into the SUV, there's a bit of luggage juggling act outside between the rest of us. Once everything's situated, my little friend looks to me, lifting his hand for a tip. After straining my foreign currency exchange math to its absolute limits, I give up, and settle on handing him all spare pocket change.

Certainly, that must be enough?

I'm jolted back into my seat as the Hilux accelerates sharply.

Apparently not. My former amigo scowls and pockets his coins, then flip me off before scuttling towards the terminal.

The ramshackle houses, graffitied billboards, discarded laundry and clusters of piled garbage finally give way to the ochre desert, making the outskirts of town feel like we're departing Mos Eisley Spaceport after a gnarly Mardi Gras at the bad end of the universe.

Panamerican Highway North is a buzzard's paradise. Parts of this hour-plus drive make the burning roads of The Mojave seem downright homey. A few crotchety pump jacks bob up and down. Elaborate crosses and makeshift shrines sporadically marking the deaths of loved ones keep company with packs of climbing goats nibbling at the tops of wizened scrub trees.

This must be Nowhere, Ground Zero.

After an hour, the desert scrub gives way to a parched Pacific coastline as the Hilux jogs to a crawl onto a pockmarked road.

Our driver yelps like a wounded polecat. "¡Carajo!" Horn blasts. A swarm of chintzy tuk tuks blaze past, a whisker's breadth from our windows. The last tuk tuk jockey spits at us, his passenger's shell shocked faces frozen in a blurred horror show. Our driver rolls down his window and shrieks out a stream of useless obscenities.

Aunti M takes off her earbuds. "You wanted your adventure."

Perking up, I squeak out, "Is this Mancora?"

Auntie M braces herself against the seat and armrests like she's riding out a medium grade earthquake. "Es Mancora Chico. Our hotel es in Vichayito. Es more tranquil than Mancora."

We hit a pothole and my head smacks hard against the ceiling. Auntie M giggles while I rub circles on the top of my head, my vision a bright medley of starbusts.

To the left, rows of restaurants. To the right, tall gates that lead to hotels. Some luxurious. Some spartan.

I think I cracked my coccyx four hotels ago. "Are we in Vichineeto?"

A soft voice from the driver's seat. "Es close."

Potholes turn to craters while we pass a wildly-painted canary-yellow hotel named 'Casa Serenity', then dip a hard right into a palm tree-lined enclosure.

The popcorn crackle of tires crunching through gravel suddenly stops. I'm bemused, eyeballing a tattered Jolly Roger flag tethered halfway up a coconut tree beneath a sign reading 'PIRATE'S COVE'.

The driver gets out, stretching his legs. I glare at Auntie M. "Pirate's Cove?"

Slowly craning from side to side to pop her neck, she opens her door. "Es less than half the other hotels."

She shrugs as the driver hoists the last piece of luggage next to me and slams the trunk. Auntie M and I stare at the life-sized plastic pirate effigy sporting a rotted life preserver with the words 'Yo Ho Ho' scribbled in black magic marker.

She scrunches her nose and starts poking around the pirate. "You can't tastes the champagne on eh beer budget, Dougito."

"Point taken. Although I didn't. . ."

Let it go. Pacing near the heavy wooden double door, I search for a doorbell. "How do you get into this place? Hello? Anybody there?"

I turn just in time to see Auntie M press a button on a rusted box attached to post partially obscured by an untrimmed bush. A speaker hidden inside the parrot perched on the pirate's shoulder squawks, "Welcome aboard, Mateys."

Footfalls advance from behind the door, then stop. The sounds of heavy locks and levers releasing. Auntie M glances at me, uncertain. I raise my eyebrows and sigh at the empty air where our ride to freedom was parked not even a minute ago. No escape.

The right door swings inward, revealing a thin, stern-faced Peruvian kid with black, curly hair, maybe just out of his teens. He greets us in Spanish. His name is Molero, the caretaker here.

Our luggage wheels slap against cobblestone as Molero leads us to our rooms.

Taking it in, the place looks better than I imagined, although the compound wall ends, giving way to shelter of banana trees only thirty feet past the big double-door entrance. Not-so-nice security.

It's a cloudless day and there's a big, inviting pool with a jacuzzi and a large thatched-roof outside bar. No people. Auntie M stops and smiles back at me, pointing to a lonely row of lounge chairs plopped in the sand facing the ocean.

After chipping a sandal on the stone path, I catch up to Auntie M playing with her phone on the front patio between the two middle rooms of a fourplex-style compound. With a heaving grunt I hoist my overpacked bags up the steps and wipe my brow. "Whew. Man, this place is dead. Where's Molero?"

The corners of Auntie M's red lips raise mischievously with an affected English accent. "You are going to loves this, Mist-ah Dougito. There es no keys at this establish-ah-ment."

I feel the folds of my forehead scrunching against the rim of my glasses when I frown.

Auntie M keeps up the facade, like she's the queen of jolly old England. "Mist-ah Dougito, accordings to my eh-source-es, the owner of this fined establish -a-ment, he got, uh, a wee bit eh-smashed at a party last night after making a fights with her girlfriend."

I turn away, chuckling under my breath. "His girlfriend."

She steps forward to get back in my face, "His girlfriend. And that is when eh-she, in a piqu-ed of fury, throws all the keys of this fine establish-a-ment onto the ocean."

Molero pops out of the door, startling me. I lock eyes with Auntie M. "What, so we're on the honor system, now?"

"The locks no work here. And even if they did, the back doors es chiquito with open eh-space at the top. Anyone only has to climb over, anyhows," she says in her regular voice.

Her face is beaming, full of herself. She reverts back to Queen Elizabeth. "Mist-ah Dougito, what are you afraid of? Someone. . . eh-scrof'u'lous?"

She laughs maniacally as she picks up her travel purse. Molero rips the lighter bag from my hands while I ponder. "Eh-scrofulous?" Great. Now I'm going to have to look up words she uses in English, too.

#

After settling into my room, I look into the mirror at the fashion squall staring back at me. Every stitch of garment, from the bright red 'Bond, Cholo Bond: Peruvian Secret Agent' t-shirt to the over-sized sombrero, to the teal cargo shorts with a big yellow cartoon alpaca's shit-eating grin absolutely screams tourist dork. Oh well, you go with what you know.

I set my backpack on a gurney, like for a masseuse or an ob-gyn, tucked against the wall. Strange? Auntie M's voice radiates from next door, playfully imitating a false baritone for a children's octopus character. I cross the room, taking in its wry charms. A king-sized bedspread beneath a wide dreamcatcher. A tasteful black-and-white portrait of a Japanese woman posing in a kimono from the play *The Mikado*. An old TV, a decent-sized couch and table with a small cloud of fruitflies swarming over a plate of overripe platinas.

The TV reverberates from next door. A telenovela. "Thin walls." I giggle and shake my head, then don my knock-off Moscot sunglasses and venture outside.

Ahhhh. Bright, fresh sunlight and a gentle sea breeze. Maybe this is what I needed all along. Move to a forgotten beach. No daily grind. No traffic noise. Get straight with life. Boil my cares away in a jacuzzi, then ooze into a lounge chair, making circles in the sand with my feet while sipping Chilcanos.

KAAATHUNK! A head-splicer of a coconut carves a deep gash in the dirt not a kindergartner's softball toss away from me. I nervously eye the batch of blurry palms towering above.

I let out a soft whistle. What a funny way to check out, being de-brained by the world's largest nut.

Shaking off the negative vibes, I shuffle past the assortment of bamboo tables. No one appears to be home, save for a white fluffball of a cat curled asleep into a ball on the rump of a mermaid statue in the corner.

My attention turns to the clamshell décor bar area with a menacing crocodile skull hanging overhead, but no bartender.

Rrrrrreeeeaaahh! I follow the scratching sound to my left. In the cubby hole next to the pickup spot, a burly figure fidgets at a small table, scratching what looks like a large protractor against a chalkboard.

The voice of a pack-and-a-half a day habit: "Ova' 'ear."

He's dressed like a disgruntled theater groupie that got bounced from the set of 'Peter Pan' for passing around quaaludes and inappropriate touching: A jizz-stained pirate's hat; a drooping right eye patch; a goofy, oversized shark tooth necklace; a fake parrot on his shoulder and a blunt in his mouth. A younger, Rubenesque Peruvian woman, adorned with a red and tan, textured bohemian poncho, is perched rigidly to his right, avoiding my gaze.

I try my best poker face. "Hey, there."

The burly pirate sizes me up. "Da name's Pirate John. Welcome 'board."

"You fuck with Pirate John, you fuck with the best! Waaaaaak!" the bird croaks.

Christ, it's real.

I offer my right hand for a handshake. The pirate pauses, then pulls up his arm from under the table. A hook. Surprised, I fumble switching hands. He reciprocates with his left. Another hook.

"Uh, what can I do ya fer?"

"Um. . ."

I sneak a glance at the woman staring into space like a puffy-eyed mannequin, like she's still in shock from being sideswiped by an emotional busride. Could be crying? Could be something stronger than a midday cocktail?

Spying a blotch of white powder over Pirate John's upper lip, I rub mine. He snarls, "Powdered donuts fer breakfast. What's yer pleasure?"

A squawk. "My coke! My coke!"

"Uhhh. Um. A Cuba Libre."

He smiles and nods. "Good choice."

Pirate John strokes his right hook through his beard and lifts his chin. "Arrrrgg! Mahhhhlly! Git yer butt ova' 'ere, boy!"

Racing footfalls. Molero dashes around the corner, bearing an armful of linens. He places them carefully on the nearest table, then stops spread-eagle next to me as Pirate John lays into him, cussing him out in gringo-fied Spanish.

I wince and watch as Molero bows his head, staring into a hole in the floorboards beneath the buzzing flies nibbling at his sandals. Probably wishes he could disappear into it.

There's been enough vile tripe posing as managers, mid-managers and lead stupervisors in my day to know the deal. A public lynching and all-around castration to let everyone know just who is boss.

Molero opens his mouth, then thinks the better of it. Ignoring me, he dashes behind the bar to whip up the concoction. Good job. Act attentive. Play busy.

The pirate relaxes, flashing a wide, toothy grin like all is right with the world again. "'Ow long ya wid us?"

My mind pops back from bad work memories. "I think three days. My. . . uh, my friend actually booked us. What is there for a tourist to do here?"

The parrot beats its wings and croaks. "Stick your head up your ass? See if it fits. Waaaak!"

"It's da beach." The pirate shrugs, then wrinkles his nose like I smell of sulfur. "Ya don't look much da surfer. Ya could go ta Nuro and swim wit' da turtles. Thar's horseback ridin' on da beach 'ere. You an' yer 'friend' could go ta Mancora an' drink 'til yer blue in da face. Ya fish?"

"Not for quite some time."

Pirate John gasps, struggling to grip the joint in his mouth with his left hook. The woman is still catatonic, a small nervous twitch her only reaction. Molero hands me my drink. Are those cigarette burns on his arm? I want a better look, but he flies off like an elite Tarahumara runner being chased down by wild dogs. Shakin' that bush, boss.

Finally, Pirate John manages to clasp the joint with both hooks before spitting it to the floor and hocking a loogie. "Some a da best fishin' in da worl' is 'n Cabo Blanco, jus' down da way. 'Ell, 'emingway caught a nine-hundre'-poun' marlin thar' back in da fifties. S'where 'e came up wit' da *Ol' Man 'n' da Sea*."

"Haaaah!" The woman blurts out what starts as a laugh, but trails off into a series of progressively weaker coughs.

For the first time, Pirate John looks at her, glowering. His mouth opens, then he changes his mind and turns to catch me transfixed at the sight of his left hook scratching his beer belly.

The doorbell sounds.

"Waaaaak!" The parrot takes off up to perch on the wall as Pirate John rises.

Holding out his arms as if he's being crucified, he bellows out, "Op'rashun Urgen' Fury. Eighta-Three. 'El'copter shot down in da battle over Fort Rupert. Both han's sheered right off in da instant."

A male voice yells from over by the 'Serenity By the Sea'. "Cut the bullshit, Shrödinger! Don't make me come over there!"

Pirate John's unfazed. "Na' ya' won'!"

"Yeah, Fuck you! Waaaaak!"

Pirate John sneers, scouring my face for any signs of disgust. "War is 'ell. But we kept da world's supply of nutmeg out da 'ands of dem commie Grenadan bastards 'n' saved Christmas fer da whorl damned free world'. Earn'd da Triple Cross a Courage fer dat 'un."

"Haaaah!" The woman looks at me, then stares straight ahead.

Pirate John sits down and scowls. "Thank ya 'ery much."

What is this?

He turns to her. "More yum yum, please."

No reaction. "More yum yum, Adriana."

A gravelly snarl. "I says 'Give Daddy 'is foockin' yum yum!'"

Adriana hesitates, then produces a lighter and a joint from underneath her poncho and turns to Pirate John, avoiding his eyes. He curls a smile. Trembling, she places the joint between his lips, then flicks her thumb on the lighter, yet fails to produce a flame. As she keeps trying for a spark, Pirate John leers and pulls her towards him with one arm. Stifling a sob, she manages to get the joint lit. They lock eyes and he inhales, the embers glowing an intense, deep red. Then, he blows a puff of smoke in her face, chortling as she pulls away.

I feel dirty all over, like I need to purge myself in a bathtub full of Drano. *Are we doomed?*

Pirate John scowls as a mousy, nervous laugh squeaks from my mouth.

Before I can reply, the puffball cat jumps on the table, leaning its face into Pirate John's gut. Its back arches as it stretches and purrs while he gently rubs his wrist behind its head. Adriana is still as a statue.

Pirate John fawns over the beast. "'Eeeees. Datsa' goods quyoootsie."

Looking back at me, Pirate John manipulates the joint towards the side of his mouth. "Ma therapy cat. Miss Whiskers."

He glares at Adriana. "Ma most prized possession." Nodding down, he allows Miss Whiskers to rub her head all over his face as he makes baby talk. "Yes ya are. O', yes ya aaaaaare."

Adriana hasn't the slightest reaction. Nothing.

His gold tooth glints as he smiles at me. "Ya got pets?"

"No."

"Didn't think so." Pirate John flares his nostrils like he's caught me ripping a squeaker from a deviled egg sandwich lunch. "Pets. That's where da shite is at. Don' listen to dem parents 'n' thay kids horseshite. Compared ta da responsibility of feedin' 'n' takin' care of a cat o' a dog o' , 'ell, even a chinchilla, raising a decent chil' is fookin' nuthin'. I'm here ta tellin' ya' right now, pet ownership. Is the mos' awesome responsibilit-eh dat God eva' gave a man o' woman in dis life. Well, dat 'n' maintainin' an incredible nuclea' first-strike cape'o'bilit-eh."

Pirate John launches a big rope of spittle that lands mere inches from my feet. "Ya should try it sometime. It'll make a man outta ya', ya' pencil-necked geek."

My neck cranes at Auntie M wandering around. Behind her Molero leads a Peruvian couple with three children across the grounds.

"Doug? Dougito?"

Waving my hands like I'm hailing a taxi, Auntie M changes course. As she rounds the corner in her straw cowgirl hat and oversized aviator sunglasses, I secret a nervous smile. "I think this insane guy's the owner."

She smiles as her eyes dart from side to side, appraising the couple. "Hola."

With his hooks hidden under the table, Pirate John perks up and performs a well-studied smile. "Hi."

All attention shifts to Adriana, still slumped over, peering down at the tabletop. Pirate John jabs her arm with his elbow.

Adriana pauses, then meekly replies, "Hola."

A screech from above. "Say hello to my little friend. Waaaak!"

Auntie M sets her sights on Pirate John. "My room es full of the ants."

Adriana breaks down, crying. Pirate John ignores her. "Molly. . . Molero will git right on dat. Git some ant traps from da town."

Auntie M looks around like she's touring the Louvre. "Gracias. Nice place you has here."

"Tanks. Ya should try our ceviche. Deee-lish!"

His words trail off into an awkward pause.

With that, I step away "Yes. Well, that sounds like quite the plan. Uh. . . it's been enchanting. Chau. Chau." I wave goodbye, then give Auntie M a gentle nudge.

Auntie M pulls away from my grip and whispers. "Aye. ¿Que pasó?" She looks me dead in the eye. "They eh-seems likes nice people."

Pirate John cheerfully waves a salutory hook. Adriana starts sobbing.

Returning the smile, I whisper at Auntie M. "Really?" Then, shrug of my shoulders in disbelief. "OooKaaaay. I'll be in the jacuzzi if you need me."

The prattle of Spanish slowly ebbs away as I shuffle off, destined for the pool area.

#

There's this thing about bees. They can really hijack a pool party.

Squadrons of them congregate at the jacuzzi's tantalizing waterline, their cacophonous buzzing fills my ears. From a safe distance, I surveil the steady stream of reinforcements as they zip back and forth from a hive hidden behind a carob tree in a thicket of bushes.

Sweating bullets, I give serious thought to turning on the bubbles and taking a leap of faith, suffering the wrath of the histamine-laced stingers while belting down shot glasses of pure pisco like I'm trying out some New-Age acupuncture treatment. But no, I forgot my epi-pen, so. . .

. . . I saunter to the outside bar, and find Auntie M seated in a white plastic chair, sipping from an Aqua Velva-colored drink glass. She adjusts her yellow sun hat from the light's rays rippling through cracks in the thatched ceiling.

I give it a go in Spanish. "Como se dice. . . Ovejas en la piscina?"

She winces. "¿Qué? English, por favor."

I shake my head. "Bees. At the pool."

Auntie M sets down her drink as Molero darts by. Sticking two fingers in her mouth, she produces a sharp-pitched whistle.

I'm apoplectic. "No. It's not that important."

Molero bounds over. A Spanish conversation goes on while I guesstimate how many calories Molero "The Running Man" burns through every day. No wonder he's so thin.

I laugh, imagining what my Spanish must sound like, malformed conjugations crashing at each other like drunken shipmates playing bumper cars on the Exxon Valdez.

Pirate John's voice cracks like a whip, summoning Molero. After he leaves, Auntie M sits down and pockets her phone. "Mist-ah Dougito, I has eh-somes bad news."

"Yes, my Queen," I say with an elegant faux bow.

"Mist-ah Molero has informs me that he no can kills your bees eh-since, uh, for the environment. Es. . . en'pro'pi'tious." She nods, regally.

"Un. . . propitious?"

"Sí."

The hazy figures of the Peruvian family, each decked out for some serious pool play time, pass by in the background.

I lift myself up and stretch. "Let's get out of here."

She smiles. "The beach?"

My vertebrae pop. A pleasurable release. "Yes. . . uh, Sí."

#

Auntie M and I walk in a sun-drenched paradise, the ocean breeze on our faces. We've been following these freshly-plopped horse turds like olfactory breadcrumbs, and now the culprit's in sight. Thirty paces ahead, a couple of well-heeled Peruvians, probably Limeños, are nestled atop two skeletal beasts. The horse whisperer, a knock-kneed waif of about fifteen, is draped in a large red soccer jersey as he hikes along next to them.

He holds a reed whip, more for show than anything else. These are poodles in horsehair clothing. The couple flirts and giggles, oblivious to the slug trail plopping between the flicking tails behind them.

Auntie M grimaces, waving the wafting scent from her nose as I sidestep next to her, keeping my eyes peeled for surprises. "Something's rotten back there."

She glances over at the sandpipers scampering from the receding wavelets, beaks pecking the wet sand for tiny morsels of snotlike crustaceans. "¿Dónde?"

"Denmark. Where do you think, my princess? 'The Manson Family Apocalypse' waiting for us back at the Bates Motel from hell."

I'd like nothing better than to march all the way to Mancora, maybe check out the reggaeton scene, then skip town like a couple of shithouse rats fleeing a dumpster fire. How to convince Auntie M?

But she's not having any of that. Her eyes roll behind her sunglasses. "I es no princess. I es a queen."

A quavering death warble, like an ostrich autoerotically asphixiating while playing the kazoo, brays for some bizarre seconds.

"Well, it's official. We're royally screwed. What's that sound?"

She raises an eyebrow. "You wanted adventure you eh-said. What eh-sound?"

A wiry diver walking towards us from out of the surf, lugging two big pails while coughing water out of his lungs.

"I do want adventure. Climbing Inca Trails. Admiring condors. Boat rides down the Amazon--"

As we pass by, I lean over and take a look. Live octopi. A mass of writhing tentacles uncoiling themselves in every direction, groping for that elusive escape route back to mother ocean.

"Ugh. Even eating a guinea pig on a stick. But not Pirate John's serial killer Creepshow Dungeon. That's too much fucking adventure."

"Forget about Iquitos, Dougito. You is being estupido."

My voice cracks. "Am I? The sick fuck's probably putting ant bait poison in our ceviches, even as we speak. There! That sound."

Auntie M pauses, then shrugs. "I don't hear anything."

I stop in disbelief. "That sound. You don't hear it?"

She shakes her head, then starts walking. "No. What's it eh-sound like?"

"I don't know!" I bound to catch up with her. "And just wait 'til tonight, my queen, when right outside your unlocked door lurks Jack 'The Ripper' Sparrow, all coked-out and braying for blood as he twiddles his chafed dork between his meathooks for hands." I throw my arms up in the air. "Sweet dreams!"

Ignoring me, she turns her attention to the ocean.

What's she looking at?

Auntie M shakes her head. "Dougito, churro, I think you es exasperated of things."

"What? No, I'm not." The sound undulates in my ears. "There it is!"

Auntie M stops, looks around, then points behind me at an antediluvian woman in a bright yellow four-wheeled pedalcart with signage, handing out ice cream to gaggles of children. "Es just the ice cream lady. You es making imachionary hills from a mole's ass, again, Dougito."

As if on cue, the aged woman stiffly mounts her mobile good cheer factory and gives the air horn a squeeze. The bombinating warble makes us both laugh and we lock eyes, searching each other's gaze for some seconds.

Abruptly, Auntie M shakes her head, sighs, then turns to glance at some specific blur on the ocean. "I don't has my makeup on. . . " Her voice trails off. "So? Gus says I look like a Basset Hound with Parkinsons. Who cares?"

She lets out a sigh. "Gus again? ¡Callate!"

"What can I say? We have a bond. . . among other things."

She moves past me then stops and places the palm of her right hand flat above her eyes like a visor. "Right."

What's so interesting? A muscular paddleboarder is out by the breakers, showing off for his female friends onshore until a rogue wave dumps him into the drink. "What's wrong with us?"

"Us?" She doesn't look at me, instead facing forward.

"All of us. We never like the way we look. We're either too fat or too thin. We never have enough friends. Even if we have all the money in the world, it's never enough. We've gotta keep moving because wherever we're at sucks. Chronically dissatisfied. . . and then we die."

"Eh-sounds charming."

In contrast to the inept paddleboarder, farther out, a Mancoran fisherman is plying his trade, gliding over the surf on two bamboo logs lashed together with a swimfin for a rudder. It's Gilligan's Island technology, but applied with a lifetime of skill.

"It's insane. Completely, horrifically insane." I step in front of Auntie M. "Well, I don't care if things keep getting weirder and we're all born to be pulled apart. I'm not about to give up."

"What?"

"Salvation. She'll come dressed in a dream and rescue me."

"O. . .kay Dougito." Auntie M looks past me. "¿Qué es esto?" She points excitedly. "Es un. . . a eh-seal?"

I turn. A black, blurry blob bobbing with the surf. Bigger than a dog. Stepping forward, I take off my Moscot sunglasses and squint. A dead seal's carcass. Riding along the waves. Big one, too. "Christ. That's a bad omen."

"You es starting to sound like your amigo Gus." Queen Auntie M heaves a sigh and starts walking. "Mist-ah Dougito, don't be. . . ob'tuse."

She chuckles to herself and strolls away. Man, I really hate it when she out-Englishes me. How is she pulling off these words? My stomach clenches as I watch the ragdoll pinniped's body carried away, lost in the merciless waves.

Bad omen indeed.

#

It's not every day you return to your hotel and find fifteen corpses floating in the pool.

The bees. Sometime after the 'We are in their environment so don't hurt them' speech, the insects had all been mercilessly slaughtered. Well, almost all. One's still clinging to life, buzzing a defiant left wing as it makes pathetic backstrokes in ever-tightening circles inside the jacuzzi's chlorinated tomb.

Auntie M and I stare at the carnage, bemused at the bodies spinning on the ground like tops, while the ice cream in our cones melts on our hands.

Why the change of heart? My hardly-earned betting money is one of the Peruvian familia's kids got a thrill playing too close to the ball of stingers. After that, the parents grabbed a couple cans of Raid! and declared an insecticide. After all, there's a hierarchy in all things in life, and the bees clearly flouted the golden rule: Thou shalt not fuck with the family vacation!

The horror of the carnage quickly wilts to irony after I look up at the sign above the pool hut:

"BE HAPPY/love one another/help others/BE SWEET/keep your promises/laugh a lot/Work Hard/but play harder/think before speaking/SMILE/say please and thank you/eat your veggies."

And another sign below that: "Happiness/IS TIME/spent with/Good Friends/."

Scanning down from the red sunset to see the platoon floating dead in the drink makes it all feel staged. A sickly, artsy-fied insect diorama preaching about the folly of man against nature.

I point in dismay. "You see. This is another bad--"

"Say Cheeeese!" Auntie M takes my picture right as I turn around. She grins, clearly happy to have caught me off guard.

"--omen."

It's quiet and we enter the bar compound warily. Miss Whiskers lazily pokes her head up, yawning from the comfort of the crook in the mermaid statue's tush.

I whisper, "I wonder where 'Here's Johnny!' is?" with visions of him hunched over in some dank trap door basement, eyes crossed as he snorts an entire family-sized box of powdered donuts up his nose.

Auntie M wipes melted lucuma ice cream off her hand with a bar napkin. "I don't know. And why es we whispering?"

"Shhh."

I'd like nothing better than to guzzle seven or eight Cuba Libres and get blottofied. Something to cave my mind in from the image of that psychopath gussied up like a goitered Captain Morgan. But, there's this voice screaming out from somewhere deep inside the primitive lizard side of my brain, "Stay sharp!"

And who am I to defy the lizard man, dispensing all that pent-up survival knowledge throughout the ages?

Even Auntie M feels the vibe, an unspoken force sagging our energies. So, we slog to our rooms, ascending the patio steps carefully, avoiding any undue noise.

Until Auntie M's eyes grow wide as saucers. "Colorado kid!"

"Colorado?"

"Es means red. You es sundburned, Dougicito."

I look down at my arms. "Aw, crap!"

Yep. The four-plus hour walk has done me in. I look like I've been sauteed and ready to join the flea market circus as The Amazing Lobster Boy.

Auntie M looks at me and giggles while she whispers. "Does it hurt?"

Inspecting my beet-red arms, I murmur. "No pain yet. That'll come later."

She gets to her room door, looks at me, and smiles. "Well, this es it."

Maybe a kiss? But no, maybe not. I look at my door, then back at her. "Yep. Just remember, we're in this together."

"Good night." A tremble then a pause. "Dougito."

We both chuckle like school children. I turn the door handle to my room. "Good night, Auntie M."

My room seems untouched. . . except for that tasteful black-and-white portrait of a Japanese woman posing in a kimono for the play *The Mikado*. Wasn't she facing the opposite way, earlier? Probably just me. I always have trouble with faces.

What's that breathing sound?

My phone's message signal chimes in. "Hello, Gus."

I head to the large bathroom and fail a toggle switch IQ test trying to get the proper lights to come on. The shower is semi-enclosed by faux wood with hanging bamboo cage lights on thatched walls.

"Duck. DuckFlucker. I just reads online. . ."

Sure enough, the back door only goes three-quarters the way up, leaving a three-foot opened drawbridge for flying bugs and petty larcenists. At least any would-be thieves or mass murderers will have to get their exercise climbing over it. That's always a plus.

". . . They just discovers another Pishtaco ring. . ."

Right above the shower there's a rusted grill in the ceiling. The water heater's up there, pulsating. Nothing like enjoying your relaxing beach stay trapped inside an iron lung.

". . . The policia says they sucked out they victim's blubber. Can you imagines that, Duck?"

"Why are you telling me this, Gus?"

After three more rounds of checking hiding places, I've convinced myself there's no Charles Manson pirate inside my room. Guard down, I head to the john.

"They stores them in a roomful of 2-liter Inca Kila bottles to sell on the Peruvian fat market. Is booming."

Sitting there, listening to the sounds from the ceiling grill breathing full bore, as if Darth Vader's my personal toilet attendant, ready to hold my hand and comfort me while I drop a deuce.

"They is coming to get you, Duck! Pfffffthththththah!"

CLICK.

#

The wheels of the gurney squeal like a stuck pig. It's heavier than I expected, but I have the half-bright idea to push it to the front door as a barricade and, damn it, I'm gonna do it. Riiiight. There. Perfecto.

I haven't even caught my breath when Auntie M opens the door outward. "Christ!"

"You okay?"

Catching my breath. "Fine. Why?"

"I kepts hearing someone outside my door."

"Not me. I've been here. . ." We check out the gurney at the same time. "Making. . . alterations. You?"

She shrugs. "Tranquilo. Just watching La Vida de Pee."

I silently mouth the translation before frowning. "The Life of Pee?"

"Pee es Pi in eh-Spanish. 'The Life of Pi', Doug."

"Oh, yeah. I was just joking. I'm glad you get my sense of humor."

She shakes her head, then motions to leave before hesitating. "You're eh-still having a good time, esn't you? I means you es eh-still enjoying. . . my country? No?" There's an uncertain timber in her voice.

I suck in air, not expecting the question. "Of course. I wouldn't be anywhere else."

Her smile radiates, before slowing evaporating as she walks away. "Bueno."

Did I just not insert my foot in my own mouth? A small victory. "Good." I lean over the gurney, waving heartily. "Um, if you need anything I'm right here. Or text me, too, you know? Okay?"

"Buenas noches, Dougito."

#

The whoosh and crash of the ocean's waves are my lodestones, my focal points for this night of fearful sleep. At first it works, but slumber ain't easy when the brain's braced itself for a white-knuckle disaster every thirty seconds.

Was that the front door handle moving? Are those foot falls in the bathroom? Or is it that iron lung thing firing up again? Mosquitoes? ZZZzzzzz.

Nope. Nothing's stabbing me in the chest. Just the sound of the waves. There is peace and serenity in the waves. Washing away all anxieties. (Yawn)

Wait. That's gotta be the front door? Wish that fucking water heater would stop. Is that squeaking the wind or is someone climbing through the back window?

Nah. That's nothing. Just the. . . (Yawn). . . sounds of the. . . (Yawn). . . Waves. . .

The waves. . . (Yawn). . . THe waves. . . (Yawn). . . THE waves. . . THE Waves. . . THE WAves. . . THE WAVes. . . THE WAVEs. . . THE WAVES! THE BIG WAVES!! TSUNAMI!!!! Crashing through the door!!! How the fuck do I get outta here? Auntie M? How fast can we run uphill on a dirt road in the middle of the night in our skivvies?

Lathered in sweat, I awake with a scream still rattling through my throat. A nightmare. What an utter failure. Time for a different tactic.

I cross the room and sift through my backpack. After hearing a muffled moan, I place my ear to the wall and smile. It's Auntie M's familiar voice from next door. She's play acting a cartoon character role, singing 'Go to Sleep Little Baby' in Spanish with passionate abandon.

Feeling around the guts of my backpack for the familiar dog-eared book. "Aha." My old childhood storybook friend. Wish I had a drink with me. 'Pig Pig' and a good, hard Scotch go hand in hand. Plopping down on the couch, I flick the TV remote for some background noise and thumb through pages.

It's not long before my eyes look up from the young cartoon pig in a diaper to the TV.

What is all that yelling about?

It's a Mexican telenovela. Some old dude with an eye patch and a terrible toupee is seated on the stairs of some luxury hacienda, beating his head against the banister while screaming his guts out. No clue why, but being a telenovela, he's probably just found out he's being cuckolded by the beautiful female lead for a brooding rich guy. Of course, being a telenovela, he concusses himself far too long and screams far too loud.

CLICK.

Oops. A porno. Turn down the volume. Strange. The sound doesn't match up. This must be reeeeally low budget.

CLICK off the TV, but the overacted sound of ardor continues. Hmmm? I tilt my head and listen. The neighbor's TV? Different movie. Must've gotten the extended package. Or are they going at it?

Oh well, back to the business at hand. From the beginning.

"Pig Pig was the baby of the family. His brothers and sisters had grown up and left home long ago, but Pig Pig refused to grow up."

Moaning. Is that my neighbors next door? You've gotta be kidding me. The neighbors are fucking at an eleven. I need them fucking at a three. I'm trying to do something important here.

No respect. Must focus.

"He still wore his sleep suit, though it was much too tight."

The disaster on TV is tawdry by even gonzo porn standards. A grimy hotel scene shot from a low angle and lit by what looks to be a replacement bulb from an 'Easy Bake' toy oven. The female lead, who's built crack-head thin, screams at the top of her lungs like she's receiving The Great Pumpkin. The male lead, a dirtbag pouring sweat with the faint beginnings of a porn mustache. . . wait a minute? Is that the taxi kid who picked me up at the airport in Lima?

Oh well, back to the book. "And he continued to sleep in his crib, even though his feet hung over the end."

I look down. Little Duck is at attention, pointing to the opened book. "Dammit!"

All right. But just this once. Some manipulation and concentration to achieve a certain clarity of mind. Puts me to sleep, every time.

Bite my lips and close my eyes, coaxing the proper visuals to complete the trick at hand. Mercifully, the audio is already provided. Now, they've switched to a shower scene. I want to yell out something like *Fucking keep moaning. I'm not finished yet*! or *Faster, dammit, faster!* but I don't want to ruin the moment. No. I've gotta go with what I'm given.

The visuals are fast and furious. In addition to what appears to be a lunging reverse cowgirl Dirty Sanchez backbend, to downward dog with the entire Swedish Bikini Team, which is an impossibility in real life but well worth trying, I'm trying to milk an extra twenty seconds from my habit by conjuring up the most boring thoughts known to man: Watching grass grow, paint dry, Dubstep, a tax audit, waiting in line at the bank. . .

Getting close. I throw the book to the side. No sense doing the money shot on that fucking pig's face. I'm not that kinky.

And. . .that's a wrap. No surprises here. I run a quick physical. Blood rushing to the temples. Check. Pulse racing but starting to taper. Good. Breathing is slowing. Excellent. Whew. Where's that damn tissue box?

"Jaaaaaaaaahhhhhhh!" It's Auntie M's voice from next door.

I jump into a ragtag assortment of clothes and race out the door.

Multiple voices scream in Spanish through the shadows of the open-air bar. Farther away a male voice yells, "Shut the fuck up, Shrödinger!"

After falling on my ass vaulting up the porch stairs, I slog over to Auntie M's unit. The light's on, but I can't make out if anyone's home. A tentative knock. "Uh, hello? Anybody there?" Silence. Then, frenetic breathing and a female scream.

What the fuck am I doing? Stepping back from the door, I shift my weight and deliver something that feels like if Chuck Norris taught Tweety Bird how to deliver karate kick. "Ow. Fuck!" I'm bouncing around in awkward circles on one foot and holding my throbbing toes when Auntie M screams. "Es unlocked. Remember*?"*

Oh, yeah. Turning the handle, I burst in. Auntie M's panicked, wet as an otter with a white towel wrapped around her, holding a curling iron like a dagger.

She stammers, "Alguien…Eh-someone is in mi baño!"

What the hell?

Double dammit. Tossing down the piece of used tissue stuck to my hand, I look around, full of adrenaline. There's a clothes iron in the closet. That'll do! I rush over and brandish the iron like overweight brass knuckles, before its cord slaps smartly against my left leg. "Ow!"

Time to be a man. My heart pounds as I rush into the bathroom, ready for battle.

"¡Cuidado!" Auntie M's voice trails behind me.

Auntie M follows me in, ready to curl our intruder's hair to the death, but no one's there.

She points at the slats in the ceiling. "Aquí."

I squint, trying to make out a figure. "You sure?"

"Sí. I saw these eyes."

Somebody's using the water heater room as their private pervert's nest? I shudder at the thought of Auntie M taking a soothing shower, then looking up and locking eye-to-eye with a twitchy-faced reprobate tugging on his joystick. Jesus.

I rush to the living room. More voices outside, in Spanish and English. The stairs to the pervert's nest must be out back.

With the reflexes of a mildly retarded jungle cat, I snatch Auntie M's curling iron with my right hand and pull back the clothes iron like I'm getting ready to play Mike Tyson's 'Punch Out' in a low-rent fashion salon.

Taking a deep breath. "I'm going in!"

"You means out?"

I think about it, then shrug. "Whatever."

An explosion rattles my fillings and knocks both of us down. The hotel grounds appear to be awash in a pulsing, magical glow. I poke my head out the front door. The property next door, 'Casa Serenity', is engulfed in flames. The Peruvian familia rushes past me, mom and dad desperately dragging their offspring in tow like fleeing war refugees.

"We're getting the fu--" I turn to Auntie M.

She's already packing her suitcases.

Looking down at my white-knuckled fist gripping the curling iron, I mumble. "Here, take this."

She snatches it from me.

I turn, then hesitate.

"Oh, and make sure to get the little bottles of shampoo."

She zips up her smaller suitcase. One more to go. "¿Qué?"

I hold up my thumb and index finger like I'm sizing a shot glass. "The little shampoos and conditioners. We're getting even."

She hoists her other suitcase onto the bed, then looks at me like I should be put to sleep. "What es wrong with you? Es like you thrives on the loco." She stuffs in more clothes from the closet and zips up the suitcase. "Where es you going?"

Giving a bold thumbs-up, I lift the clothes iron like a medieval mace. "Don't you worry. I can take care of myself. I've got a mind like a steel crap. . . uh, trap." I point to the bathroom like a man possessed. "Just get the shampoos and stay calm. It's a Gringo thing."

I bolt out and feel the heat of the flames against my face. People are screaming from the 'Casa Serenity' conflagration next door, but with the hotel grounds cloaked in black, acrid smoke, I can't tell what the hell is going on. With one side of my brain coolly reciting *This is stupid.* and the other yelling *Fuck yeah!* I jump off the patio and start running, flicking falling embers off my arms.

Past the mermaid at the bar, I slow down, looking out the corners of my eyes for signs of movement.

"Fuck you, you fucking cock-a-roach! Waaaaak!" The parrot buzzes just past my face and flies away into the night sky.

"Shit!" Surprised, my grip gives way, sending the lethal clothes iron crashing onto my foot. "Ow!"

"Arg!" The familiar guttural voice. "Leavin' so soon?"

A lit tiki torch outlines Pirate John's silhouette. With my arm covering my nose and mouth from the smoke, I limp forward into the breach.

He's shitfaced, sitting unsteadily on a bamboo stool with a joint wedged between his lips and a cradling a shotgun. He's snorted so many powdered donuts his face looks like an addled caricature of a kabuki actor. A rocket launcher lies on the artificial mini-putt turf behind him.

"I wouldn' 'ear a it. Ma lil' party is jus' beginnin'."

A flickering glow. I wipe the floating orange-yellow embers away from my face, catching a glimpse of the palm tree above us. Its fronds have burst into flames.

Pirate John points his cleft chin to a bowl on the table. "Wan' sum Ceviche?" He belches a guttural laugh..

Wait? Wasn't his eyepatch on the other side this morning?

His crooked smile gives way to a sad clown frown, bursting into a sobbing fit. "Jus' got back from da vets. Turns out da Miss whiskers is 1/16th lezbeen."

The shotgun accidentally fires, jolting us both. "Arggghh!"

I want to back away, but my feet are frozen, both from fear and a bad bunion. This is it. I'm trapped liked a shithouse rat.

Dropping the weapon, he seizes at a fifth of Jack Daniels, lifting it off the table with his hooks, pressing it to his lips. Before his first gulp, a hook cracks the bottle and it explodes on his lap. "Fuck! Oh Lawd, I shoulda seen dis a comin'. She's par' Scorpio 'n' par' Calico 'n' anyone wit' a whit a sense 'bout pet astro-ology

' GUS' S PERUVIAN GUIDEBOOK' PROUDLY PRESENTS:
Chapter Six: Peru's Color-fullest Characters

Aye, Peru no is the biggest dog in history's fight. She was founded on the exploitation of her natural wealths: gold, jewels, slaves, cotton, bird poop, and coca. Lots of bird poop and coca.

But, if there is one area where she pound-for-pound punches above her height, it's in the colorful cast of characters.

Makes the pisco! Not the wars!

It's 1880 and the Peruvians and Chileans is enjoying in they War of the Pacific, also known as the Saltypeter War, when Colonel Francisco Beolognesi speaks the most badassified words ever recorded by a Peruvian: "Tengo deberes sagrados que cumplir, y los cumpliré hasta quemar el último cartucho--I have a sacred duty, and I will carry it out until the last bullet is fired."

Truth to his words, he got gunned down like a mange-inflested dog with rabies by the Chilean invaders. Cool speech, though. Not one to be outmartyred, fellow Peruano Alfonso Ugarte decides to kick it up a notch and rides his horse off a cliff to keep Peru's flag from getting captured. A tad dramatic and a bad last day in the life for one of Peru's true heroes, but you do what you has gotta do to get into them historical books, man.

Poor horsie.

But that's just how Peru rolls. Open up any book on Peru's military heroes, and if your name is there, chances are you has died a gnarly death: cast from a battlement, beheaded, drawn and quartered, run through with a lightsaber, shot, shot at the stake, propelled from a cliff, gettin' shot again, blown up, assassinated, y maybe killed by friendly fire just to spice things up. And that's just on page uno. Dying for a lost cause is all part of the fun en Peru. Is the thoughts that counts!

I have but one life to. . . aye carajo!

Not only did them Peruvian war heroes die gnarly deaths. The big-time hero of Peruvian medicine is Daniel Carrion. In them 1870s a bunch of dudes building the railroad from Callao to La Oroya starts dropping like shit-eating flies, dying by the thousands from an epidemic of fever and warts. The doctor dorks ain't ever seen nothing like it before. The only thing they gots to go by was an increased cases of verruga peruana, which is a disease that causes fug ugly wart-like breakouts in all kinds of nasty shapes and sizes.

On August 27, 1885, at the tendered age of twenty-six, Daniel decides it's time to take his shots at Peruvian medical immortality and find the cure. Only problema is Danny Boy ain't got no lab coat, let alone a lab. He can't even find a test subject to play guinea pigs with. But that's no problema. Since Daniel's a badass, he gets his closest compadres to injects him with blood taken from the eyebrow wart of an infected fourteen-year-old. Then, he just chills out to see what kinda cool shit will happen next so he can writes about it in his dear diary. "What importance is there to the sacrifice of one's life if I am serving humanity?" He dies thirty-eight days later, provings through his self-experiment that the Oroya Fever and them verruga peruana are two phasers of the same, inoculatable disease. But, on the cool side of things, they renamed the Oroya fever Carrion's disease.

A few years on the go, the Peruvian Congress gots into a big debate team about a bill that would elevate Carrion from "martyr" to "hero." Some peoples say it ain't much of a promotion, but that's all pussy talk. After alls, they has no idea how tough it is to die. They hasn't tried it, yet. Any hows, the bill passes, and Carrion's remains gets to moves to the official Heroes Crypt.

Vamos a Peru!
"My three years in politics was very instructive about the way in which the appetite for political power can destroy a human mind, destroy principles and values, and transform people into little monsters." --Mario Vargas Llosa

But if they is one guy who The Gus must give a special color-full character shouts out to, it would be good, ol' Vladimiro Montesinos.

Big, Bad Vlad

"Montesinos and Fujimori maintained the facade of democracy, but drained its substance," --John McMillan, Stanford University economics professor.

The Vlad is So Bad he's The Rad. Montesinos' life reads like if Ian Fleming imagineered a cartoon Henry Kissinger who channeled his inner James Bond, except that 007 would definitely be playing the bad guy.

Back in them days, The Vlad got cadet training at the U.S. Army School of the Americas. In 1976, he falsifies a blank form, and flies to the U.S. as a guest of the U.S. government. According to Peruvian smartie pants journalist Gustavo Gorriti, once in the United States, Montesinos starts chillin' out with the poindexters in the CIA.

When he returns to his ol' stompin' grounds in Peru, Bad Vlad gets arrested and convicted of lying and being a little stinker in May 1977. He's expectorated from the army and sentenced to one year in jail. While behind bars, Montesino figures out that if he's gonna go to all the trouble to break the law he might as well becomes a lawyer. In them roarin' 1980s, he is making a fortune helping drug traffickers with their unpaid parking tickets.

By 1990, Vlad is exchangin' cookie recipes with the CIA station chief in Lima and payin' visits to CIA headquarters in Langley for Sunday morning Bingo.

In 1991, Montesinos' Dr. Evil wet dream finally comes true and he takes charge of the joint Peru-U.S. anti-drug unit in the National Intelligence Service (SIN).

And sin they do. Through former President Alberto "El Chino" Fujimori's 10 years in office, from 1990 to 2000, Bad Vlad and SIN enjoy unlimited fluck you power.

At first, the Fujimori government was muy popular in Peru for pledging to kick ass on inflation, foreign investment and the Shining Path. But by 1992, the corruption was gettin' out of his hands. According to the Center for Public Integrity in Washington, D.C., the CIA gaves the narco division of Montesinos's SIN services a guesstimated $10 million. Some of this cash, the Center alleges, ends up in Montesinos' personal coffers. I is sure it was just an accident.

A former U.S. intelligence agent, who spoke to FRONTLINE/World on the condition of oh shit, don't say my name! said that during the mid-1990s, the CIA was getting spooky vibes from the State Department that "the U.S. government should not deal with him or meet with him." This MENSA intelligent agent dude still thought Montesinos was a valuable asset. "Was he a bad guy? Yes," he said, explaining that intelligence comes from "all sorts."

Others saw Montesinos in a shittier light, calling him "Rasputin, Darth Vader, Torquemada and Cardinal Richelieu," in the words of a 1997 U.S. Army intelligence report released under the Freedom of Information Act.

At the end of the Full Montesinos power grab in Peru, his tax records shows he is making $600,000 a year, even though his official salary is $18,000.

Maybe he was doin' the bake sales thing on the weekends?

The Vladi-videos

On September 2000, 'bout 3 months after Fujimori's re-election, Peruvian TV broadcasts a video of Montesinos bribing a congressman to support Perú 2000, Fujimori's party.
In them next few months, more "Vladi-videos" starts to making the rounds. One shows the owners of Channel 4 gettin' $1.5 million a month to ban the political opposition. Others show Montesinos counting out $350,000 in cash to Channel 5's big wig, and the owner of Channel 9 got a piddly $50,000. What a dumbass.
Aye. The magic of the "show me the moneys bidness."
Baddy Vladi's videos cause Fujimori's supports to go poof like a fart in the wind. He hands Montesinos his well-earned pink slip and thanks him for his genocide. . . uh, services. Then Fujimori gets his ass on the first flight outta the country and faxes his resignation when he hits the ground runnin' in Japan.
But you can't kick a good James Bond villain in the dick forever and just expect him to stay down. Vladi the Baddy slips out of Peru on a luxury yacht, scams them Costa Rican border patrol Nazis with a wacky beard and fake ID like the ones 16-year-olds likes to use on spring break, then goes on a six-week 'Where's Waldo?' Odysseus trek around Latin American and the Caribbean 'til he winds up in Caracas, where he gets facial reconstruction surgery--then skips town without paying the bill.
At these points, he's even managed to piss off the FBI, who takes up the search for Bad Vlad. In June 2001, they pinpoints Montesinos in Venezuela where he is arrested and sent back to his beloved Peru.

The trials of being The Vladinator

Montesinos is convicted of embezzling, illegal assumption of his post as intel chief, abuse of power, under the influence peddling, bribery, and just being a dick. Aye, not bad for a career in government, to be honest.
Now, he enjoys himself at the maximum security naval base prison in Callao--which he helped design during the 1990s. Betcha he wishes he added in that luxury rec yard with an Olympic-sized pool and ping pong tables when he had the chance. In totals, he got himself accused of sixty-three crimes that derange from drug trafficking to murder.
"Maybe Mr. Montesinos didn't need to be influenced," said former French ambassador to Peru Antoine Blanca, who was representing French government interests in the case at the time.
"He knew exactly where his interests were, he worked for the CIA."

IQUITOS

The Shaman:

Ingredients:

1 1/2 oz. Salers Aperitif
1 oz. pisco, preferably Macchu Pisco
3/4 oz. fresh pineapple juice
1/2 oz. cinnamon syrup
1/2 oz. fresh lime juice
8 dashes Angostura bitters

1/2 oz. mezcal, for topping

Preparation:
Combine Salers, pisco, pineapple juice, syrup, lime juice, and half the bitters in an ice-filled shaker. Shake vigorously and strain into a chilled coupe glass; top with mezcal and remaining bitters.

The Iquitos Airport restroom: A man-bun eco-traveler bearing a backpack with designer pot leaf sticker, plays Candy Crush on his iPhone while taking a piss.

Unbelievable, I muse, darting to a stall for privy time and a quick game of Angry Birds. Ahhh. That's better. Business is done and my birds are still angry.

As I emerge from the airport, I find Auntie M waving at mototaxis with her pink 'DISCO BITCH' folding hand fan. A stylish multi-tasking technique to beat the mid-day heat. A quick jaunt to our nearby hotel, where, owing to my bank account's magical disappearing act, we wind up sharing a room.

Entering, I casually plop my backpack on the double bed and inspect the room. It's a quaint, green room with all the necessities. "This is cozy."

Auntie M looks around and smiles. "Sí." She slings my backpack over her shoulder, then tosses it into the other room. "Two double beds. I'll take the view of the garden." I spring up with a big sigh. Oh well, it's the thought that counts. After ditching our travel gear and gulping down a couple of Cañazos, we head off to see the 'Venice of the Amazon.' Belen's marketplace is like no other. Located on the floodplain of the Itaya River, thousands of families live cheek-by-jowl in this shanty town on stilts. Everything's built for life on the water. A floating church. A floating school. Even floating gas stations.

I follow Auntie M as she swats flies away. We walk the planks, ducking under drooping electrical cables slung between corrugated roofs and low-hanging laundry straining to dry in the sun-drenched humidity. Like many locals here, she's dressed rainstorm casual with a poncho. I'm trying my best to rock a full-on jungle badass adventurer motif, but feel like I'm coming across as Indiana Jones meets Alfalfa.

Auntie M stops to assess my garb, then screams over lively music banging out of an old boombox in a window. "Did you take your meds?"

She watches me standing there slackjawed, like I've been assigned an algebra problem in Cantonese. "For Malaria. Yellow Fever?"

Pressing my brown felt outback fedora down above my eyebrows, I try to act suave. "Oh! Oh yeah. I got 'em." Holy shit.

Funky smells invade our nostrils at the rows of vendors' booths, with locals hawking freshly chopped pieces every type of thing-once-living, including caiman legs and a huge Amazonian fish called a paiche. Auntie M dodges darting children, defiantly shaking her head 'No' as locals offer up exotic jungle fruits, mollusks, insects, and freshly-hacked animal parts as delicaciesI mouth Thank You to the waitress.

"Namaste." She briefly bows, cradling her hands to her chest, then bounds off.

Is this what I've been waiting for all this time? Waiting to walk on a life's moments edge. I had done this to myself, but didn't have the strength to see it all the way through. I needed an ally, someone like Linda. Someone to watch me set the trap, then kindly watch me fall into it.

"Thanks for the truth. Thanks for being kind and caring, Linda."

"Well, sometimes kind and caring Linda has to be a witch."

"A good one or a bad one?"

"Bad, but it's for your own good, Dougie."

It's like making silly faces at myself in front of a firing squad, then asking a dearest friend to pull the trigger. So sorry about Old Duck's demise.

My magic marker drops. I stare at my fingers, smudged in dead black ink.

What will this be?

A longtime, patient wait off my shoulders or an economic death sentence?

Linda's tone ticks up a notch. Impatient. "Well?"

Peering at my notebook wrinkled pages, the only excuse left unscratched out in big, black lettering: Cargo Cult.

At this point why not? Nothing to lose. My mouth curls to a smile. "Ah, funny story. I, ahhhh, you see. . . I'm on an island in the South Pacific."

"An island?"

"Yes. You see, I. . . I've been abducted by a cargo cult--"

The frenetic gum-chewing stops. "A cargo cult?"

Shaking my smudged fingers, I stare at my hand likes it's been dismembered. "This is legitimate. I swear."

"Let me get this straight: you want me to go into Larry's office and tell him you absolutely, positively can't come into work today because you're trapped on Gilligan's Island? Is this a joke?"

I gulp. Doomed. "Shit, shoot. Forget about that last one, Linda. Please. I haven't joined a Cargo Cult. For what it's worth, I think the tropics are overrated!"

CLICK.

"Linda? Hello, Linda?" The harshest delusions to give up are the ones we create for ourselves. "Crap!"

Swaying my head around, I scan the oogling stares of the customers before their faces return to their meals. The final remnants of a social disaster.

"My, you're a live one."

A Brazilian-esque woman, brightly dressed and in her early thirties, walks towards me from her seat at the bar next to a ferocious-looking, bug-eyed red Puno dancing devil mask used as a tip jar.

"Who, me?"

She plops down her 21 Raices brandy snifter and dips into the empty chair next to me. "Of course, silly, who else would you be?"

Way, waaaay outta my league.

Taken aback, I give my best Humphrey Bogart smile and try to will my sweat glands to grind to a halt. No such luck. "Hi."

She takes a big, lazy drag of her homemade cigarette, giving me the once over, like I'm some exotic tropical pumpkin the tourists haggle over at the Belen marketplace. She blinks while puffing clouds of smoke. "You looking for Dimitri?"

I squint. What's she getting at? "Never heard of him. Sorry." This damn tropical shirt is riding high, and my armpits are itching something fierce.
Undaunted, she sips her drink and tilts her head.

What is this?

"You look like you're ready to run with the Deemsters?"

Run with the Deemsters? In this heat? I don't have time for that.

"No." I shut my notebook, the pages folding on themselves limply from the humidity.

After gulping more brandy, she stares again. "So, you're not looking for Yage?"

Yage? Is that a local rock band? Dammit, I need to ditch these dorky glasses. They make people think I'm smarter than I am. "Ayahuasca. I'm looking to score some Ayahuasca, lady."

Her glossy lips pucker as she taps cigarette ashes into the lumpy clay ashtray. "Welcome to Iquitos."

Now we're getting somewhere. "And maybe do some camping in the jungle." I can't take it anymore and start scratching my armpits.

"Okay."

Really? "Oh, and I'd like to fondle a pink dolphin! With my friend."

Bobbing her head back, she gives me the look of the leper. Dammit. Pet. I meant pet a pink dolphin.

She tells me a price. A high price. Very high. She belly laughs watching me spit out my drink, covering the table in foamy droplets. Recovering, I tell her about my born-again frugality, recently acquired from burning through my savings like a newly-minted lottery winner on crack ever since I touched down here. She says she's got me covered. Her father has a buddy whose nephew who owns a ship. . . Uh, oh. This is dodgy.

#

With the thirst for psychedelic adventure drowning out the alarm bells in my head, I'm off to see the good ship 'Cato'. I swat away mosquitoes while walking down the long wooden plank towards the dilapidated hulk moored unceremoniously in an overgrown bog.

The guard rail creaks when I hoist myself up to the main deck and peer around. Not a soul in sight except for some tropical birds perched on the pilot house, squawking furiously.

Gus' ringtone, Charly Garcia's 'Botas Locas', plays from my phone.

CLICK.

This is not the time.

Heading towards the bow, I step around large patches of rotting floorboard, nervously stroking my M.C. Escher Angels/Devils necklace. This is gonna float us down the Amazon? There's no way Auntie M goes for this.

Very faint sounds. Turning my head, I guide my ears for some echolocation. The noise seems to be floating from the upper deck. I take in some spongebath air, then let out a heavy sigh. Well, Doug, in a lifetime of stupid things, this is the stupidest. And with that fine thought, I head up the stairs. With every step, the wayward noises congeal to a melody. Unmistakable. Even here, some 2,300 miles upstream from the Atlantic Ocean, in the largest city in the world that can't be reached by car.

Toto's 'Africa'.

'THE GUS'S PERUVIAN GUIDEBOOK' PROUDLY PRESENTS:

Peru's Divine Moments of Truths

"The cost of sanity in this society, is a certain level of alienation."
—**Terence Mckenna**

In the lasts 25 years or so, Ayahuasca touring-ism has been in the bloom. Thousands of foreigners comes to Iquitos to get they medication on, with Ayahuasca jungle lodges becomings all the rage.

So, why is everybody so crazy for this stuff? The Ayahuasca tea has been in ceremononies since forever, with some smartsperts making bold-ass claims like it's some kind of cure all: depression, mental and emotional issues, alcoholism, tobacco and drug addictions, arthritis, diabetes, flatulence, skin disease, and possibly even the big C.

Sounds nice.

Or maybe some people just wanna gets high as fluck and dream about the nature of the universe floating outta they belly buttons?

So, get comfy all you lotus-eating heathens, time for some smartie-pants drug talk.

The trippy-assed fluck substance in Ayahuasca is dimethyltryptamine. DMT is a powerful fluck-with-your-brain-o-gen, kinda like the good ol' LSD. Want another trippy fact about DMT? Nature-formed DMT has been found in the precious bodily fluids of people found suffering from severe non-reality interpretating mental diseases like schizophrenia, kinda like when Duck flips out in Lima traffic.

Richard Strassman, a clinical Psychosmartie pants at the U of Mexico, was the Big Daddy Blunthead on the psychonaut campus for DMT research. In 1990 to 1995, he injects 60 subjects with the DMT joy juice during 400 wacky sessions. Aye. Here is hoping these poor schmucks is volunteers and Strassman ain't just going around school stickin' random people for the jollies of it. 'Haha. Try to study for mid-terms, now, fluckhead!'

Aye. Higher education. Is a blessing and a curse.

So what did Strassman find out about all these wastoids tripping they gonads off? 'Many subjects claimed "they sensed the presence of a powerful, god-like being or that they dissolved into a radiant light.' Sounds like fluckin' science to me.

'Meanwhile, about 25 subjects says they witnessed alien robots, reptiles and/or insects and even when the hallucinagenic "trip" ended, they could not be convinced that these images weren't real. After these bad experiences and negative effects, Strassman stopped his research, but he writes about all these good 'n' high times in his book tittled, "DMT: The Spirit Molecule."'

So, now you've read all this smartie pants drug talk, and you're like, 'Alien Robots? Hell, yeah! Where do I signs up?' What's an Ayahuasca ceremony actually like?

Chances is good you will be sitting in a crowded circle smoking a tobacco pipe with a shaman burning sage next to Ayahuasca sludge-filled Fiji water bottles and puke buckets.

And after you've stepped up to the psychonaut Amazonian brunch special and pissed the points of no return?

After enjoying some delightful bouts of vomiting and diarrhea, you gets the visual honeypot you came for: a six-hour hallucination.

But, Gus, my life is trippy enough as it is. How wills I tell the difference?

Aye, you will.

"This is the most powerful drug I have ever experienced. Yage is not like anything else. It produces the most complete derangement of the senses." – William Burroughs, The Yage Letters

This is what's on the DMT menu: Meaningless Visual "noise"; Strong visions, especially snakes, big cats, insectoid aliens, and goddesses; hearings and sound distortions; altered sensings of the space and time. And if you is really lucky, you get to meets "the mother" in the plant. Word is she's in the form of a snake, and she will answer your questions about the demeanings of life right as you is shittings your pants.

And if you has a "bad trip"?

LOTS of diarrhea; LOTS of vomiting; body aches; sweats and the chills; food poisoning-like symptoms; fear and paranoia; feelings that you is lost in your mind; all this fun mixed with the feeling as if you gonna die at any second.

Oopah!

I told Duck he mights just get a little case of the sniffles.

My bads.

Pffffhhhthththaahhh!

'Only those who attempt the absurd will achieve the impossible. I think it's in my basement. . . let me go upstairs and check'

– MC Escher

The song purrs softly through the room in what must be a galley, but looks like a demented biology professor's hoarding attic and smells like a fouled-up port-a-potty after a weeklong chili cookoff.

Assorted two-liter Inca Kola bottles, filled with a thick, yellow-brown sludge, sit on a metal table next to mounds of green snail eggs piled on a bookshelf. A veritable jungle of impressive ferns and tropical plants hide an Easter egg farrago of dried piranhas, fake shrunken heads, animal skulls, snakeskins, giant turtle carapaces, and store window mannequins in various stages of undress.

Wild human figure paintings with faces scratched out, haphazardly occupy the room.

And over to the—Crap! A cockroach the size of a cat scurries over my Keen hiking sandals.

The hum of frenetic music switches songs, landing on Kansas' Dust in the Wind, then stops. Sounds of movement, then metallic clanging noises from behind the doorway curtain with the design of a two-headed green anaconda. One head eats its tail. The other points up to the sky.

On the emerald-green lintel above a wild scrawl in black magic marker:

'TOYNBEE IDEA
IN MOVIE '2001
RESURRECT DEAD
ON PLANET JUPITER
"MEANINGLESS! MEANINGLESS!" SAY THE TEACHER
"EVERYTHING IS MEANINGLESS!"

Meaningless?

"Ah sheee-it!" A male voice.

Sucking in a big gulp of air, I take a step inside a disheveled kitchen. Chahk. Chahk. Chahk. Chahk. I poke my head in a bit further, primed to flee.

Beyond the refrigerator, with his back to me, a gaunt male figure with a shaved head chops thick tree bark at a cutting board near the sink. Stern strokes.

CHAHK CHAHK CHAHK CHAHK. . .

Pots and pans clang and swing to and fro from the ceiling rack. A lazy white cigarette cloud billows above him, then streaks from the open window's breeze.

Has he heard me? A tiny step. The floorboard creaks. I stop, barely breathing. Only the toylike ringing of the wind chimes in the window.

He lifts his head, revealing a bony staircase of vertebrae atop his ivory Guaybera shirt collar. The cleaving halts.

Without turning to me. "There's beer in the fridge." The chopping recommences.

Why not? Complying, I open the fridge door, keeping the man and his knife in my line of sight while poking inside.

A fat carboy filled with white sludge sits on a rack, 'Boa Grassa' felt-penned on its label in wild script. A smaller bottle reads 'Dolphin Sperm'.

Gingerly clearing space from a rancid forest's worth of unidentifiable edibles, I spy a couple bottles of Iquiteña beer in the back.

"The opener's on the table."

I wend around a knotted wood table in front of a thicket of potted plants and a large painting of a tortured woman, scarred to disfigurement, blindfolded and bearing a torch against a black storm cloud background. Its inscription is wildly scrawled in black felt pen: E Pluribus Unim.

The bottle opener's sterling silver, with some pre-Incan figure of a sun god baring teeth at me. The beer cap pop off easily. "Thanks."

"Just mixing some Levántate Lázaro. For some clients."

After balancing my backpack on a chair, I take a swig. He scrapes pieces of fruit into a large metal bowl, then impales the knife blade halfway into a tropical gourd on the counter.

After smearing his hands on a cloth towel, he walks barefoot towards me, picking up his beer bottle.

"Fuck it." He inspects me with hollowed-out eyes. A flash of recognition, then he catches himself. "So you're?"

Does he know me? "Doug."

"Marcello." We exchange a bony handshake as he sits down.

I look around. "Nice ship."

He crushes his spent cigarette into a faux, I hope, shrunken head ashtray, then plucks a joint from his shirt pocket, lights it, and takes a drag. "My uncle's." After a sigh, Marcello pulls out a glass pipe, a baggy, and a pirate skull lighter from his other shirt pocket and sets them on the table. "Want a little tokie pooh?" I shake my head.

Marcello nods at a digital vaporizer nestled between two banana plants on the table. It looks like Mount Saint Helens after the eruption. Underneath some blinking read out lights is a label: Vülcano ᑫong 5000! "How 'bout some DMT?"

"Uh. . .um, I'm pretty new at this."

"It's just a vaporizer. I got some fresh balloons as well." He carefully reaches over the mess and pulls up a large balloon with a stick figure stamp with a weird scowl.

"Uhhh. . . I'm not sure how that works."

A smile. There's something familiar about him, right up to the face. I always have trouble with faces.

He puffs away on his joint like it's the finest Cuban cigar. "Suit yourself. Magdalena tells me you're looking for an Ayahuasca trip."

"Is it safe? I've heard people have died."

He looks at the joint twirling between his cadaver-like fingers. I can't place him. He's like a Colonel Kurtz-type who got lost in the Amazon and was forced to survive off LSD-laced weed.

"Aye. One guy died in a motorcycle accident after a ceremony. Another, tobacco poisoning. . ."

I tilt my head.

". . . another guy choked on his own vomit. . ."

Wait a minute. Wasn't the light on in the other room? Did I turn it off?

". . . another guy named Stevens, poor bastard. He did a private Ayahuasca ceremony in his room. Around nine PM, this dude named Gomez left the group ceremony and went to Stevens' room where he attacked him. . ."

Can't be.

"According to witnesses, Gomez appeared "possessed". It all came to a head in the kitchen. With Stevens fearing for his life. . ."

It's 'Troy.'

"He stabbed Gomez with a kitchen knife. Killed him dead right there on the floor."

I take a gulp and fake a smile. "I'm guessing they ate out that night?"

He leans back in his chair and chuckles. "Don't worry, they've been doing this for thousands of years. Getting in touch with their spiritual selves. All that crap."

Searching through the tabletop leaf litter, he uncovers an ornate jewelry box the size of Leor's son's lunchbox. "Mind if I finish my breakfast? It's the most important meal of the day, you know."

I shrug. "Sure." What a metamorphosis. From chrysalis into a malformed dung beetle.

"Anything to cut this nutmeg bender I've been on for the last three weeks." Marcello opens the box, revealing. . . another box. "You know, between the smallpox and the violence, nine out of ten natives died during the conquest." With mouthful of decayed teeth, he grins and opens it, revealing a smaller box, this one with a lock. "Over two-hundred-billion-dollars were sent back to Europe from the Americas. So, what's a poor country like Peru to do? Excuse me."

He pulls out a small key hidden in a turtle shell by my arm. "Most of the cocaine comes from regions where a farmhand earns less than ten dollars a day."

Marcello fidgets until he finally unlocks the box.

"Cazzo!" After a bit of tugging, he takes out yet another box, the size of a cigarette pack. This one has a combo lock.

There's clanging from the room next door. Is that furniture moving?

Raising his voice to get my attention. "It takes three to five days to backpack the coca paste to the traffickers. One hundred miles or more. High altitudes. Very dangerous."

Marcello taps the mouth of a mannequin's head on the table, and it opens. He grabs a small vial and a folded piece of paper.

"Armed gangs. Crooked policia. Even rival backpackers will steal their load. But for the poor farmhands, the gamble's worth it. It's like a lottery, really."

He spreads some of the vial's worth of cocaine on a small mirror, then snatches a pair of reading glasses off the mannequin's head and works the numbers on the combination box.

"They might earn $150 to $400 per trip, depending on the load. The 11 pounds of coca paste are worth about $3,500 in Peru—and 16 times as much wholesale in Los Estados Unidos. As powdered cocaine, sold by the gram in New York City, it can fetch up to $250,000."

It opens and he whips out a small leather pouch. Unzipping it, out comes a. . . black permanent marker. I tilt my head in disbelief.

"Most farmhands haven't finished school. They don't know they're the vital first link in the drug-trafficking chain, all the way up to us hopelessly addicted assholes up North."

He twists the permanent marker, revealing a hidden compartment with a small, glass snuff pipe.

"But living down here, I cut out the middle man."

I fake a grin. "What a world we live in."

"The best. ¡Bienvenidos a Peru!" Marcello leans in and snorts a huge line. "Figlio di puttana!" He clutches his chair as his eyes lurch to the back of his head like he's doing a 2,000 volt galvanic shuffle, then goes catatonic.

Should I flee now? Maybe scoot my chair over just a bit for a head start? He's trapped in his own world until the squeak of the chair on the floor wakes him and he switches gears. "I know you assholes. You cocky fucks strutting in here from the safety of your first-world bunkers."

"Bunkers?"

"Bunkers!" He lifts his arms and sneers. "Just smart enough to know you can't do a shit-ass thing without your fucking technologies."

He throws his cell phone like a baseball, smashing it against the wall as he stands up. "So you live your life like a helpless, little shitty mouse. Frightened."

"That's not me."

He waves me off. "Yes it is, Mister Shit Mouse. You shitty assholes have come and gone through here since forever. That's what you are. A revolving door of frightened mouse assholes. Shitting all over themselves!"

He's too close to that big knife in the gourd to make a run for it.

"And the older you get, the less comfortable you feel about your shitty little lives."

I unfold my arms and shrug. "You've got me."

"So whatcha waiting for, Mister Shit Mouse? What's your end game?"

Fear-ridden, I force a smile. "You're so smart. You tell me." Stupid to provoke him, but I only need to get out that damn door.

"You?"

"Yes. Me."

Marcello looks pensive for a second. "All right, Mister Shit Mouse." He scoots over and stares at me, pointing his joint at my pineal gland.

"You're easy. You'll die all alone, trapped in some smelly old folks home. Bored to a passionless death from watching nonstop shitcom hell. Your last breath inhaling the full stench of shit piling out of your bed pan that hasn't been changed for days because your beat-off death grip broke the nurse's call button."

He twirls his joint hand, making circles in front of my eyes. "Your last batshit-crazy thought is a lifetime's worth of regret from your wasted, frightened, and shitty life."

My eyes dart to the exit, then back at him. Does he know that I know? Is it drugs? Madness? Something worse?

He stammers something in Italian, then laughs. "You'll enjoy this trip. Someone with your mind."

My mind? A nervous laugh trickles from my mouth. Be strong.
I manage a weak smile. Marcello gesticulates, excitedly, like we're old friends.

"Three-fifty. That'll be for three nights down the river and the Ayahuasca ceremony."

It's my play. I furrow my eyebrows. The tinny chimes fill the silence. Finally, I relent, forced to decide on a non-decision. "Okay."

Marcello gives a strong thumbs up, then looks me up and down. "Aye, Mister Mouse. First we'll have get to you on the Ayahuasca diet."

He cleverly produces a badly handwritten note from his shirt pocket, passes it to me, then groans out another huge line of coke.

It's a list:

'Absolutely NO Alcohol! NO Red meat! NO Drugs! NO Marijuana! NO Dairy! NO salt! NO avocado onions! NO sex! NO non-fresh fish! NO artificial sweeteners! NO sugar! NO coffee! NO medications! NO banana spices!'

Then down below:

'FOR TWO WEEKS!'

My jaw drops as my legs shoot up from the chair. I look up from the note at Marcello. "No alcohol and coffee for two weeks? That's insane!"

Marcello's stuck to his chair, eyes rolled all the way up, locked in a gaze at the ceiling. Is he even breathing?

I want to make a dash for it, but I'm curious. With baby steps, I tiptoe over, quietly waving my hand in front of his face. Nothing.

And that's when the half-naked dwarf in the Dancing Devil mask comes running at me with a big butcher's knife.

I jerk the chair up like a lion tamer just as he stabs with a fierce, downward arc. A grunt and a sick, thwacking blade-on-bone sound. Expecting to see my guts falling out, I glance down. The knife's embedded in the wooden chair, the tip poking right through, aimed at my belly button.

With a growl the dwarf bowls into me like a psychedelic wrecking ball. The little bastard bites my biceps. "Ah! You little fucker!" My knees blow out into a perfect 3-7 split, cranking me to the floor.

With a deranged junkyard dog howl he jumps on my chest. His low-slung center of gravity feels like being sumo wrestled to death by a rabid fire hydrant, sucking out every ounce of air from my lungs. Rotted fish breath and saliva spews from the red Dancing Devil as he tries biting my face off.

I push away with both hands.

Stout little fucker. And me? Thick glasses. Lax muscles. Pencil-thin wrists. Too much video game keyboard time lost in a virtual lifestyle. Yet this is no game. This is all too real, and the hopeless thoughts are creeping in again. I hear a preconscious wail before I realize it's me, a last summons of strength from my ancestor's DNA, then grab his elbow and twist, rolling him over to straddle him next to my backpack. We crash against the knotted wood table, knocking over potted plants and clinking beer bottles.

Dirt-stained fingernails scratch my cheek as he tries gouging out my eyes. But let me tell me something. This time, I'm dead wrong.

Instinctively, I grab his elbow and twist and roll over on top of him next to the splintered chair. We bang into the knotted wood table, knocking over potted plants and beer bottles. He gropes for my face, again.

With a spastic neck jerk I bite down on his fingers. Hard. A sick, metallic taste. The deep, guttural wolf howls turn to wailing pig squeals. He rips his bloody hand away, lowering his guard. I drop my forehead square into his nose, full force. A sharp crack and a dribble of blood.

He's a goner. . .

Not. . .

"Ow!" That damn mask is harder than it looks.

In these push-comes-to-shove moments in life, we're stronger than we think.

Wresting the knife from his hand, I heave my entire buck-fifty of fighting weight onto him. The crack of ribs. His eyes bulge open. He reaches out to me, grunting and baring teeth like a stuck swine. I wrap my hand around his throat.

Gravity and weight start to prevail, and my knife hand slowly descends towards his collarbone, aiming straight for his Adam's apple. "SHHHhhhhhhh."

Panicking, he tries ripping at my face, but I push down for the death blow, puncturing his throat with a deep stab. "SHHHHHhhhhhhh. SHHHHhhhhhhhh."

Blood gushes out the devil mask. He gurgles up a pathetic final, feeble cry. I twist the knife for good measure. His arms convulse before all strength leaves him. "SHHHhhhhhhh."

I spring up, rubbing the pain from my forehead and gasping for breath. A quick scan to my right at the disheveled kitchen strewn with plastic 2 liter Inca Kola bottles and glass carboys filled with gelatinous sludge.

What the hell?

To my left, beneath the large painting of a disfigured woman, blindfolded and bearing a torch against a black storm background, Marcello's pathetic, skeleton frame is stuck in its chair. His eyes are rolled up, locked in a distant gaze towards the ceiling. Yellow bile sloughs from his twitching lips as he finishes O.D.ing.

Catching my breath, I creep over the the dwarf's lifeless body, carefully avoiding the pooling blood, and kick at his foot. "No. No. No! Can't be! This can't be. You can't be. . . real."

Yes, it's true. Really. There is so much more we can do in our world. All it takes is the right. . . frame of mind. I don't know where his soul is now, but I'm sure as hell looking forward to that old folk's home.

#

The dwarf's doll eyes, lifeless yet omnipresent, stare at me, judging like some sort of grand inquisitor from the beyond.

Vicious and guilty thoughts swirl as tropical rains pummel from outside.

Liquidating does sound like as good a plan as any. Let nature's brutality and sweet, savage time wash away all sins. With a splat in the bog.

My body can't handle the adrenaline. Breathing won't slow down. Fingers shake in a spastic, palsied fashion struggling to shut his peepers. Keep that gaze away from me. Finally, both eyelids close. "Sweet dreams."

After a brief, screaming freak out, I get a grip. A desperate search throughout the ship, all the while playfully chanting "Will you help me hide a body?" Frantic rummaging of cluttered cargo holds yields bupkis. Until, a curious present. Deep in the bowels of this doomed boat, a cache of rain ponchos and blue tarps. Finally, something to latch onto.

Fine. In my mind, this is how it should be. A pair of neatly-wrapped blue ghosts, sucked down in the brackish ether of the Amazon's bog. Assimilated. Lost forever.

Elated, I hoist my precious cargo up to the room of the dead and pull out a Marcello-sized rain poncho. Time to get to work.

I'm not entirely sure how long I'm transfixed on operation 'Wrap the dead bodies', but I suddenly find myself humming "Go to sleep little baby." Minutes? An hour? This should neat and quick little survival gig, but the damn folds of the tarp won't match up. Not even a tiny bit. Every time I try the stupid dwarf's left arm falls out and I have to corral it, push it back in and try to make as tight a fucking fold as possible. If I'm going to do something this important, I might as well do it right.

Waving away a buzzing fly, my grim reality hits me like a bullet through my spine. I'm out of my depth. What am I going to do? Turn myself into the authorities and beg for mercy? How much do lawyers cost in Peru? Should I tell Auntie M when I get back to the hotel? It seems like a cruel joke to wake her up from a restful sleep and lay this shit on her.

Here goes. I suck in a breath, wrap my arms around the dwarf's armpits and squat deep to hoist. It's like trying to fireman's carry a gunny sack filled with bowling balls. Surprising. After straining to gain a minuscule couple of feet towards the outside door, his arm falls back out of the tarp again. "Fuck!" Exhausted, I drop him with a thud.

While catching my breath, I look over at Marcello, still locked in his death pose sitting at the table, blue tarp wrapped around him like he's an undead extra for 'Singin' in the Rain'.

I desperately need my mom. She was always good at this sort of stuff. Nice, clean pleats. Somehow, I never got the hang of it, whether it came down to making my bed or getting that cool look in dress pants. Small hands. No dexterity. What if I've completely snapped? What's next? Bouncing my head off a padded hotel room with no check-out times?

I grab a beer bottle from the table and raise it towards Marcello in a mock toast. "Here's to a complete clusterfuck." A frustrated sip, then I flip the bottle upside down. No more beer. "Crap."

Snatching a Iquitaña reinforcement and the opener, I stomp outside and lean against the steam ship's guardrail for a wide gander at the Amazon's ocean of vibrant green. The fresh, drenching rain and oxidized air feel good. Anything to disinfect this case of the willies infesting my mind with wild thoughts. With gut-wrenching Alpine Butterfly Knots twisting a möbius band in my stomach, I pop open the beer.

"Crap." Warm beer fizzes all over me and the pre-Incan bottle opener falls overboard.   Leaning over the rail, I watch helplessly as it sucks down into the bog. "Fuck." Lowering my head, I slump over, completely drained. "I can't do it. This is impossible."

Then, I twist upright. Charly Garcia's 'Botas Locas', plays from my phone inside.

Gushing sweat, I rush in, tripping over the dwarf's dead body.

"Sorry." Why the hell'd I say that? Oh well.

Snatch my ringing phone on Marcello's table. Check the caller ID. My innards feel like a folded, dirty diaper. Gus. Dammit. The last thing I need right now is this cackling drunkard asshole. Let it go to voice mail and avoid responsibility like it's some parasitic jungle worm? I could, but. . .

Stay calm. Act casual. "Yes."

"Hola, Duck. How goes the it? I thoughts you was ignoring me."

"I was. Every time this phone rings bad things happen."

"You sounds stressed."

"Me? No. Things couldn't be better." I pan at the menagerie of grotesque junk all around me, then over at Marcello still staring into the blankness of the ceiling. Fuck it. "After all, I just strangled and stabbed a naked Pishtaco in self defense on a cocaine boat full of dead people's fat cells."

The hyena laughs. "JesuCristo, what a horrible vacation. I can't take you anywhere, Duck."

"I take it that's illegal in this country?" My guilty stomach sure thinks so.

"Aye. I'd say so, Duck."

"Yeah, well, I'd like to give my angst-ridden confession to the proper authorities, but blabbing about Andean vampires in crappy Spanish is a sure-as-shit-fire way to get the electric chair. Maybe I should make an Olympic-sized sprint and pole vault over the fortified fence at the U.S. Consulate while screaming 'Fuck it all! My bad!' at the top of my lungs? What do you think?"

"Pffffhhhthththaahhh! Tranquilo, Duck. I don't thinks the electric chair has caught on down here."

"No?"

"Nah. Is a flucking terrible waste of energy. They probably just going to beat you into the living death with large rocks, then chop your head off. You know, quick, cheap and easy. Is the way of the brave, new world, nowadays, Duck. Now, I'll be right over."

"Be right over? Gus, you sly-like-a-fucking-fox piece-of-shit. You're here?"

I pace over to the window with the tinny chimes and look outside. Just the jungle. No boats on the river. Nobody.

"I is close."

"May I ask what the fuck you're doing here?" Flush with goosebumps, I shut the dirt-stained curtains, then pace about the knotted-wood table.

"I is spying on you."

"Spying on me? What the fuck?"

I take a seat next to Marcello, sneaking a glance at him like he might wake up any second.

"Sí. Is what's I do. And what is it with all the flucks, Duck?"

"What the f--? Unbelievable."

I look over at the leather pouch.

"Sí."

Well, shit, Gus. . . Please, tell me you at least know the name of a good lawyer down here?"

Unzipping it, I pull out the DMT pipe, lighter, and baggy.

"Pffffhhhthththaahhh! Duck, I didn't comes all this way to helps you. I cames here to make fun of you."

"What the fuck, Gus!"

The laugh is unmistakable. The uninhibited sounds of Fantastic Mister Flucks, drunk and gorging on his own power. "Aye, Duck, I likes the carnage. It relaxes my soul. Remember? My answer to you is oblivious. Just smokes a slow boat's load to China of whatever you got, then after you is so high you is pissing your pants, just turns yourselves into the policia. Is easy. Now, I be right over."

"You've gotta be shitting me?"

"Gus?"

"Aye, Duck?"

"Keep the fuck away from me. I mean it. Forever!"
"No problema. I be right over."
"No. You're not listening to me. Stay the fuck away."
"Aye. Aye. Captain Duck. I'm heading right over."
"No, Gus. I'm not answering the door. You fucking hear me?"
A slight pause. "Duck?"
"Yeah?"
"What's with all the flucking?"

CLICK.

"Fuck! Fuck-edy! Fluck! Fuck! Gus, I'm not going to jail!" I wind up like a gangly carny dunk tank pitcher and heave the phone across the room, knocking over the portrait of the blindfolded lady with no face and a bleak background. "Shit!"

It's even uglier on the floor. Somehow. More helpless.

"Dammit." Uncertain steps evolve to strides. I carefully lift the gauche artwork and gingerly place it on its wall hook. Nice and straight. Satisfied, I take two steps back like an art critic soaking in the nuances of an old master. No face. Bleak background. Mesmerized.

A quick, electric tingle down my spine and a shudder. One last look, then a shrug. "Shmuck!" With a big exhale,I rub my temples while spying that DMT pipe, lighter, and baggy staring back at me, innocent like children's toys.
Should I?

There's The Vülcano Bong 5000! and the vaping balloons over there on the dining room table.

Giddy thoughts for pure experience fill my mind. Why not? "If I'm not completely fucked by now. . ."

So true. But, in my admittedly fragile state of mind, is this the absolute best thing to do? And in a foreign country? With no knowledge of their drug laws?

What the hell, we live but once. . . except for the reincarnationists. Those greedy, little fuckers can get high for thousands of lifetimes.
So, let the visions begin. . .

After perusing the user manual a few times, the vaporizer actually seems fairly straightforward, in an obsessive garage stoner's demented chemistry set sort of way:

Congratulations on your purchase. The Vülcano Bong 5000! represents the absolute cutting edge in multi-purpose glass convection bong technology and can be used as a vaporizer, digital synthesizer, hookah pipe, and 6-quart slow-pressure cooker. . .

. . . Followed by twenty pages filled with enough esoteric gibberish and unreadable diagrams to make a sober person's head spin: Four one-touch cook functions allow you to slow cook, pressure cook, brown and sauté, or steam, sequential bonghit venturi extraction chambers, aftertouch-enabled, 88-note Balanced Vülcano Hammer Bong Action Keyboard ©, peak vaping delivery efficiency, multiple note parameter modulation, Ultimate specimen density filling chamber, Temperature/storage time ratio alarm clock, Eight one-touch digital meal settings make it easy to create meats and stews, beans and chili, rice and risotto, poultry, dessert, soups, yogurts, and multi-grains. . .

. . . The Vülcano ꓷong 5000! is dishwasher safe, and includes 20 customized vaping balloons, a recipe book, steaming rack, and serving spoon. . .

**** in addition, The Vülcano ꓷong 5000! uses state-of-the-art quantum encryption. Finally, jack off to internet porn and share psilocybin mushroom brownie recipes without Big Brother looking over your shoulder. Remember, The Vülcano ꓷong 5000! has got your back. . .

. . . The Vülcano ꓷong 5000! The Gold Standard in 21st-century ꓷong Technology!

The manual ends with a no-nonsense, stern warning written in five different languages:

Caution: Do not attempt to use psychotropic drugs in The Vülcano ꓷong 5000! without the supervision of a licensed physician, pharmacist, or at least the express, written consent of a dope dealer with a MINIMUM of TEN years verifiable street cred.

MissBeatrizGlassworks Technologies, LLC
P.O. Box XXXX
Ashland, OR 97520

Well, there you have it. I'm satisfied. With all that paperwork, it must be safe.

Once it powers up, a funride version of White Zombie's 'More Human than Human' blares through its speakers and the top of the volcano lights up like a fiery, blood-red lava lamp. The yellow stick figure faces on the balloons turn out to be custom lenticular stamps, with the weird scowl morphing into a smiley face as the balloon fills up. All I can think of is This is one helluvan engineering marvel.

I lean back and line up for that first, fateful hit. "Oh well. So much for reality. I'm gonna miss it."

The faintest smell of burning hair and melted rubber. . .

"There's no place like. . ."

I can't hold back the coughing and then it hits me. I'm off and running away. Far away. Full force. From zero to What The Fuck? in two seconds flat.
Was that a knock on the door?

LIMA

Pisco Sour:

Ingredients:
2 ounces pisco
1 ounce fresh lime juice
1 ounce simple syrup
1 ounce egg white
Angostura bitters

Preparation:
Add pisco, lime juice, simple syrup and egg white to cocktail shaker. Dry shake to emulsify egg white. Add six ice cubes and shake vigorously for 15 seconds. Double strain and garnish cocktail with dashes of Angostura bitters.

'Islands in the Stream.' What kind of sick bastard plays that song? At this hour? Rolling over, I fumble for my phone. Eleven AM? Already?

Easing off the hotel bed, my skull feels like a egg cracking. Too much blood throbbing to the temples. Whatever happened, it was rough. I've got a bad case of the blurries, but when I reach for my glasses, they're broken in half. Strange.

I pull on my wrinkled 'Lake Titicaca: making immature geography students giggle since 1538' T-shirt, and slip into the bathroom. I've found the culprit. The maid did it. She looks like someone's kindly aunt, lost in her job, swaying her hips happily to The Bee Gees while whistling and wiping down the mirror. How did she get in here?

Must've forgotten to put out the 'Do Not Disturb' sign.

Rummaging through my toiletry bag, I find my back up-pair of ugly, horn-rimmed glasses. There. That's better. Dammit! The white blur on the counter is the blow-up 'Love Ewe' doll. I stuff it behind my back just as the maid turns to me, startled.

I smile and wave with my free hand, innocently. "Hola."

"Hola."

"Uh. . ." Facing her, I shuffle my feet and point towards the bedroom area. "Vamos a. . . Chau. Chau."

She looks at me while dusting and politely smiles, then turns to dump the bathroom trash bin. I bolt away, passing the egg-shaped jacuzzi, filled to the gills with a green, brackish boiling cauldron of liquid soaps, shampoos, and conditioners.

Still cradling the 'Love Ewe,' I'm shocked as I head out to the open living area and bedroom. Bananas, placemats and cutlery have been tossed around like I decided to play an impromptu game of disc golf by braille. The curtains and chairs are piled up on the sofa like a children's play fort, flanked by a massive beeramid. The only item left in the minibar is a half-eaten jar of peanut butter.

But the bed is of particular concern. Pillows are wrapped inside sheets, raising the suspicion that during last night's blackout I had asphyxiated a small body there, right next to an unidentified wet spot.

The maid's moving about in the bathroom. Probably checking out the Guernica tableau around the jacuzzi by now. Gotta ditch this 'Love Ewe' bomb. I pull back the clump of bedsheets.

What the f--?

It can't be!

The dwarf is lying buck naked, his face a deep blue with an evil expression staring back at me. What the hell? "You can't be! Fuck! Fuck! Fuck! Fuck! Fuckedy, Fuuuuck!"

Hearing the maid coming, I stuff the love doll next to the dead dwarf and cover them up just as she rolls her cleaning cart into the room. She nods at me then looks around, her smile fading as she sees the Fukushima disaster she's been charged to clean.

Time to do damage control. "Uhhh. . . Limpiar, uh, clean, uh, mas retarde. Mas retarde por favor!"

She raises her voice, yelling at me in Spanish.

I grab the cleaning cart and race towards the front door. She follows at my heels screaming, "No. No. No. No. No! ¡Ya pues!"

"Sí. ¡Yeah piss! Sí. Sí. Sí. Sí!" I brace my whole less than buck-fifty and give a mighty heave. The door slams against the wall, knocking off pieces of drywall as I push the cart out into the hallway with all my might. The kindly maid catches up, cuffing me in the back of the head while cursing at me in Spanish. As she struggles to turn the cart around, I give a wave and veer back towards the room. "Sorry. Gracias." Secure that damn door shut.

Whoops. Open up it back up again. Gotta turn that 'Por Favor, No Molestar' sign around. Back inside with the door bolted shut, I wanna give Gus a swift kick in the balls for convincing me I'd be fluent in a month.

A deep sigh as I make unsteady, anemic footfalls towards the bed.

With a burst of energy, I pull back the sheets like I'm taking the corpse by surprise. Nothing new. Dead dwarf. Freshly drowned. A gaping knife wound in his throat.

I place my hand over my mouth and gag as the smell hits me.

"Can't be." It's repulsive, but against every cell in my body screaming at me to keep away, I bend down and reach out. Lightly touching the right cheek with my fingertips, the dwarf's head bobs to the left. Phlegm and bile ooze between my fingers as I stare blankly. That settles it. This is real.

"Fuck me."

Unmistakable. The buzzing starts. Whether it's inside my skull out or somewhere out in the world, it doesn't matter. It's there. My face twitches as I stare at the shadow emerging from the dwarf's right ear. I'm clawing at my own neck, my face consumed in a bout of nervous tics.

The noise grows, a shrill symphony of feasting bugs buzzing on violin strings throughout my ears, beyond my reach.

I want to turn away from the face, but can't. Yellow bile retches from my mouth. All's I can think about is piercing my fingers through my cheeks and scratching my skull clean out.

The fly emerges from the dwarf's ear. Pounding decibels engorge my ear canals. I feel my eardrums ripping apart. Briefly, I shut my eyes and turn in circles, but the hell won't go away. I give in to a final stare at the dead dwarf as the fly takes off like a jumbo jet turbine overpowering my ears and frying my brain.

#

I'm sleeping sound as a pound on my side like a fetus on a throw rug when the distinctive sounds of Lima's cooing doves and honking traffic wake me up. The hotel room's spartan, darkly lit, with none of the luxuries of the previous one. No gaudy furniture, TV sets, or artwork. Not dingy. Spartan, really. This must be the first floor, the car horns sounds coming through the window seem so close.

Rubbing my temples, my parched throat guides me off the floor.

Smacking my lips while shuffling to the bathroom, I pass The Vülcano Song 5000! resting peaceably on the small dining set. Nerves jangled, I fumble taking the plastic off a small glass on the counter, fill it with water, and take a test sip. Then, a pleasing gulp as I rub my temples.

A refreshing "Ahhhhhh" then I rubberneck at the man in the mirror. The same, reassuring caricature: wafer-thin lips, greying hairline, bony nose, pufferfish face. Pressing the glass to my lips for a second sip, I freeze. Through the bathroom mirror, to the bedroom on my left, I spy the anaconda lump in the well-made bed. "Fuck me."

Turning around, I wish it would just disappear, but it hasn't. "Ughhh!" That's the trouble with Pishtacos. I always kill 'em. Even in my dreams.

Or have I? I've got to step back and look at this logically, like with Occam's razor or even Pirate Shrödinger's one-sixth lesbian therapy cat. Did I really strangle a dwarf in a drugged-out reverie, or am I just hallucinating? Both?

I choose neither. But whatever reality is, it's fucked up my vacation. The best laid plans of Pisco and Peru. . .

My heart's palpitating like a Adderall-addicted ferret as I crouch over the bed. Who made up the covers? I know I didn't. Too neat. With a grim look of resignation, I slowly peel back the sheets hiding the offending bulge.

It's Big Boy. My biggest piece of luggage. Revivified, I turn it around and unzip, revealing all my travel gear, packed neat and tight like a snare drum. I start haphazardly piling Big Boy's contents onto the bed.

How did I pack all this crap? A bottle of Crema de Chirimoya. A bottle of Crema de Lucuma. Two bottles of Tabernero Pisco Sour, Maracuyo flavored. Twelve snarky, armpit-stained Peruvian T-shirts. A half-eaten jar of peanut butter.

An opened pack of black magic markers.

That's it. I've snapped. It can't be real. Bad nerves.

More crap. Three pairs of Moscot knock-off sunglasses. An amazing collection of thirty-seven econo-sized hotel shampoos bottles. A half-drunk bottle of Bismotol. Two bottles of Frutti Flex, one cherry, one anise; One chipped pair of sandals; The list goes on. Might need another suitcase. . .

My anxieties slide back to my future prospects. If I make it home I've got nothing. No signs of victory. Not even a job to latch onto. I'm unmoored, with a sudden freedom that feels like an emotional high wire act on acid while wearing roller skates and juggling blindfolded.

What was this trip all about? An alcoholic flunky's attempt at being a writer? A dark bar sucker's bet to make Gus some extra video poker cash at my expense? Or did I scam myself on another one of my self-sabotaging benders, again?

Even if the answers are elusive, the trip felt super necessary. A re-launching of mental lifelines. Dead dwarves or hallucinations notwithstanding, a good trip feels like being blasted out like a cannonball into a completely different reality. A new way of seeing oneself. Another high-priced shot to the ego plexus to prove that, yes, indeed, I am still alive.

I pull out one dried llama fetus in a clear jar filled with liquid gunk, just like the one Merlina teased me with at Gamarra.

A knock at the door.

"Fuck it." The jar goes back into my luggage.

This is almost over. With each tourist relic being tossed into Big Boy I feel the full weight of all my fears and possibilities staring back at me, for good and ill. After failing at trying to wipe the black magic marker smudges from my fingers, I zip up the beast and race to the door.

I brace my whole less-than-buck-fifty-something and give a tug. The door slams against the wall. It's Auntie M, dressed up smartly like she's either ready to sponsor me for an AA meeting or an exorcism. "We es late." Her broad smiles disappears in concern as she reads my face. "Es you okay?"

Trying to put on my best smile. "Couldn't be better. Now, let's get the fuck outta here!"

#

Auntie M jams the Yaris past a Volvo-driving soccer mamacita with a giant bumper sticker of Peru's flag shaped like a pair of flaming lips. Unsure, I gently tap Auntie M's shoulder.

She gives me an annoyed look. "Why es you poking at me?"

"Just checking." She's real, alright.

I recognize the Modern Art Museum as Auntie M bites her bottom lip, barreling down the curves on Quebrada de Armendariz. We descend past the chic high-rise condos flanking us for a stunning vista as the Pacific's deep blue fades out, unfurling into the gray of the horizon.

"¡Eso!"

Wow! With both hands I clutch the bottom of my seat as she speeds past traffic into a gravity-fed right turn running north onto Circuito de Playas. I stare helplessly at the crowds of surfers and power joggers along Playa Makaha and Playa Waikiki, knowing full well we're going the wrong way.

But things aren't always as they seem and Peruvians definitely have their own way of doing things. I look over, wanting to tell Auntie M to ease up, that we'll make better time going the wrong way at a slower pace. But she's locked in, doing what Limeños do best: driving like a ceviche-eating bat out of hell.

She glides through traffic like a World War II bombardier ready to drop the Big One. The Yaris, "El Tigre", has enough dents, bumps, dings, scratches and stripes to ward off potential passing predators.

Without warning, she busts left into a nook for a turn-out. Ignoring the honking, she stares at the onrush of cars whizzing by. A large Subaru capers in behind us, trying to keep its ass end out of traffic. The driver faithfully applies the one-second rule and blasts his horn.

Auntie M grits her teeth. "¡Ya Pues!"

I follow her eyes as she calculates the slim distance between us and an oncoming taxi. No! That's not enou--

Her foot pounds the gas pedal. We burst into the imaginary safe space in front of the charging cab driver, bracing for impact. A horn blares. . . and then. . . I guess we have enough room.

Auntie M stares back from her rear view mirror and squeals "¡Ya Pues!" in a high pitch. It's a flexible word combo. I've learned it can mean any of about five things, ranging from exasperation to disbelief.

Stretching my neck, I look back just in time to see the cabbie punch his steering wheel and flip us off. Hmmmph. I've been in Lima too long. I'm enjoying this.

\#

We lane-lurch south on Circuito de Playas de la Costa Verde before Auntie M pretends to signal then jams a hard right into the parking area of La Rosa Nautica, home to what some consider the best traditional pisco sour in Peru.

Judging by all the empty spaces, I'm not sure we had to sweat the reservations, but at least it's a gorgeous day with a stunning view of this old-school Lima landmark.

The faded-blue roof reminds me of my condo back home, flooding me with fears for my future.

Do I head north to re-join the rat race or stay here and start from scratch? Either way I'm completely screwed.

A very Kierkegaardian Why the/Fuck not?

I shudder, then look over at Auntie M as we amble along the restaurant's pier, popping into small boutique shops selling tourist doodads along the way. The seagulls feel at home on the roofs here, their white washed poop stains marking favorite perches.

My cell phone erupts with a buzz as the mustachioed maitre d' greets us at the entrance, guiding us up the short steps past an expansive atrium filled with ferns. For once, it's bigger than I imagined.

Auntie M chats in Spanish as we're led past the surprisingly packed bar area. Did all of Lima's lunch hour alcoholics take taxis here en masse?

"HOoooooooool-aaaah!" It's Auntie M's friend, Gabi, seated at the bar, across from a young, slicked-back Lothario type extending a three-martini lunch break from his account executive job in San Isidro.

Gabi leaps from her chair, a small dynamo of blonde energy, embracing Auntie M with a flourish. They exchange hushed tones in Spanish before she looks over at me. "Daaaaahhhhgg-ah!"

Our mesero, having lost track of his guests, walks himself back into the fold, waiting patiently at the periphery.

Auntie M and Gabi smile, articulating in the muted symphony of tones and double-meanings shared by women in the company of men since the dawn of feminine thought. The ubiquitous sisterhood.

After symbiotic nods and smiles, Gabi decamps back to her company and our waiter shepherds us into the dining area towards a corner table.

Auntie M shakes her head, pointing outside. Without skipping a beat, the Maitre D' improvises a one-eighty, making a tack towards the patio door with a sly nod and a grin.

It's the perfect location for wave watching. A shoal of surfers bob up and down, snaking a line in their coal-black neoprene wetsuits like an order of monks performing daily devotionals.

My phone buzzes in my pocket. Let it rest. Probably another telemarketer.

"Ayyyye." Auntie M lets loose a long, satisfied sigh, soaking in a lungful of salted sea air while admiring the view.

I can almost hear the waiter thinking, This is gonna be a good tip as he hands us menus, glancing at us in a reverent, controlled manner. "¿Qué quieren tomar?"

Auntie M smiles and looks over at me. I return the favor, shrugging as if the answer is self evident. She winks. "Dos pisco sours, por favor."

"Buenas selecciones." He nods approvingly, then executes a well-rehearsed turn and bounds off.

Auntie M glows. "They gives me a rose at the ends of the meal. ¡Que lindo!"

Damn phone's buzzing off the hook as I scan the menu's prices, hoping for something cheap and tasty. "Everything looks so good."

"How abouts the ceviche limenito?"

I move my eyes around the menu. Might they have a Value Meal, like McDonald's?   Probably not. Oh well. "Ricko."

"Rico."

Auntie M gets up and chuckles.

I grimace at my accent. "Where you going?"

"Al baño."

"But what if the waiter comes back for our order?"

She puckers while dabbing her lips with balm. Loading up for a kiss when she gets back, perhaps? "Then order."

Order? In Spanish? Me?

"Y watches my purse." She strides off.

More phone buzzing. Uh oh. It's my work. "Hello Linda."

"Doug?"

Oh, shit. "Yeah?"

The sound of the phone changing hands. A gruff, familiar voice. My boss.

"Glad you survived the cargo cult. I don't give a shit about your condition. You're fired! Good luck on the funny farm, you screwy piece of shit!"

CLICK.

And. . . BLOCKED.

How rude. Apparently, the cargo cult excuse was the last straw for the ADA's reasonable accommodations clause for the mentally ill.

Oh, well. Now I have an ex-boss. . . finally. Good riddance. No more excuses.

I power off the phone, set it down on the table and lean waaaay back. Ahhhhhh. Free air again.

I'm broke, and broken, but it was one helluva trip.

Out with the old boss. A tired slogan of hopeless change. In with a new boss. Different faces. Same trope. It's a factory. A perfect bullshit factory for extracting money. Once you wake up to it, it's like fighting a shit tsunami armed only with hip waders and a dixie cup. A completely self-delusional machine.

Hell, I'm probably the most sane person there. . . or at least I was. But I've seen the error of my ways, twenty years too late. So now, whatever drib drabs of life I have left traversing this impersonal blue dot, I'm done wasting it. Nobody puts Duck in the corner.

I close my eyes and lift my head up, feeling the sun's warmth caressing my face. "Or maybe I should just take it easy and check myself into an institution of mentally ill repute?"

"Disculpe." The waiter surprises me as he places both pisco sour glasses on the table with affected care. "¿Listo?"

I mouth the word while making the connection. I'm not really ready but I guess I am.

"Uhhhhh. . . sí."

Pressing my horned-rimmed glasses up the bridge of my nose, I place my forefinger down on the menu confidently for my way out. "Aquí."

He bends his head down to look. Wait. Pointing's cheating. Give it a shot. "Civiche leminito." Slurred and under my breath, but audible.

He rises up, stone-faced. "¿Y para la señora?"

"Uhhh. Nada. Uh, vamos a. . . share--"

"Compartir."

". . . Si. . . compartimos la. . . no, el civiche leminito."

With a firm grip, he smiles and takes the menus from my hand. "Excellent choice, sir."

"You speak English."

"Of course."

As he marches with a snap-kneed gait, I can almost hear him lowering his tip expectations.

I raise my pisco glass to my lips.

First contact. Ahhhhh. Yes. That's what I'm talkin' about. "Ahhhh."

Oh! Do I have enough cash on hand for a tip? I open my wallet and count out the dirty, wrinkled Peruvian Soles. It won't be spectacular, but it should be enough. What's this? I pull out the neatly folded paper that's been in my wallet since I last set foot in the Dark Bar.

Neat and Flowing and Feminine Cursive:

Here's Auntie M's contact info. She's a kind person and speaks English, so you're in good hands.

Enjoy your Peruvian Adventure, Dougie!

Have fun!

Gayle

P.S. And for God's sake, don't tell her about Gus. It might weird her out.'

I pocket the note and seep luxuriantly into my chair, closing my eyes. The sun feels beautiful. Listening to the Pacific's steady heartbeat of rilling waves.

This could last forever.

Who's insane, now?

Ringing noises from the not-so-smartphone. Strange. The screen is blank and the power is definitely off, but, somehow, that never bothers guys like me.

I place it up to my ear. "I've been expecting you, Gooseman."

"Aye. Of course you have, Duck. How goes?"

"Great. You should have joined me. 'Course you were too busy being somewhere else."

"Did you enjoy Iquitos?"

"Yep."

"Pfffffffththththtth. I always knew you would. Just remembers, Duck, no matter where you go, there you are. Meaningless!"

"Excuse me?"

The laugh of a hyena downing shots at the whiskey bar. "Meaningless! Everything is meaningless!"

I hear the clink of icecubes as his mind incubates a thought. "Just like them Pishtacos you is always runnings from, Duck."

"Nah. I'm done running from ghosts. It's exhausting."

"Bueno. Everyones makes a past to forget."

"Indeed they do."

His high-pitched whistle, then a whisper. "So, then helps me wins my bet."

"Bet?"

The clink of ice rattling around his drinkie poo. "Aye. You is the talk of the walk in the whole Dark Bar. Java. Gayle. Even Timmy and Jon. Everyone's got a big wager on how many days you will last on yours own down there. So comes back home pronto and, you and me, we will wins me a great, big pots of money."

I pause and listen to the familiar sounds of video poker. "You wanna know when I'll come back?"

He gulps his drink. "Aye."

"Whenever I damn well feel like it. Pfffffffththththtth!"

CLICK.

And. . . BLOCKED.

Ahhhhh. At last, the final word champion has met his match.

"Hola, Dougito." Auntie M's back, sniffing at a red rose she's holding while she stares at me. "Es was Gabi's. Her boyfriend gaves it to her, but they got into a huge blowup."

"So, now it's yours?" I nod.

"Síííí."

The voice from above. "Your ceviche." Auntie M and I exchange smiles while the waiter carefully sets the ceviche spread between us. "Can I get you anything else right now?"

Auntie M shakes her head. With that, he bows and walks off.

We both gawk at the feastival of octopus, mussels, shrimp causitas and drunken scallops in a key lime tomato sauce.

I smile. "Rico."

She smiles back and winks. "Ricko."

Auntie M places the rose into the water vase on the table, sniffs it once more, then stabs a healthy forkful of octopi and shrimps onto her plate.

A lull lingers, remaining for much more than a moment before Auntie M laughs and shakes her head. "Well, this es. . . en'com'mo'di'ous."

"I know how you're pulling that off." I shake my head, self-satisfied.

"What?"

"Your big vocabulary. You're looking up words on your brain of an iPhone, beforehand."

A very stylish, coy hair tousle. "Bueno. Y how did you crack the case, eh-Sherlock Holmes?"

My hands extend out like a magician casting a spell. "It came to me in a dream. We were on a tour bus. In the center of Lima."

"That was no dream."

"No?"

"No, we did that, Dougito."

"Really?" I take a pisco sip and shudder. "It felt like a bad dream. Anyways, that's cheating."

A hearty, "Hah." Then she glances around before staring at me. "Me? That's no cheating. That's learning. There es a difference. Y besides, my English es. . . ¡Asombroso!"

"Maybe."

Another incommodious silence, then she smiles. "I read your notebook."

"Really? Now that's cheating."

"Maybe." She shrugs. All innocence. "You know some things didn't happen exactly likes that."

"It did for me."

More forkfuls for the lady. "Y your eh-spelling eh-sucks, by the way. I thought you eh-should know."

I pull a big sip, trying to look casual and laugh. "That's probably just me trying to sound like Gus."

"Ah, your special friend, Gus, again." She dabs her mouth with her napkin and observes me, seriously. "You es gay, esn't you?"

Managing to turn my head away, spraying pisco on the floorboards as I gag and cough. "What the hell?"

"Sorry." She hands me her cloth napkin, but I wave her off.

"No. It's okay." I dab my lips, reconciling fractured thoughts. "I wish. That would be simpler. I'm. . . mentally ill. Schizotypal personality disorder according to the psychiatric experts, whatever that means."

A soft, "Oh," then she straightens in her seat, dropping her fork to her plate. "Oh!"

"Yeah. So I may be going away for a while." I bite my lip, then fish out my wallet and plop it on the table. "I've blown through all my cash. We'll be lucky to pay for our last meal, together."

"Is everything excellent?" Our waiter smiles in a well-rehearsed, pleasant tone, but his eyes betray concern.

Auntie M and I share a secreted glance, then flash him the fakest smiles he's seen in all his years of customer service, before answering in unison. "Sí."

He bolts off, even more worried about his tip. Probably heading to inform the manager that he's got a couple of potential dine-and-dashers on his hands.

I flick at the frayed wallet on the table. "I did a real fine job of pissing away all my money in record time."

Auntie M looks over at me, thoughtfully. She roots around in her purse, then produces a half-bent envelope and passes it to me. "No you hasn't."

I put down my glass of pisco and tear into the paper. It's a check for twelve-thousand dollars. Leaning back, I read it in wonder before staring back at her.

Auntie M takes a sip. "I took out eh-some of your money before you could eh-spend it all. It es yours."

Still in shock, I read it again, snap out of the spell and gaze towards her. "Thanks."

"De nada. Less my plane ticket to L.A. For my tour eh-services, of course."

"Of course."

"Es no much, but es will get you re-eh-started."

We look into each other's eyes. An impulse calls to me. Say it now. The words leave my mouth in a disembodied, self-conscious mumble. "You know, I know it isn't in your plans. . . but when you're in L.A., would you wait for me? I may need to get a little extra help."

Auntie M puts down her fork and dabs her lips with her napkin. "You know, eh-someone once told to me that a brilliant man once says, Time has a way of dealing with all our best laid plans. It just doesn't give an. . . eh-shit."

We both laugh, then a silence hovers, needing some words.
Why not? Crazy to contemplate.
Here goes. "Te llamo."
Uh. Oh. The pained expression. "¿Qué?"
A little piece of me just died. I swallow hard. "I said, "Te llamo.""

She places the rose down on the table and shrugs. "You will call me? Why? I es right here?"

Arggh.

She tilts her head. "What is you trying to say?"

Everything's in flux. "I love you."

The faintest smile. "Oh. Te amo."

Whoops. That failed miserably. How can I disappear from this situation?]

The awkward pause lingers. . .

Microplastics have now been found in mother's milk. So erotic. A species that can't pick up after itself gets the wooden spoon.

But, even with all the world's problems, right now I'm alive. I raise my gaze into the day's warm glow and draw another taste of pisco sour to drown these negative thoughts.

. . . And then I see it. The signal. Auntie M sets down her glass, then furtively yet unmistakably leaves her hand at the center of the table.

Reality-challenged or not, I'm still dead sexy, dammit. So I pick up my drink and sip. Sneak a glance down. Hand is still there. So far, so good.

It's go time. I slide my hand over, near the center line, then casually grasp her hand. We look into each other's eyes, smiling like damned fools.

Finally, I sip the perfect pisco sour and watch a gull drifting on an air current above the nearby guardrail.

What is love but a pleasant insanity in an indifferent world? Maybe I should reach out? Or will I just let the moment pass by? It's happened before. Many times.

And so we sit, admiring the protean marble of the sea, sipping pisco sours. Surfers perch themselves patiently, waiting for the next wave rising from its own profundity, folding in on itself, only to collapse in a burst of flecking seafoam when it reaches the rocks ashore. Then the sucking and gurgling of its retreat.

Auntie M's thumb playfully taps the inside of my palm. I feel this fragile moment and turn away, admiring the tiny green plants sprouting over the rocky escarpment in the distance, the fogbank obscuring Lima up above.

Somehow, it's perfect. I can't describe it. To be deliciously lost is like that. I'd love to describe it all. But these fleeting, lucid moments on my lovely path to perdition are far too fragile. I finally understand that.

I've finally learned to live, despite myself.

In Peru.

THE END

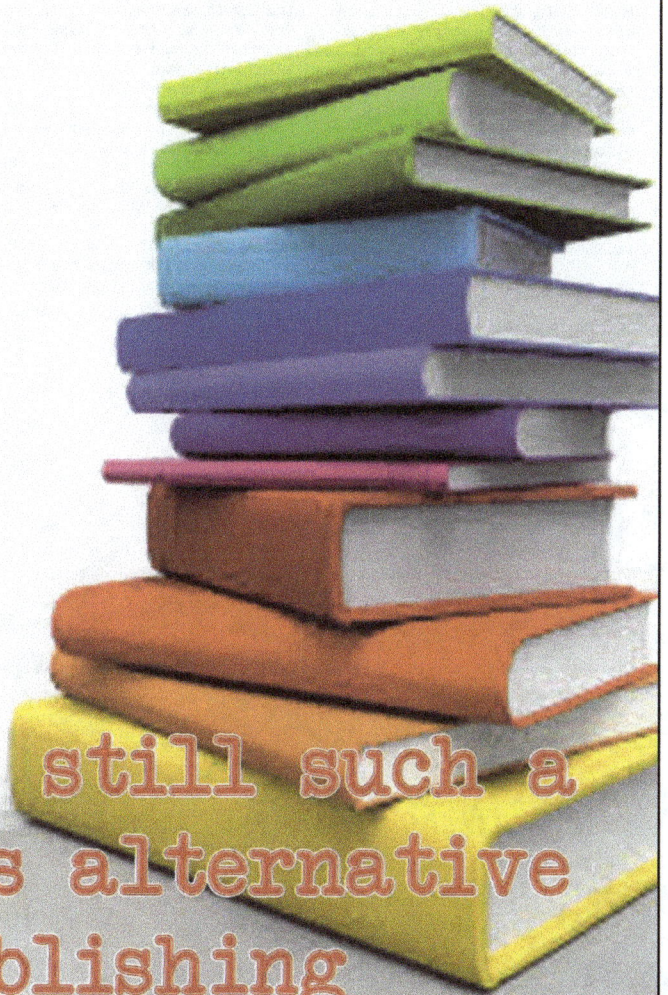

GONZO Books

There is still such a thing as alternative Publishing

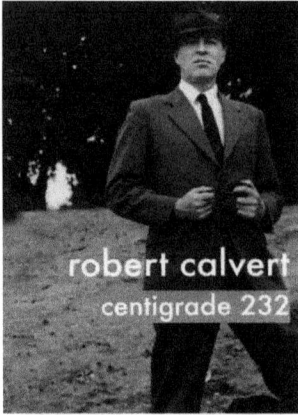

Robert Newton Calvert: Born 9
March 1945, Died 14 August 1988
after suffering a heart attack.
Contributed poetry, lyrics and
vocals to legendary space rock
band Hawkwind intermittently on
five of their most critically
acclaimed albums, including Space
Ritual (1973), Quark, Strangeness
& Charm (1977) and Hawklords
(1978). He also recorded a number
of solo albums in the mid 1970s.
CENTIGRADE 232 was Robert Cal
vert's first collection of poems.

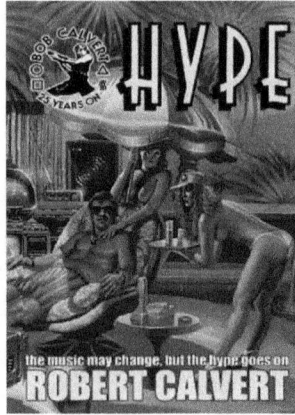

Hype   'And now, for all you speed
ing street smarties out there, the
one you've all been waiting for, the
one that'll pierce your laid back
ears, decoke your sinuses, cut clean
thru the schlock rock,
MOR/crossover, techno flash mind
mush. It's the new Number One with
a bullet ... with a bullet ... It's Tom,
Supernova, Mahler with a pan galac
tic biggie ...' And the Hype goes on.
And on. Hype, an amphetamine hit of
a story by Hawkwind collaborator
Robert Calvert. Who's been there
and made it back again. The
debriefing session starts here.

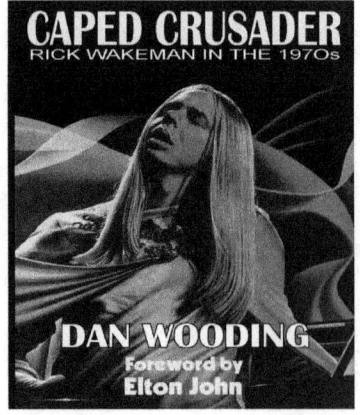

Rick Wakeman is the world's most
unusual rock star, a genius who has
pushed back the barriers of electronic
rock. He has had some of the world's
top orchestras perform his music, has
owned eight Rolls Royces at one time,
and has broken all the rules of com
posing and horrified his tutors at the
Royal College of Music. Yet he has
delighted his millions of fans. This
frank book, authorised by Wakeman
himself, tells the moving tale of his
larger than life career.

"So many books, so little time."
Frank Zappa

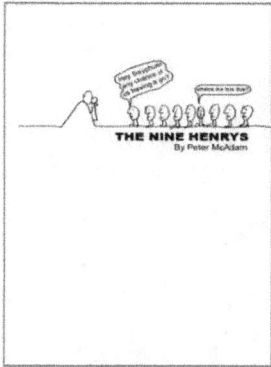

THE NINE HENRYS
By Peter McAdam

TERRY DENE: BRITAIN'S FIRST ROCK & ROLL REBEL

DAN WOODING

King Squealer

MAURICE O'MAHONEY WITH DAN WOODING

There are nine Henrys, pur ported to be the world's first cloned cartoon charac ter. They live in a strange lo fi domestic surrealist world peopled by talking rock buns and elephants on wobbly stilts.

They mooch around in their minimalist universe suffer ing from an existential crisis with some genetically modified humour thrown in.

Marty Wilde on Terry Dene: "Whatever happened to Terry becomes a great deal more comprehensible as you read of the callous way in which he was treated by people who should have known better many of whom, frankly, will never know better of the sad little shadows of the past who eased themselves into Terry's life, took everything they could get and, when it seemed that all was lost, quietly left him … Dan Wood ing's book tells it all."

Rick Wakeman: "There have always been certain 'careers' that have fascinated the public, newspapers, and the media in general. Such include musicians, actors, sportsmen, police, and not surprisingly, the people who give the police their employ ment: The criminal. For the man in the street, all these careers have one thing in common: they are seemingly beyond both his reach and, in many cases, understanding and as such, his only associ ation can be through the media of newspapers or tele vision. The police, however, will always require the ser vices of the grass, the squealer, the snitch, (call him what you will), in order to assist in their investiga tions and arrests; and amaz ingly, this is the area that seldom gets written about."

"Outside of a dog, a book is man's best friend. Inside of a dog it's too dark to read."
Groucho Marx

LUNAR NOTES
ZOOT HORN ROLLO'S CAPTAIN BEEFHEART EXPERIENCE
BILL HARKLEROAD with BILLY JAMES

THE EMPIRE OF THINGS
SELECTED WRITINGS 2003 - 2013
CJ STONE

The Time of Feasting
mick farren

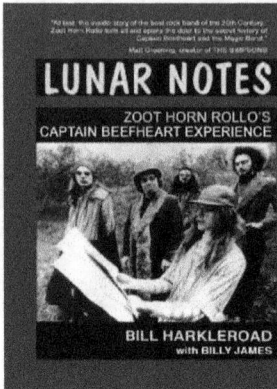

Bill Harkleroad joined Captain Beef heart's Magic Band at a time when they were changing from a straight ahead blues band into something completely dif ferent. Through the vision of Don Van Vliet (Captain Beefheart) they created a new form of music which many at the time considered atonal and difficult, but which over the years has continued to exert a powerful influence. Beefheart re christened Harkleroad as Zoot Horn Rollo, and they embarked on recording one of the classic rock albums of all time Trout Mask Replica - a work of unequalled daring and inventiveness.

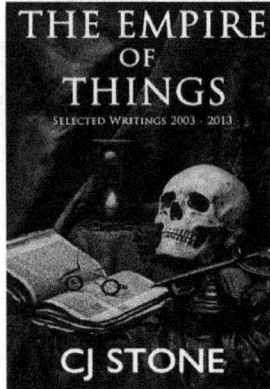

Politics, paganism and .... Vlad the Impaler. Selected stories from CJ Stone from 2003 to the present. Meet Ivor Coles, a British Tommy killed in action in September 1915, lost, and then found again. Visit Mothers Club in Erdington, the best psyche delic music club in the UK in the '60s. Celebrate Robin Hood's Day and find out what a huckle duckie is. Travel to Stonehenge at the Summer Solstice and carouse with the hippies. Find out what a Ranter is, and why CJ Stone thinks that he's one. Take LSD with Dr Lilly, the psychedelic scientist. Meet a headless soldier or the ghost of Elvis Presley in Gabalfa, Cardiff. Journey to Whitstable, to New York, to Malta and to Transylvania, and to many other places, real and imagined, polit ical and spiritual, transcendent and mundane. As The Independent says, Chris is "The best guide to the underground since Charon ferried dead souls across the Styx."

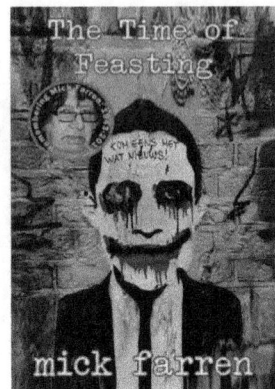

This is is the first in the highly acclaimed vampire novels of the late Mick Farren. Victor Renquist, a surprisingly urbane and likable leader of a colony of vampires which has existed for centuries in New York is faced with both admin istrative and emotional prob lems. And when you are a vampire, administration is not a thing which one takes lightly.

"The person, be it gentleman or lady, who has not pleasure in a good novel, must be intolerably stupid."

Jane Austen

Los Angeles City of Angels, city of dreams. But sometimes the dreams become nightmares. Having fled New York, Victor Renquist and his small group of Nosferatu are striving to re establish their colony. They have become a deeper, darker part of the city's nightlife. And Hollywood's glitterati are hot on the scent of a new thrill, one that outshines all others immortality. But someone, somewhere, is med dling with even darker powers, powers that even the Nosferatu fear. Someone is attempting to summon the entity of ancient evil known as Cthulhu. And Ren quist must overcome dissent in his own colony, solve the riddle of the Darklost (a being brought part way along the Nosferatu path and then abandoned) and combat powerful enemies to save the world of humans!

Canadian born Corky Laing is probably best known as the drummer with Mountain. Corky joined the band shortly after Mountain played at the famous Woodstock Festival, although he did receive a gold disc for sales of the soundtrack album after over dubbing drums on Ten Years After's performance. Whilst with Mountain Corky Laing recorded three studio albums with them before the band split. Follow ing the split Corky, along with Mountain gui tarist Leslie West, formed a rock three piece with former Cream bassist Jack Bruce. West, Bruce and Laing recorded two studio albums and a live album before West and Laing re formed Mountain, along with Felix Pappalardi. Since 1974 Corky and Leslie have led Mountain through various line ups and recordings, and continue to record and perform today at numer ous concerts across the world. In addition to his work with Mountain, Corky Laing has recorded one solo album and formed the band Cork with former Spin Doctors guitarist Eric Shenkman, and recorded a further two studio albums with the band, which has also featured former Jimi Hendrix bassist Noel Redding. The stories are told in an incredibly frank, engaging and amusing manner, and will appeal also to those people who may not necessarily be fans of

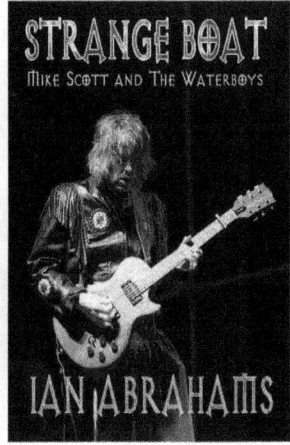

To me there's no difference between Mike Scott and The Waterboys; they both mean the same thing. They mean myself and whoever are my current travel ling musical companiona" Mike Scott Strange Boat charts the twisting and meandering journey of Mike Scott, describing the literary and spiritual references that inform his songwriting and explor ing the multitude of locations and cultures in which The Waterboys have assembled and reflected in their recordings. From his early forays into the music scene in Scotland at the end of the 1970s, to his creation of a 'Big Music' that peaked with the hit single 'The Whole of the Moon' and onto the Irish adventure which spawned the classic Fisher man's Blues, his constantly restless creativity has led him through a myriad of changes. With his revolving cast of troubadours at his side, he's created some of the most era defining records of the 1980s, reeled and jigged across the Celtic heartlands, reinvented himself as an electric rocker in New York, and sought out personal renewal in the spiritual calm of Findhorn's Scot tish highland retreat. Mike Scott's life has been a tale of continual musical exploration entwined with an ever evolving spirituality. "An intriguing portrait of a modern musician" (Record Collector).

"A room without books is like a body without a soul."
Marcus Tullius Cicero

500 ALBUMS
You Won't Believe until You Hear them

NEIL NIXON WITH THOM NIXON

The Way to(o) Weard

A Musical Memoir of (not) growing up in the Sixties (or since)

ROY WEARD

Luca Ferrari

OUT OF NOWHERE
the uniquely elusive jazz of
MIKE TAYLOR

An erudite catalogue of some of the most peculiar records ever made. We have lined up, described and put into context 500 "albums" in the expectation that those of you who can't help yourselves when it comes to finding and collecting music will benefit from these efforts in two ways. Firstly, you'll know you are not alone. Secondly, we hope that some of the work covering the following pages leads you to new discoveries, and makes your life slightly better as a result.

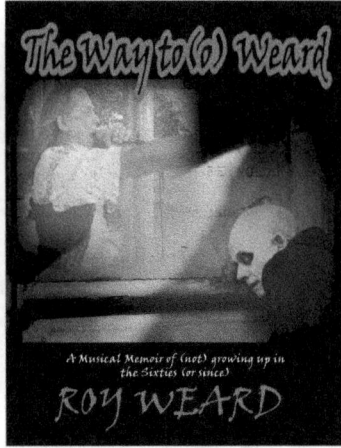

Roy Weard was born in Barking, then a part of Essex, in 1948. He spent most of the mid-sixties through to the mid seventies involved first in folk music and then in the psychedelic hippie scene. He toured with many bands in various capacities from T-Shirt seller to sound engineer, production manager and tour manager. He was involved in several bands of his own, played at many of the iconic free festivals, made three full length albums and two singles, wrote for music magazines, computer magazines and produced copious MySpace blogs. He has lived all over London, spent four years in Hamburg, Germany and finally settled in Brighton where he now resides. He still sings in a rock and roll band, promotes gigs, does a weekly radio show and steadfastly refuses to act his age. This is his story.

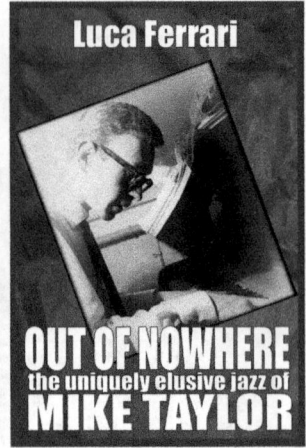

Michael Ronald Taylor (1938 - 1969) was a British jazz composer, pianist and co-songwriter for the band Cream.

Mike Taylor drowned in the River Thames near Leigh-on-Sea, Essex in January 1969, following years of heavy drug use (principally hashish and LSD). He had been homeless for three years, and his death was almost entirely unremarked. This is the first biography written about him.

"I have always imagined that Paradise will be a kind of library."
Jorge Luis Borges

THE TRIALS OF OZ

TONY PALMER

With contributions from RICHARD NEVILLE, FELIX DENNIS and JIM ANDERSON and other veterans of the OZ Obscenity Trial
40TH ANNIVERSARY EDITION

CALLING FROM A STAR

THE Merrell Fankhauser STORY

THE REAL PORN WARS

EXPLICIT CONTENT

RECORD LABELING
HEARING
COMMITTEE ON COMMERCE,
SCIENCE, AND TRANSPORTATION
UNITED STATES SENATE

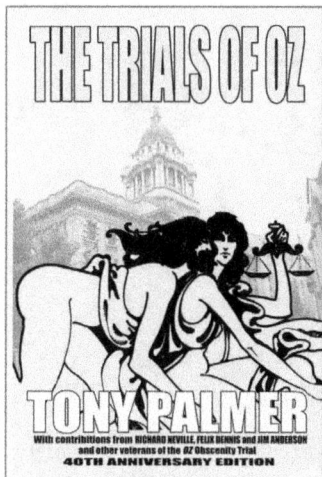

The OZ trial was the longest obscenity trial in history. It was also one of the worst reported. With minor exceptions, the Press chose to rewrite what had occurred, presumably to fit in with what seemed to them the acceptable prejudices of the times. Perhaps this was inevitable. The proceedings dragged on for nearly six weeks in the hot summer of 1971 when there were, no doubt, a great many other events more worthy of attention. Against the background of murder in Ulster, for example, the OZ affair probably fades into its proper insignifi cance. Even so, after the trial, when some newspapers realised that maybe something important had hap pened, it became more and more apparent that what was essential was for anyone who wished to be able to read what had actually been said. Trial and judgment by a badly informed press became the order of the day. This 40th Anniversary edition includes new material by all three of the original defendants, the prosecuting barrister, one of the OZ schoolkids, and even the daughters of the judge. There are also many illustrations including unseen material from Felix Dennis' own collection...

Merrell Fankhauser has led one of the most diverse and interesting careers in music. He was born in Louisville, Kentucky, and moved to California when he was 13 years old. Merrell went on to become one of the innovators of surf music and psychedelic folk rock. His travels from Hollywood to his 15 year jungle experience on the island of Maui have been documented in numerous music books and magazines in the United States and Europe. Merrell has gained legendary international status throughout the field of rock music; his credits include over 250 songs published and released. He is a multi talented singer/songwriter and unique guitar player whose sound has delighted listeners for over 35 years. This extraordi nary book tells a unique story of one of the founding fathers of surf rock, who went on to play in a succession of progressive and psychedelic bands and to meet some of the greatest names in the business, including Captain Beefheart, Randy California, The Beach Boys, Jan and Dean... and there is even a run in with the notorious Manson family.

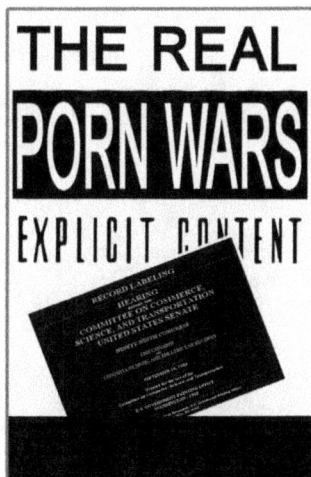

On September 19, 1985, Frank Zappa testified before the United States Senate Commerce, Technology, and Transportation committee, attacking the Parents Music Resource Center or PMRC, a music organization co founded by Tipper Gore, wife of then senator Al Gore. The PMRC consisted of many wives of politi cians, including the wives of five members of the committee, and was founded to address the issue of song lyrics with sexual or satanic content. Zappa saw their activities as on a path towards censor shipand called their proposal for voluntary labelling of records with explicit content "extor tion" of the music industry. This is what happened.

"Good friends, good books, and a sleepy conscience: this is the ideal life." Mark Twain

www.ingramcontent.com/pod-product-compliance
Lightning Source LLC
LaVergne TN
LVHW022011080426
835513LV00009B/667